LOOPHOLES

LOOPHOLES
READING COMICALLY

JOHN
BRUNS

Transaction Publishers

New Brunswick (U.S.A.) and London (U.K.)

Library of Congress Catalog Number: 2008050741
ISBN: 978-1-4128-1017-3
Printed in the United States of America

Library of Congress Cataloging-in-Publication Data

Bruns, John.
    Loopholes : reading comically / John Bruns.
        p. cm.
    Includes bibliographical references and index.
    ISBN 978-1-4128-1017-3 (acid-free paper) 1. Comedy—History and criticism—Theory, etc.   2. Comic, The.   I. Title.

PN1922.B78 2009
809'.917—dc22

                                                                2008050741

This book is dedicated to the memory of
my grandparents,
Lew and Lucien.

Contents

Acknowledgments   ix

Introduction   xi

1. Reading Comedy Comically   1

2. Laughter, Affect, and Power   21

3. Comic Perception   49

4. The Mind of Stanley Cavell: A Comedy   79

5. Get out of Gaol Free, or: How to Read a Comic Plot   97

6. Reading and Repairing the Grotesque   127

Epilogue: Last Words   163

Bibliography   189

Index   197

Acknowledgments

I am pleased to acknowledge the support and encouragement I received while I was a graduate student at the University of Southern California, most importantly from Judith Grant, Peter Manning, Margaret Russett, and Lynn Spigel. I am grateful for the heated arguments, casual exchanges, and lengthy conversations I've had with people over the last several years. Many of these people have read parts or all of this book with varying degrees of indifference. Those who had the courage (or artlessness) to speak up have provided me with valuable criticism, especially Leo Braudy, Elizabeth Brown, Arnab Chakladar, David Eggenschwiler, Michael Frisoli, Paul Hansom, Valerie Karno, Mike Reynolds, and Peter Stokes.

Versions of three chapters of this book have appeared in print elsewhere. Chapter 2 first appeared in *Studies in American Humor*, Special Issue: Humor and Ethnicity in the Americas. New Series 3, No. 7 (2000), 5-24. Chapter 3 appeared in *Texas Studies in Literature & Language*, 47.1 (Spring 2005), 1–30. Chapter 5 appeared in *Journal of Narrative Theory*, 35.1 (Winter 2005), 25–59. I am grateful for permission to reprint this copyrighted material. I presented a version of what became this book's epilogue to the faculty of the Program in Writing and Rhetoric at Stanford University in 2005. I'd like to thank Andrea Lunsford and Marvin Diogenes in particular for their comments. Their kindness, too, is not forgotten. Special thanks go to Ned Schantz, who gave me invaluable comments after reading a version of Chapter 4.

I developed and substantially revised much of this book while benefiting from the generous support of the College of Charleston. Specifically, I wish to thank the Department of English, the dean of the School of Humanities and Social Sciences, and the provost. Because of their generous financial support during my first year, I was able to generate the necessary momentum that carried this project to completion. Thanks, too, go to my colleagues—especially Chris Lamb and Joe Kelly for their wise counsel.

I've been most fortunate in receiving guidance from two distinguished scholars: my father, Gerald L. Bruns, and James R. Kincaid. Considering all they've done for me, I find it impossible to thank them enough. They both know this, although the latter insists that I try all the same. My mother, too, deserves mention. I am the beneficiary of her enduring wit and wisdom. Finally, I'd like to thank Alicia for her love, support, and comradeship.

Introduction

The argument of this book is that comedy can be understood as a mode of thought that undertakes to bring an object of study to some sort of unscrupulous irresolution. From this point of view, comedy is a way of understanding, not just something to be understood. Much of the writing about comedy in the last twenty years has tended to present us with exhaustive taxonomies (wit, puns, jokes, humor, satire, irony, nonsense, etc.) and pointless political endgames ("Is comedy liberating or does it simply reinforce the status quo?"). But never, it seems, is comedy understood *comically*. Often subject to the disciplinary control of other discourses (particularly the discourse of power), comedy is seldom understood as a mode of meaning in its own right. Take, as an example, the work of Susan Purdie who, in her book *Comedy: The Mastery of Discourse*, draws an explicit analogy between the politics of comedy and the politics of gender, "Comedy occupies a position in the structure of traditional literary discourses which is precisely parallel to that of 'female' in gender constructs: comedy is the 'different,' lesser, subordinate genre: credited with forces not intrinsically possessed by the centre, but allowed as valuable from the centre" (120). In less intriguing though equally suggestive terms, Purdie refers to comedy as the mastery of "joking discourse," a "mode of meaning which negotiates both psychic and cultural restraints; while its use always flavours any communication, this is less because it utilises a 'dictionary' of forms (as does a register like academic discourse) than because it manipulates the social relationship of the participants. However, joking, precisely because it offers immediate individual psychic pleasure, is very likely to be at the service of entrenched social power" (126). Although it is surely not Purdie's aim to show that comedy is nothing more than the aggressive exercise of social power, it is nevertheless difficult to distinguish Purdie's description of comedy from her description of the workings of power.

Similarly, in Paul Lewis's *Comic Effects: Interdisciplinary Approaches to Humor in Literature*, one finds a definition of comedy that is inextricably linked with the discourse of power. Lewis refers to studies in sociol-

xii   Loopholes: Reading Comically

ogy that have shown "that, because it expresses shared values, humor can be a social lubricant and a tool or force in the exercise of power in social groups" (36). Among the "social groups" to which Lewis refers are sexist senior staff members and Nazis. At best, according to Lewis, the world of comedy is a corporate world, one in which "characters jockey for position in a hierarchy of acceptable values" (37). At worst, comedy is a tool for human brutality; it is a means by which social groups can "support and advance destructive ideologies and political programs." Because we so often find ourselves fully engaged with the workings of power in an effort to undermine its otherwise transparent strategies, the politics of comedy has remained suspect: comedy can be oppositional to, participating in, subversive of, but nevertheless remaining within the terms of power.

What we may do is what Stanley Cavell does in order to understand his personal "discovery," the genre of the Hollywood comedy of remarriage, which is "to let the object or the work of your interest teach you how to consider it" (10). Fair enough. Many of us, however, are too easily persuaded by the idea that to speak *of* an object is to speak *for* it. Cavell says he would not object to the charge that his anti-theory advice is theoretical, so long as it is called practical as well. He would not object, it would seem, so long as our experience of an object guides us rather than dictates to us. I cannot begin to argue, as Cavell and others admirably do,[1] how we might approach an object of study without some sort of theoretical procedure dictating to us, but I do strongly believe that criticism has made little or no effort to understand the comic on its own terms. The question is, "What does it take to get into the spirit of things so that one might frame the question open-mindedly within our current critical discourse?" We have an abundance of knowledge about comedy, but we have acquired most of it by *not* getting into the spirit of things and by maintaining that comedy isn't something worth knowing about. Although W. K. Wimsatt's claim that critics "have tended to assign comic theory its own special and inferior place, apart from serious poetics" (106) is from an essay written nearly fifty years ago, it's about as true today as it was then—and about as true then as it was one thousand years ago. That comedy has an inferior place in any branch of criticism is hardly an authoritative statement in need of proper citation. It's common talk even today. For example, Margaret Rose argues in her excellent analysis of the history of parody that critics have tended to define parody in ways that avoid the comic altogether "in order both to save parody from such denigration and to stretch its meaning and func-

tion to cover other fashionable meta-fictional and 'intertextual' forms"
(28). Of course, Rose isn't giving us much more than a modern remix of
Wimsatt, who doesn't do much more than sing an old song that's public
domain. Nevertheless, there *is* something sweet and new to be found in
Wimsatt's essay, something that's worth citing properly: "to be yet more
inclusive and venture a concern even for the comic...may be the most
urgent requirement for a progressive criticism of poetry today" (106).
As conventional as the critical discourse on comedy may often appear, it
can take surprising and unfamiliar turns by raising questions we seldom
ask, "Sure, we know comedy is inferior and to be avoided whenever
humanly possible, but what sort of knowledge is it when the knowledge
of something is that it is inferior and to be avoided whenever humanly
possible?" According to Wimsatt and others, whose voices are lost in
the familiar buzz and hum, there is much to be gained by assuming that
comedy is superior, even sovereign.

The guiding assumption of *Loopholes: Reading Comically* is that
comedy is sovereign. It is not simply a literary or theatrical genre—something to be differentiated from tragedy or from romance—but a certain
way of disclosing and perhaps undoing the way the world is organized.
If we look at the world from the standpoint of what is incongruous with
it, we are reading the world comically and, in the same stroke, arguing
that the world is essentially open and incomplete. Comedy in this sense
is outside the alternatives of tragic and comic—indeed, it is outside the
alternatives of inside and outside, high and low, serious and frivolous.
Comedy sides with the heteronomous or with whatever is subject to the
control of binary structures. My working definition is this: comedy can
be understood as a mode of thought that undertakes to bring any fixed
state of affairs to some sort of unscrupulous irresolution, including settled
views as to what counts as comedy, starting with the idea that comedy is
a form of relief from the difficulties or constraints of life.

Indeed, what I aim to study in this book are some of the critical and
cultural suppositions that block, limit, and suppress our understanding
of comedy. This book questions the trivialization of comedy (as cheap,
as quotidian, as temporary distraction from things that "really matter")
and argues that this trivialization is related in some way to the fear that,
if left to its own devices, comedy will tell us what we simply do not
want to hear. Our allegiance to the rigid and often bumbling discourse of
seriousness is due to our fear that comedy addresses our anxieties with
greater honesty and resolve. For this reason, I will assume that comedy
is found in the quiet fidelity of Cordelia, not (or not simply) in the noisy

xiv   Loopholes: Reading Comically

histrionics of the Fool. In doing so, I hope to show how comedy is a mode of thought with a *cognitive* function—what Simon Critchley calls "philosophizing in action." But Critchley doesn't give any considerable weight to this mode of thought. For Critchley, and for just about everyone else, comedy is still a form of relief. It gives us "a bright silvery thread in the great duvet of existence. And one can easily engage in it for an hour or two every day." The *thinness* of the language here (comedy is *threadbare*, something that occupies our thoughts for only a fraction of our day) reveals less about comedy than our attitude towards it. *Loopholes* tries to thicken things up. Comedy is indeed a domain of human understanding, but a domain far more troubling and certainly more available than we care to acknowledge.

The purpose of the first two chapters is to highlight our obsession with the question of power, and to show how it shapes our theories of and traditional approaches to comic forms. In the first chapter, I wish to offer a critique of what I call the new orthodoxy of representation of comic discourse within literary criticism of the past twenty years, specifically the study of carnival in the work of Peter Stallybrass and Allon White. This new orthodoxy does virtually nothing to undo the old orthodoxy's hierarchical arrangement (tragedy high, comedy low) borrowed from Aristotle's *Poetics*; rather, it has employed a far more complex, though similarly biased, arrangement in which carnival, as both a political and analytic category, is but "one instance of a generalized economy of transgression and of the recoding of high/low relations across the whole social structure" (19). It's no coincidence that the rise of the new orthodoxy marks, to a large degree, a decline in the reputation of the Russian philosopher and literary critic Mikhail Bakhtin. In my view, this "decline" is measured not by the degree to which critics began to avoid Bakhtin, but by the manner in which they began to use him. In a chapter entitled "Reading Bakhtin Dialogically"—a chapter which has been a great influence on this present work and not in name alone—the authors M. Keith Booker and Dubravka Juraga discuss the ways in which critics have read *Rabelais and His World* through theoretical frameworks complying with post-structuralist thought. To read Bakhtin's concept of carnival through the Foucaultian metaphor of power is to choose not see its fundamental ambivalence (7).

The chapter concludes with a reading, performed in the spirit of carnival ambivalence, of Elisabeth Cohen's "Kids Who Died in My High School Last Year." The reading is, in a sense, a rehearsal for what follows—an attempt to understand, not comprehensively but in piecemeal fashion, the ways that comedy can reorganize the world for us, make it strange and open. A comic understanding of comedy begins with Bakhtin's idea that laughter and seriousness are not separate aspects. Rather, they "coexist and reflect each other, and are indeed whole aspects" (*Rabelais and His World*, 122). The challenge is to sustain this idea as we engage with other, more familiar and comfortable ways of organizing experience.

In Chapter 2, the second part of my reply to power-centered accounts of comedy, I imagine the social expression of laughter in more open and indeterminate ways. If laughter can be understood, as I argue in Chapter 1, as a way of expressing the point of view of the whole world, it should stand to reason that laughter has something to say about suffering. Using the case of the Castlemont High School students' putatively inappropriate laughter during a screening of Steven Spielberg's 1993 film *Schindler's List*, I explore the ways in which truth, the natural, and the serious have become theoretically amalgamated in contemporary cultural inquiry. The widespread moral disapproval that followed the students' response to the violence in Spielberg's film reveals an underwhelming curiosity about the phenomena of laughter, as well as an overwhelming desire or compulsion to bring the laughable to a hasty and unambiguous resolution. In addition to Bakhtin's writings on festive laughter, I use Bergson's theories of the comic, Freud's writings on humor, and Eve Sedgwick's and Adam Frank's work on affect, in order to fill in the theoretical space all but emptied by the serious/frivolous binary—a binary that has been granted so much explanatory power in our culture.

Chapter 3 is a move away from our traditional interpretations of laughter (as an explosive guttural response to the ridiculous, as Saturnalian excess, as the transgression of culturally prescribed boundaries, or simply as an interesting theme), to a less well-known conception of "reduced laughter" formulated by Bakhtin in his book on Dostoevsky, as "form-shaping." In *Late Modernism: Politics, Fiction, and the Arts between the World Wars*, Tyrus Miller shows us that Bakhtin's concept of reduced laughter is provocative and can help identify the loosening of symbolic unity characteristic of late modernist culture. What sort of utterance, wonders Miller, does a subject that is denied any stable place in the universe, any firm ground from which to judge the just and the true, make? The answer is, though it comes not without some reservations, laughter—not satire, since the satirist's views of the world depend upon stable positions in both ethical norms and in knowledge, but mirthless, self-reflexive laughter. But for Bakhtin, "reduced laughter" is not mirthless, it is the general attitude that "nothing conclusive has yet taken place in the world" (*Problems of Dostoevsky's Poetics*, 166), an attitude built into the very structure of the literary work. No longer understood negatively, "reduced laughter" is now a form-shaping ideology, an artistic visualization of the world. I demonstrate the continuing importance of Bakhtin's idea by addressing a particularly troubling issue in literary criticism—the seemingly indefinable character of Henry James's comic sense. In James, reduced laughter is a means of critical reflection; it is a form-shaping, meaning-bearing attitude. If we are to understand anything about James's comic sense, it's that it is extremely quiet. So rather than associate Jamesian laughter with the atmosphere of the carnival or marketplace, we might instead associate it with a certain mode of moral and philosophical reflection, one that understands our world to be open and incomplete. I find this idea to be thoughtfully worked out by Martha Nussbaum in her writings on James and moral philosophy and, to a greater degree, by Bakhtin in his writings on Dostoevsky and the dialogic principle. May Bartram, from "The Beast in the Jungle," can be read as an ideal Jamesian agent—one whose "finely aware and richly responsible" character, whose comic distrust of falsifying abstraction, may shed light on the margins of our readings.

My reading of James is part of a larger effort to locate comedy's place in the sphere of moral reflection and philosophical perception. The next chapter, which is devoted to the writings of Stanley Cavell, continues this effort. In this chapter I explore the comic character of Cavell's thinking. Comedy, I'd like to suggest, is everywhere in Cavell. It can be found in his writings on skepticism, the distinguishing feature of which is this moral: "the human creature's basis in the world as a whole, its relation to the world as such, is not that of knowing, anyway not what we think of as knowing" ("Disowning Knowledge," 241). What we can learn from this moral is the value of the ordinary, the value of acknowledging the world rather than knowing and mastering it. Cavell's doubt, then, is a comic's doubt. That is, the comic, too, understands that the world is not to be known but accepted. I argue that comedy teaches us precisely the same moral (a moral that, in the previous chapter, May Bartram embodies); the human creature's relation to the world is openness, flexibility, and acceptance. I examine Cavell's major works on skepticism, namely, *The Claim of Reason* and *Disowning Knowledge*. But I also examine Cavell's fiercely contested writings on film, *Pursuits of Happiness: The Hollywood Comedy of Remarriage* and *Contesting Tears: The Hollywood Melodrama of the Unknown Woman*. I try to show that Cavell's thoughts about film, particularly the screwball comedies of the 1930s, is not a diversion as some critics have implied, not a temporary retreat from serious matters (Wittgenstein's puzzles, Shakespeare's tragedies, Emerson's essay on self-reliance), but of central importance to his overall philosophy. I'd like to suggest that few other philosophers (in our time, anyway) have given us as full an account of what might be called comic thinking as Cavell has. Whereas most can say, with comfort and confidence, that comedy provides us with nothing more than temporary relief, it is Cavell who reminds us that "the temporary might be as good as the permanent if it lasts long enough or recurs reliably enough" ("Pursuits of Happiness," 183). There is no question that Cavell is drawn to the comic. But comedy in Cavell's writings has yet to be fully and extensively indexed. I will pursue the comic in Cavell's writings on Shakespearean tragedy, Screwball comedy, and the Hollywood melodrama of the unknown woman and, in the bargain, show what insight we gain by following a philosopher's comic thought to its absolute threshold.

By emphasizing the extent to which situations in culture and literature we deem serious are repeatedly deprived of the rich and valuable insight a comic point of view can offer, I risk neglecting how even those things we deem comic are often subjected to distorted, largely negative, and powerfully un-comic interpretations. With Samuel Pickwick, we are given a philosophy of laughter in its least reduced form. Why, then, are we still unable to accept his terms? The fifth chapter is an attempt to suggest that modern readers share certain culturally constructed assumptions about what constitutes the comic plot, and these assumptions, in turn, shape the way we construct Dickens's *Pickwick Papers*. In other words, our modern sense of the comic allows us to attach a set of rules to this book, rules which guarantee all that is regressive, indulgent, slippery, incomplete, and overflowing in the book is contained, disciplined, straightened out, and wrapped up. In *Reading for Plot*, Peter Brooks argues that plot is "best conceived as an activity, a structuring operation elicited in the reader trying to make sense of those meanings that develop only through textual and temporal succession" (37). Traditional narratology, with its emphasis on paradigmatic structures, fails to take into consideration the dynamics of reading. For Brooks, psychoanalysis forces us "beyond pure formalism" into an active reengagement with narrative desire. Brooks's insights are useful here because, in our attempt to go beyond conventional (and formalist) readings of Dickens's book that give absolute authority to some locatable shift, mid-way and to how we need to turn an eye toward "our compulsions to read," to our own "competence," and how in our performances, good and bad, we animate "the sense-making process…that carries us forward, onward, through the text" (36-37). From this point of view, one might say that the comic plot is not a particular type of narrative; it is an activity. The comic plot of *Pickwick Papers* is not to be found, it is to be made; it is, like any other plot, to be "actualized in the reading process" (36).

Using the insights of Walter Benjamin, Frank Kermode, Garrett Stewart, and John Glavin, among others, I attempt to make sense of our sense-making processes and show that the differences between reading for a novelistic plot, a legalistic plot, and a comic plot are not differences of value, but of kind. In other words, the idea is not to discover new ways of producing heretical readings, transgressive readings, or misreadings. Such critical posturing would belie the extent to which we are dependent on the stability of meaning, the coherence of plot, and the Aristotelian constraints of logical form. Rather, the idea is to simply call attention to the differences between various types of plotting. Those who choose to read a novelistic plot are animated by what Brooks calls the "suspense of final prediction" (19). Those who choose to read a comic plot are animated by a desire for what might be called Shandy-esque, anarchic, non-linear accumulation. One might say that the comic plot shatters all sense of order—including even the familial paradigm that governs the way we classify Mr. Pickwick and Sam Weller (as child and parent, respectively). I'm able to make good use here of Freud's essay on humor, which revisits some of the themes of *Jokes and Their Relation to the Unconscious*—though, and this is what is quite remarkable about this lesser-known work, it is far more indulgent of the liberatory possibilities of comedy.

A paranoid skepticism about the liberatory possibilities of comedy informs several of the problems this project seeks to address but no more so than our modern construction of the grotesque—the subject of the sixth and final chapter. Once treated as an extravagance of imagination or style no matter the literary genre or artistic medium, the term "grotesque" has, since the late nineteenth and twentieth century, come to express a world of radical alienation in which all that is familiar becomes hostile, in which all hope of liberation is foreclosed by trappings beyond our control, in which laughter is the implicit expression of fear. No literary figure, apart from Samuel Beckett, has been exploited more than Franz Kafka in the service of this idea—which is just to say that there exists a general consensus that one must take Kafka seriously. In this last chapter, I exploit Franz Kafka for very different, more comic reasons. Using the work of Mikhail Bakhtin, Frances Ferguson, Wolfgang Kayser, Mary

Russo, and Eve Sedgwick, I explore the ways in which we use modern definitions of the grotesque to judge Kafka and vice-versa.

I begin with a reading of John Ruskin's *Stones of Venice*, in which he defines several different categories of the grotesque (the fearful, the sportive, the frivolous). One cannot, with any degree of confidence, separate these categories so neatly. Even the least indulgent reading of Dickens's *The Old Curiosity Shop* will produce a Quilp who is capable of moving in and out of each at any given time. One might argue that the reader's agility owes itself not strictly to Dickens's genius, but also to the full extent to which the various kinds of the grotesque reflect on one another. Ruskin's grotesque, in what Frances K. Barasch calls its "all-embracing proportions," offer us considerably more freedom than more recent critical investigations, and serve us well if we care to put them to use in our readings of Kafka (lv). But the definitions of the grotesque that circulate widely tend to disregard the laughing, playful, frivolous forms. Nowhere are the social dynamics and political implications of this choice more keenly put than in Peter Stallybrass and Allon White's *The Politics and Poetics of Transgression*. In it, the authors argue against nostalgic treatments of carnival history that mourn the "disappearance" of grotesque forms by claiming that the grotesque has not disappeared at all, that it has been "re-territorialized" within the symbolic domain as the political unconscious. Since the Enlightenment, powerful forces have sought to exclude the grotesque from official identity and to reject all transgressive and excessive invocations of the body. The reward for their efforts came in the form of a stable, bourgeois democracy. What I hope to show, however, is that Kafka's grotesque images are as frivolous as they are fearful, if not more so, and that it is precisely this neglect that has disabled our senses from catching whiffs of Kafka's comedy—particularly in the stories "A Report to an Academy," "The Hunger Artist," "The Metamorphosis," and "The Burrow." This particular neglect, however, is only symptomatic of a much wider-reaching phenomenon endemic to our current critical practices: the fear of frivolity.

It is not in the spirit of comedy to reach a conclusion. In the words of Mikhail Bakhtin, from whom I take the term *loopholes*, "[t]here is nei-ther a first nor a last word and there are no limits to the dialogic context (it extends to the boundless past and the boundless future)…Nothing is absolutely dead: every meaning with have its homecoming festival" ("Toward a Methodology for the Human Sciences," 170). What insight can this spirit of irresolution give us? The aim of the book's Epilogue is to, if not for all, for once curb our suspicions of comedy, respect its presumed sovereignty, and accept its premises. One of the most neglected of comedy's premises is that there are no limits, only unlimited, unforeseen possibilities. In this way, comic thinking is far more rhetorical than analytical. Indeed, there are family resemblances between comedy and rhetoric, notably the willingness to postpone adjudication indefinitely. I'd like to end *Loopholes: Reading Comically* with an examination of these resemblances and the ways in which comedy and rhetoric might join forces in order to stir things up a bit. I will even take our case, that the world is essentially open and incomplete, to the highest court in the land.

Note

1.   See, in particular, Michel De Certeau, *The Practice of Everyday Life* (Berkeley: University of California Press, 1984).

1

Reading Comedy Comically

One would expect a fairly sensible definition of comedy to appear *somewhere* in the opening pages of a book devoted to that subject—typically here, in the first paragraph. For the purposes of this chapter, however, I do not wish to answer the question, "What is comedy?" I wish instead to explore why we have been unwilling to answer this question comically. Rarely is comedy allowed to speak its own name, set its own terms, and represent itself. Instead, comedy is bound to a seemingly timeless hierarchical arrangement: tragedy is high, comedy is low. As James R. Kincaid argues, this arrangement "betrays an acquiescence to the most smothering of political conservatisms. By coupling tragedy with the sublime, the ineffable, the metaphysical, and by aligning comedy with the mundane, the quotidian, and the material, we manage to muffle or even erase the most powerful narratives of illumination and liberation we have" (*Annoying the Victorians* 92). The old orthodoxy, inherited from Aristotle's *Poetics*, is both the origin of comedy and its problem. Comedy has its place, and its place is determined by its other: tragedy. But how does one go about redefining comedy without compounding the problem? Surely it is in our scholarly interest to reject any superciliousness attitude towards comedy. But in doing so, we bind ourselves ever more tightly to the orthodoxy against which we revolt. To paraphrase Michel de Certeau, scholarly interest no longer understands that in searching out comedy, it is repeating its origins, and is thus attempting to elude the comic.[1] To do away with the old orthodoxy, one must recognize that the choice between silliness and superciliousness is no choice at all.

Many critics have cautioned against the belief that one can simply "do away" with the old orthodoxy. In their seminal work on carnival, as both a political and analytic category, Peter Stallybrass and Allon White argue that although the terms "high" and "low" have no intrinsic meaning, they are, as symbolic terms, essential to social formation. For instance, the grotesque body exists not simply in opposition to the classical body, it *produces* the classical body. What Stallybrass and White do is replace the old law with the new. The old law belonged to the Ancients, and it existed in the minds of the gods. The new law belongs to the bourgeoisie, and it exists "where ideology and fantasy conjoin." This new law is no less powerful than the one that was given to us by the gods. The new law, which Stallybrass and White call the "law of exclusion," works a kind of "secular magic": the grotesque body "is not simply a powerful image but *fundamentally constitutive* of the categorical sets through which we live and make sense of the world" (emphasis added 25). In other words, the "new orthodoxy" would have us believe that comedy's assumed inferiority is still with us, still used to preserve theoretical models of power and culture. The emphasis, as I will explore further in the following chapter, is no longer on the "literariness" of comedy, the way its status as a "low" form of art was based entirely on its unique structures and patterns, but on comedy's instrumental role (which is never unpredictable, never undetermined) within the power-relations of a given social structure. For our purposes here, I wish to suggest that there remains a possibility—one that has been entertained only occasionally—that we risk seriously misrecognizing comedy by viewing it strictly in binary terms. One could ask, "What do we gain by assuming comedy is not inferior but superior?" But as Kincaid has noted, "such a move...would maintain unchallenged the assumptions which prop up the opposition in the first place" (93). Kincaid certainly isn't the first to warn against artless table turning, but he is among the few to propose an entirely different set of terms with which we can understand how comedy functions. Rather than thinking in terms of opposites, Kincaid instead thinks in terms of inclusiveness. Comedy is no longer half the story—whether that half is high or low. Rather, "it is the *whole* story, the narrative that refuses to leave things out" (93). The question we need to begin asking, then, is this, "What do we gain by assuming comedy is neither inferior nor superior, but sovereign?"

My initial step on such a journey will be to turn to Charles Lamb who, in one of his essays written under the pseudonym of Elia, offers us a set of comedy's (loving) demands—demands we should agree to if we are to proceed with any measure of success towards a satisfying answer to the question at hand. Put another way, on the side of comedy is where we want to be. Part of what is going on in the Elia essay, as I will show, is the unconventional deployment of an anti-satiric assumption: a review of a performance of *School for Scandal* cannot really proceed unless one first fully embraces the world that Sheridan's play invites us into.

Much can be learned from Elia's words, not the least of which is just how often comedy in general is defined negatively and just how strong these definitions are. As we haven't the courage to judge Sheridan's (or Wycherley's, or Conreve's) comic characters except by our usages (rather than theirs), also we do not have the courage (or more likely, the energy) to judge comedy in general except by the usages of powerful and powerfully un-comic assumptions. Specifically, I want to undertake a reading of Mikhail Bakhtin's "carnival sense of the world" and the debates it has generated as a paradigm for our understanding of comedy—one that is closer in spirit to Elia's than to any of the paradigms used today, many of which are examined in Margaret Rose's useful study, *Parody: Ancient, Modern, and Post-Modern*. Finally, I will suggest that a crucial and often forgotten aspect of comedy is its critical function. What can be said of Bakhtin's concept of carnival—that it allows us "to creatively extrapolate from our own socio-historical milieu and to visualize alternative solutions" to the harsh conditions that prevail (Gardiner, 260)—can also be said of comedy. Yet our criticism of comedy remains, even today, largely negative. Invoking the possibility of devising "alternative" solutions rarely moves us to creatively extrapolate from our own socio-historical milieu. On the contrary, it moves us to insist, all the more urgently and with astonishing methodological power, the very impossibility of alternatives. We must curb our suspicions of comedy, respect its presumed sovereignty, and accept its premises. The first step on our way to reading comically, then, is a step back. Put another way, we must get back into the spirit of things.

Elia and the Artificial Comedy

In April of 1822, Elia lamented the extinction of comedy in his own age. But even the least indulgent readers would have been able to detect rather quickly that the author of "On the Artificial Comedy of the Last Century" was in no mood to soothe them with genteel rhetoric that sidestepped the question of whether or not, in fact, comedy had died of natural causes. Before they turned a single page of *London Magazine*, readers surely would have felt as if they were being charged with having participated in a series of brutal murders: Congreve, Farquhar, and Wycherley have been unjustly, and quite pitilessly, beaten down. Why? "The times cannot bear them. Is it for a few wild speeches, an occasional license of dialogue? I think not altogether. The business of their dramatic characters will not stand the moral test" (161). So it stands: comedy cannot survive the "perpetual moral questioning" of its audience. "We dare not dally with images, or names, of wrong," continues the author. "We bark like foolish dogs at shadows. We dread infection from the scenic representation of disorder; and fear a painted pustule. In our anxiety that our morality should not take cold, we wrap it up in a great blanket surtout of precaution against the breeze and sunshine" (162). Elia is swift to point out that he ("with no great delinquencies to answer for") doesn't fear a little misrule now and then; in fact, a perusal of one of Congreve's or Wycherley's comedies does him a great deal of good: "I come back to my cage and my restraint the fresher and healthier for it. I wear my shackles more contentedly for having respired the breath of an imaginary freedom" (162). If we weren't huffing and puffing like hotheads every time we stepped into a theater, we'd find that comedy makes it easier for us to breathe, that it offers some sportive relief from our dim and stale lives.

Elia's words would seem to us comforting and familiar were it not for the odd shift of emphasis from comedy as the "passing pageant" to the less flattering point that the "real life" experiences we take seriously when the pageant has passed are but the products of our own villainous moral judgment. One wonders if some readers may have missed Elia's point when he insisted that he "could never connect those sports of witty fancy in any shape with any result to be drawn from them to imitation in real life" (163). Although Elia scolds those who are startled and incensed by the "loose pranks" of a stage libertine, he does so not to reassure us of comedy's basic impotence, but to separate comedy, once and for all, from the world of right and wrong. Place one of Congreve's characters in a modern play, says Elia, "and my virtuous indignation shall rise against the profligate wretch as warmly as the Catos of the pit could desire...But in its own world do we feel the creature is so very bad?—The Fainalls and the Mirabels, the Dorimants and the Lady Touchwoods, in their own sphere, do not offend my moral sense; in fact they do not appeal to it at all" (163). Unlike so many of us, Elia is willing to grant that artificial comedy exists in "its own world," that its characters conduct business "in their own sphere" and "in their proper element." These creatures cannot be judged, only embraced.[2] Understood this way, and comedy seems mere shadow play only in the glow of those "fire side concerns" we insist on bringing with us to the theatre.

Of course one could say that Elia doesn't really *believe* audiences confuse a stage libertine with a real one; he is simply drawing our attention to the fact that people go to comedies not to engage with them, but to tie themselves more securely to the world of seriousness. "We do not go thither, like our ancestors, to escape from the pressure of reality, so much as to confirm our experience of it; to make assurance double, and take a bond of fate" (162). If people are really incensed by the villainy in Sheridan's *School for Scandal*, says Elia, "I must needs conclude the present generation of play-goers more virtuous than myself, or more dense" (165). One wonders which of these two conclusions Elia's readers would have preferred. It doesn't matter because the point of Elia's essay may be this: unless you get into the spirit of things, you might just as well stay at home. Critics tend to view Lamb's essay as a nostalgic look back at that "sequestered fairyland world" (Gurewich, 26) to which we flee in order to escape the "painful necessities of shame and blame" (Lamb, 164) rather than as a warning to its readers that comedy cannot be measured by anything but itself. The police are the measure of political justice, not of comedy.[3]

What is meant by "comedy" here is no easy riddle to solve.[4] For Elia, it appears as if comedy is a worldview characterized by disorder and disinhibition. Such a definition has its roots in Aristotle's *Poetics* where it is pointed out that characters in comedy are not to be taken as necessarily bad, but are nevertheless morally inferior.[5] Elia's revision of this classical interpretation might be this: characters in a comedy appear morally inferior only from a certain point of view. This point of view, one could say, is serio-tragic. One could also say that Elia's audience must suffer ridicule and reproof for coming to the theater expecting a tragedy, or at least, for expecting a comedy to function like a tragedy. Although Elia never accuses his audience outright for confusing the one for the other, he does claim that his audience holds comedy to a set of standards that it simply cannot live up to. "All that neutral ground of character," says Elia, "which stood between vice and virtue; or which in fact was indifferent to neither, where neither properly was called in question; that happy breathing-place from the burthen of a perpetual moral questioning—the sanctuary and quiet Alsatia of hunted casuistry—is broken up and disenfranchised as injurious to the interests of society" (162). What is thought of as "healthy" to society, fears Elia, is that form of drama that perpetually calls into question the line between vice and virtue. The plot of tragic drama is the struggle to solve a social or epistemological problem, even when solutions are clearly beyond reason.[6]

Comedy, following Morton Gurewitch's line of thinking, celebrates the irrational and can therefore accept human suffering without trying to work though it in order to transcend it. Comedy functions, continues Gurewitch, "as a disorderly arena in which restraint, rationalism, and responsibility are swept aside by the anarchic winds of farce" (232). In some respects, comedy appears to be in a place that tragedy longs to be, but at which it cannot arrive. Tragedy toys with the idea of abandoning reason for good, but it cannot let go. This is why Donald Caputo argues that the tragic hero, in this case Othello, "is a pawn in the hands of those know how to play the game of power" (286). A tragic hero walks a fine line between reason and unreason, and he is often tempted by those who play the game of power to forego the latter once and for all. Iago plays the game of power brilliantly and just for the fun of it; Othello is a perfect foil because, when faced with the question of Desdemona's fidelity, he feels he must choose knowing over not knowing. Comedy, however, is happy with not knowing or not caring—not just about fidelity or infidelity, but about all matters. Especially, argues James Kincaid, the high and mighty ones:

> Tragedy's focus on the high and mighty, sustains the value systems propping up our most conventional thinking—tragedy asks us not to depart from that thinking; tragedy thus insists that we not think at all. Comedy does not shift the focus, you see, does not substitute the low for the high, though that is what some would have us believe. Comedy doesn't exchange the focus but gets rid of focus altogether, substituting a blur or an impossibly wide-angled lens. By doing so, it subverts the means tragedy and the political right have for gluing our allegiance to them: tragedy and the right flog us into paying attention, focusing, believing that certain things and ways of looking at things are *serious*, deserve our concern. (94)

Nothing, says comedy, is so deserving of our attention—certainly not the high and mighty. Take, as Gerald Bruns does, the high and mighty thought, sung by the chorus in *Antigone*, that "nothing very great comes into the life of mortals without disaster." "Tragedy," says Bruns, "is the traditional medium for reflection on this question, or say this insight that human greatness—maybe the human good—is tied to catastrophe. Comedy, let us say, does not dispute the truth of this insight, but declines to participate in it, play it out, confirm it, bring it home. The task of comedy, after all, is to elude greatness and to accept the ordinary" ("Tragic Thoughts at the End of Philosophy," 112). The operation of comedy, let us also say, is to look into the face of death not to say, "it is nothing," for the operation of comedy is not negation.[7] Comedy does not turn the tables on death but dances with it.[8] Judged this way, comedy is not so much a worldview characterized by disorder and dis-inhibition but one characterized by a laughing disavowal—not of death, nor of suffering, disaster, or wounds of the flesh and mind, rather, of the finalizing, meaning-giving force we grant these matters.

Yet, we seem unable (or unwilling) to talk about comedy this way. We speak of disorder and dis-inhibition as abstract negations. Thus, we never grant comedy the sovereignty it claims. To put it another way, our discourse on comedy belongs to what Derrida, following the writings of Georges Bataille, calls a "restricted economy," a binary economy in which everything is viewed as either positive or negative.[9] Margaret Rose, in her impressive *Parody: Ancient, Modern, and Post-Modern* (1993), claims that structuralists and post-structuralists have either described parody and its comic character in entirely negative terms or not deemed them or their examples "important enough to warrant extensive or thorough analysis" (1). Even *positive* reinterpretations of comic forms rely on oppositional definitions that undermine the comic's enterprise. For instance, the typically modern view might celebrate parody as a positive literary and cultural style only because it opposes the seriousness and originality of the independent human subject. As playful as parody may seem in this modern definition, its *purpose* (to split off the serious and original in order to destroy it) remains negative (Rose, 189-190). But comedy is neither positive nor negative. It is sovereign—in Bataille's sense of the term.[10] That is, comedy does not *lord over* the serious, the tragic, and the solemn. Rather, comedy is everything—including the serious, the tragic, and the solemn. Banish comedy and you banish the world. What do we risk by believing such a claim? How do we overcome criticisms of comedy that, as Charles Lamb beautifully puts it, indict our very dreams (164)?

What we may do is what Stanley Cavell does in order to understand his personal "discovery," the genre of the Hollywood comedy of remarriage, which is "to let the object or the work of your interest teach you how to consider it" (10). Fair enough. Many of us, however, are too easily persuaded by the idea that to speak of an object is to speak *for* it. Cavell says he would not object to the charge that his anti-theory advice is theoretical, so long as it is called practical as well. He would not object, it would seem, so long as our experience of an object guides us rather than dictates to us. I cannot begin to argue, as Cavell and others admirably do,[11] how we might approach an object of study without some sort of theoretical procedure dictating to us, but I strongly share Rose's complaint that twentieth-century criticism has shown virtually *no* interest in understanding the comic on its own terms.[12] Again, one could argue that comedy does not have its own terms—that no object of study comes to us with a set of instructions as to how one must properly assess it. Besides, even if a set of instructions were available, there is no guarantee every critic would interpret it similarly. The point I wish to make, however, is that there has been an overwhelming tendency among critics to define comedy in strikingly similar, and ultimately conservative, ways. Lamb's "On the Artificial Comedy of the Last Century" is on a certain view dominated by the indignant Elia, who believes some tyranny must be afoot:

> We have been spoiled with—not sentimental comedy—but a tyrant far more pernicious to our pleasures which has succeeded it, the exclusive and all devouring drama of common life; where the moral point is everything; where, instead of the fictitious half-believed personages of the stage (the phantoms of old comedy) we recognize ourselves, our brothers, aunts, kinsfolk, allies, patrons, enemies,—the same as in life—with an interest in what is going on so hearty and substantial, that we cannot afford our moral judgment, in its deepest and most vital results, to compromise or slumber for a moment. (161-162)

My suspicion is Elia's: *something* is teaching us how to study comedy, but it isn't comedy. Whatever it may be, it appears to be quite powerful. On the one hand, it seems to be nothing more than a way of looking at things—call it an endemic suspicion that predisposes a public to expect the worst. On the other hand, paranoia of this scope ("exclusive and all devouring") demands constant vigilance. Note how Elia's prose appears to play a subtle calculation: the line "we recognize ourselves, our brothers, aunts, kinsfolk, allies, patrons, enemies" could be (mis)read as "we recognize ourselves, our brothers, aunts, kinsfolk, allies, patrons *as* enemies." This line of thinking, Elia doesn't hesitate to say, is tyranny. There's no doubt that Elia gives us an ugly portrait of a society whose harsh but therapeutic message is, one might say, that we are anti-comics of the worst sort. We are snobs with unreal distinctions and vicious self-delusions.[13]

Yet, Elia is no satirist. Although he is concerned with attacking that which is considered normative (contempt for artificial comedy) with the rhetorical devices of rich satire, such as ridicule ("I must needs conclude the present generation of play-goers more virtuous then myself, or more dense") and mild castigation ("We bark like foolish dogs at shadows"), the subject of his quarrel is precisely the same sort of smug superiority one generally associates with this literary form. Elia's essay takes issue with the public's *detachment*—its lofty declamations, its refusal to fully engage with the world of comedy. By doing so, he denies the satirist his bread and butter. "The satirist whose laughter is negative," argues Mikhail Bakhtin, "places himself above the object of his mockery, he is opposed to it" (*Rabelais and His World,* 12). Elia's attitude uses the logic of inclusion, not exclusion; he urges us (we moral spectators, we calculators of right and good) to re-inhabit and restore the world, not hover above it in stern and stupid mock superiority. The crucial point of this useful distinction between satire and comedy is that the latter belongs to the social in its entirety; its wholeness is expressed through festive laughter, not stinging, vituperative laughter. That is, Bakhtin understands festive laughter as the "ever changing, playful, undefined forms" of the social (11). Festive laughter is not oppositional; it is the intermingling and, thus, the denial of opposites—of high/low, sacred/profane, death/rebirth, purity/filth. In Elia's terms, "[t]here is no right nor wrong,—gratitude or its opposite,—claim or duty,—paternity or sonship" in the comic world (164). In his book on Rabelais, Bakhtin submits to us two world-views: the first, which (according to Bakhtin) emerges with modernity, is unequivocal, closed, and stable. The second is extremely ambivalent, open, and changing. A conventional schematic representation might look something like this:

Table 1.1

The Official (seriousness)	The Unofficial (laughter)
Unequivocal	Equivocal
Monologic	Dialogic
Closed	Open

Yet, laughter is not mere negation; the "unofficial" that Bakhtin praises cannot be fixed as the mere flipside to the "official." So the schematic, as it is represented above, is not sufficient at all. The second order of life ("the unofficial") is not distinct from the first ("the official") as white is to black or Ø is to 1. Rather, the first is incorporated by the second, subsumed by it in the same way the equivocal "maybe" subsumes both "yes" and "no." The first, in effect, *belongs* to the second. What characterizes the first order is *exclusion*; what characterizes the second order is *inclusion*. "Carnival laughter," argue Emerson and Morson, "is neither negative nor unidirectional and does not pass authoritative judgments: valuing the unfinished in everything, it is always ambivalent" (444). Although Bakhtin's argument in the *Rabelais* book is highly polemicized in that it proposes two radically different ways of experiencing and understanding the world during the Middle Ages, this really must be understood as its only binary formulation. One might say carnival laughter opposes categorical opposition but can oppose nothing else. In other words, unless the reader acknowledges the exaggerated language of inclusion, openness, and ambivalence that characterizes carnival laughter, she will likely be misled to think that categorical opposition governs the logic of Bakhtin's analysis at every turn. Yet, Bakhtin is certainly clear enough about the point of view he wishes his readers to adopt. In several passages, time is taken to carefully distinguish carnival as seen through the lens of official history and as seen through the lens of carnival laughter.[14]

What seems more familiar to us, however, is a Bakhtin who speaks exclusively of carnival laughter as oppositional. In their influential book *The Politics and Poetic of Transgression* (1986), Peter Stallybrass and Allon White are able to develop an extremely powerful theory of symbolic polarities by emphasizing Bakhtin's "exploration of the *relational* nature of festivity, its structural inversion of, and ambivalent dependence upon, 'official culture'" and by assuming that one finds, in Bakhtin, "a model of culture in which a high/low binarism had a fundamental place" (16). Mary Russo puts a similar reading of Bakhtin's carnival to use in *The Female Grotesque: Risk, Excess, and Modernity* (1994). Katerina Clark and Michael Holquist, in their well-received 1984 biography, make dismissals of Bakhtin's celebration of folk culture look as easy as changing a baby's diaper: "while opposing one idealized conception of the folk, Bakhtin's own counterimage is no less idealized, dripping with urine and feces though it be" (310). Umberto Eco, in an essay entitled "Frames of Comic Freedom" (1983) says, "[c]arnival is the natural theater in which animals and animal-like beings take over the power and become the masters." Such a definition of carnival will naturally yield the cautionary claim that "[t]he hyper-Bachtinian [sic] ideology of carnival as *actual* liberation may, however, be wrong" (3). In *Comedy: The Mastery of Discourse* (1993), Susan Purdie expresses a similar skepticism of carnival's political efficacy: "it has been argued that [carnival's] operation fundamentally calls into question the 'normality' of Symbolic hierarchies, revealing them through its inversion as arbitrary constructs, not eternal truths. However, its appearance only on sites which are permitted by the culture which is operating these hierarchies as norms leads us to see carnival's long-term effects as constraining rather than liberating" (126).

What these charges against Bakhtin's carnival reveal is that we tend to understand carnival best, or perhaps exclusively (or predictably), at its most vulnerable.[15] However, the ease with which we dismiss carnival's potential to liberate and transform owes less to the so-called impotency

of a specific cultural phenomenon than to the ways in which carnival, as
a *metaphor*, is regulated by our contemporary critical epistemologies.
M. Keith Booker and Dubravka Juraga open their *Bakhtin, Stalin, and
Modern Russian Fiction* with this useful observation on the matter:

> Conventional readings of Bakhtin's figuration of the carnival merely as a metaphor
> for revolution and emancipation…encompass only one side of carnivalesque ambiva-
> lence. Such readings, in fact, rely largely on a notion similar to what Michel Foucault
> has called the "repressive hypothesis" in relation to the work of Sigmund Freud on
> sexuality and society…For Foucault…sexuality can be a tool of official power rather
> than being inherently transgressive, just as the carnival for Bakhtin can be an image
> of oppression as well as liberation. (7-8)

What happens when we read Bakhtin using metaphors of power? *Rabelais
and His World* seems overly optimistic, an idealistic treatise with a not-
too-small dose of the panegyric. Thankfully, most Bakhtinian critics add,
the Rabelais book is an aberration, "a temporary phase through which
Bakhtin quickly passed" (8). Yet Booker and Juraga argue, quite persua-
sively in fact, that the Rabelais book and Bakhtin's other studies of carnivalesque forms (which are regarded with far less skepticism) can be seen
as consistent. The difference between, say, the Dostoevsky book and the
Rabelais book "can to a large extent be attributed to differences between
Dostoevsky and Rabelais themselves. It is our belief that Bakhtin's own
highly dialogic critical practice was such that he often adapted his voice
to fit the material at hand, allowing his style in the Dostoevsky book to
be influenced by Dostoevsky's own, and likewise for the Rabelais" (9).
If the study of festive forms in the Middle Ages seems too exuberant,
it is perhaps because Bakhtin adopted (consciously or not) a style that
bore a suitably festive spirit—one that would not translate properly to a
study of a nineteenth-century Russian literary figure. Perhaps, but what
applies principally to this current book is not the consistency of thought
throughout a major philosophical figure's career, but the ways in which
we can begin to understand how a comic discourse can teach us how to
organize experience differently than a power discourse can in order to
question the latter's "success" at forming the only serviceable basis of
understanding representation.[16] Though by no means the only way to
read him, to read Bakhtin through the metaphors of comedy (free play,
openness, initiation) rather that the metaphors of power (discipline, opposition, resolution) may provide us with an opportunity to experiment
with different ways of complicating, making strange, and restoring
irresolution to cultural forms—forms which, if left to the devices of
our current theoretical models, will appear to us always as something
already known.

Dark Laughter

I believe Bakhtin's philosophy of laughter gets us into the proper spirit of things and allows us to embrace the comic world in a way that would satisfy not just Elia, but the most skeptical of literary and cultural critics. Among the more impressive and exhaustive of works by one such critic is Margaret Rose's *Parody: Ancient, Modern, and Post-Modern,* which seems to underestimate Bakhtin's ability to restore the ambivalence and complexity of laughter within a modern critical context. Rose argues that by associating comic forms such as parody with "ridicule" and "burlesque," Bakhtin undermines his own efforts at showing how they are not specifically negative, but universal. Rose explains: "One reason why Bakhtin's depictions of comic carnivalistic parody often reduce parody to the burlesque despite his more complex stylistic analyses of parody is that both analyses remain based on a largely negative modern view of parody as destructive or hostile to its target text" (169). According to this line of thought, the Russian thinker is too much a product of his era to be able to do anything more than refer to comic forms in largely negative, destructive terms. Julia Kristeva, who follows Bakhtin and Bataille, suggests that carnival laughter cannot be put into a dialectic, despite its negative (or what she calls "dramatic") aspects: "The laughter of the carnival is not simply parodic; it is no more comic than tragic; it is both at once, one might say that it is *serious*. This is the only way that it can avoid becoming either the scene of law or the scene of its parody, in order to become the scene of its *other*" (80). By describing carnival laughter as neither comic nor tragic, Kristeva is granting carnival laughter a sovereignty that cannot be reclaimed by a dialectic (such as comic/tragic).[17] She is, however, also moved to describe this sovereignty as *serious*—a term that suggests, to Rose at least, a feature endemic to late-modern structuralist and post-structuralist thought: "the overall emphasis in Kristeva's essay is on the intertextual and 'the serious' *rather* than on the parodic and the comic...Kristeva's reference to the laughter of the carnival being both comic and tragic is also made at the same time she separates parody from the carnival and its serious aspects on the apparent, and modern, assumption that parody is only largely comic, and that its comedy cannot also be 'serious'" (179). One might say that Kristeva's sovereign carnival laughter makes something subordinate to itself (the comic) and, in so doing, allows itself to be retaken by dialectics.[18] As a result, claims Rose, we are left with no key to understanding Bakhtin's emphasis on both the negative and positive aspects of carnival laughter, no sufficient point of view with which to grasp his appreciation for the complexity and ambiguity of carnivalistic forms. We are no closer, it seems, to understanding comedy on its own terms. By invoking the term "serious," we forfeit the denial of opposites—which we assume, at Bakhtin's behest, is fundamental to comedy's point of view.

However, Rose need not (nor need we) assume that by invoking the term "serious" we necessarily invoke comedy's opposite. What if we were to understand "serious" from the point of view of carnival laughter? What would this mean? Bakhtin himself struggled to answer this question, and used the context of folk humor to do so. Take, for instance, the following passage from *Rabelais and His World*:

> The historically determined culture of folk humor…was not opposed to all seriousness in general. It was opposed to the intolerant, dogmatic seriousness of the Middle Ages which also presented a historically determined form. But the history of culture and literature knew other forms of seriousness…The sphere of belles lettres itself and its various stages of development—epics, lyrics, and drama—presented many forms of deep and pure, but open seriousness, always ready to submit to death and renewal. True open seriousness fears neither parody, nor irony, nor any other form of reduced laughter, for it is aware of being part of an uncompleted whole. (121-122)

That the world is essentially open and incomplete is a point of view not exclusive to the most exuberant of comic forms but to forms in which outright laughter is either muted or absent (those of Plato's early Socratic dialogues, Erasmus, Dostoevsky, or Henry James). Bakhtin, in the above passage and elsewhere, insists that seriousness can be expressed with laughter not because comedy and seriousness exist oppositionally (as if laughter can be *either* comic *or* serious), not because laughter enjoys safe passage into two different worlds (one comic, one serious), but because a philosophy of laughter expresses the point of view of the *whole* world. It may be useful, here, to turn to a suggestive passage in the Rabelais book in which Bakhtin reveals himself to be acutely aware of the trappings of historical criticism about which Rose is so concerned. On the critic Lucien Febvre's *Le Problème de l'incroyance au XVIème siècle, la religion de Rabelais*:

> He hears Rabelais' laughter with the ears of the twentieth century, rather than with those of the sixteenth. This is why he could not read *Pantagruel* with their eyes and see that which is essential to this book. He misses the main point of Rabelais' laughter, its universal and philosophic character. He does not understand that a philosophy of laughter, a universal comic aspect of the world are possible. He looks for Rabelais' philosophy when the latter is not laughing, or more correctly, whenever Rabelais seems to *him* to be entirely serious. When Rabelais laughs, he is merely joking in Febvre's eyes, and these jokes seem to him innocent enough. Like all jokes, they say nothing about philosophy, which can only be serious. Thus Febvre endows the

sixteenth century with the concept of laughter and of its functions in culture as they appear in modern times, especially in the nineteenth century. (133)

Febvre's understanding of laughter, one gathers from the passage above, is the product of what Rose describes as a "one-dimensional, or negative, and, in this sense, typically modern view" (191); it is incapable of imagining the comic and the serious as part of a whole, incapable of putting itself beyond the opposition of the comic and the serious.

To assume comedy is sovereign is to assume we live in a world in which nothing is excluded. James Kincaid suggests as much when he asks us to imagine comedy not as the opposite of tragedy, but as the whole story. The tragic view of things is especially sad because it demands moral conflict and sacrifice (Langer, 332). What is sacrificed, generally, is our willingness to embrace surprise, to welcome secrets, to rest easy with unknowing, to be satisfied with paradox. Tragedy assumes that moral conflicts are too important not to be resolved, and that their resolution always comes first. For Hamlet, resolution comes before everything and everybody (including Ophelia, Polonius, the Queen, himself). For Groucho, there is no answer to "Why a duck?" and there never will be, and that's just fine. "With comedy," suggests Kincaid, "nothing is sacrificed, nothing lost; the discoordinate and discontinuous are especially welcome. Tragedy protects itself by its linearity, its tight conclusiveness; comedy's generosity and ability never to end make it gloriously vulnerable" (93). This generosity extends even to tragedy, for comedy could not possibly express, in Bakhtin's words, the point of view of the whole world without it. So strong is this line of thought in Bakhtin's philosophy that one cannot easily distinguish the two. From *Rabelais and His World*: "Tragic seriousness is universal...it is infused with the spirit of creative destruction. Tragic seriousness is absolutely free of dogmatism. A dogmatic tragedy is as impossible as dogmatic laughter, and the classical tragedies rise above it. Both authentic tragedy and authentic ambivalent laughter are killed by dogmatism in all its forms and manifestations" (121). Bakhtin seems at times so determined to eliminate diacritical opposites from his philosophical views of festive laughter that he makes it virtually impossible to define comedy as that which tragedy is *not*, and vice-versa. The two do not oppose each other, though they both oppose dogmatism. "True ambivalent laughter," says Bakhtin:

does not deny seriousness but purifies and completes it. Laughter purifies from dogmatism, from the intolerant and the petrified; it liberates from fanaticism and pedantry, from fear and intimidation, from didacticism, naiveté and illusion, from the single meaning, the single level, from sentimentality. Laughter does not permit seriousness to atrophy and to be torn away from the one being, forever incomplete. It restores this ambivalent wholeness. Such is the function of laughter in the historical development of culture and literature. (123)

Though such a term may be too closely associated with the rich tradition of satire, which, as I have shown above, differs considerably from the tradition of comedy, one might say that "dark laughter" may also well describe what the world sounds like to those with the sort of perception Bakhtin describes above. Like Bakhtin's true ambivalent laughter, dark laughter is neither cynical nor naïve; it emerges from the sometimes sudden recognition that ours is a complex, paradoxical, and absurd world.

In a note to a collection of humorous fiction and non-fiction entitled *Dark Laughter*, editors Jonathan Safran Foer and Bradford Morrow supply the following commentary on Horace Walpole's claim that, "This world is a comedy to those that think, a tragedy to those that feel… But what of those that thoughtfully feel or feelingly think? Those to whom the globe is a lump in the throat—just south of the intellect's cool laughter and just north of the heart's dark sentiment? What of all of us, like Lear's faithful Fools, who, seeing the blasted heath for what it is, a universe of contradictions and fateful inversion, laugh so hard we cry?" (114). What the authors suggest here is that experience is not a matter of choosing the comic over the tragic (which is as unnatural as choosing thought over feeling), but of bringing the two together in a single body fraught with contradictions and puzzling biological motives. In a remarkable piece by Elisabeth Cohen, entitled "Kids Who Died at My High School This Year," we hear about Mary Pamela Riker, who shot Windex into her veins. "For a couple of weeks afterward some girls pinned turquoise ribbons on their backpacks. 'She loved teal,' the student council president said, and the local paper ran that quote as their headline" (200). We also hear about Stephanie Ziekov from drivers ed class who slit her wrists. "Stephanie was the fattest of the popular girls, and it was that tension which had made her interesting" (200).

Such events upset the notion that ours is a normal world, one based on cause and effect, one in which nothing appears to us as strange and unfamiliar. They remind us how poorly equipped we are to face what Susanne Langer calls the "ineluctable future" (331). At one point, the narrator of "Kids Who Died" tells us of the relief everyone felt that Orville Lee's death was not random at all, but the result of his habit of "selling stolen automatic weapons off the loading dock of his parents' restaurant" (200-201). As weak as this logic is, it's just enough to protect us from the very real possibility that ours is an absurd world.[19] But what causes Orville to sell stolen automatic weapons? And what causes Bryan Kreider to drive his parents' Buick LeSabre when his blood alcohol is five times the legal limit? "We have had a rash of bad luck this year," says the school's principal. "But together, we Fighting Mallards are still the best!" After comforting his students with these moving words, the principal shows an AIDS-prevention film starring a cartoon fish wearing a fedora. And *still*, Tim Moyer eats furniture polish, and Jeremy Ryan Greenburg douses himself with gasoline and lights a match. "Why?" asks the narrator. "We don't know" (201). Throughout Cohen's story, the narrator drifts breezily from what Susanne Langer would call philo- sophical, or comic, "acceptance of mischance" (330) to feeble reasoning borrowed from social science film strips (Orville died because he sold stolen automatic weapons, you get AIDS from kissing). Which leaves readers to suspect that although neither acceptance nor reasoning can prevent random, horrifying events from happening, perhaps the former allows us more flexibility, more responsiveness. In the following chapter, I wish to analyze another random event at a different high school—this one in Oakland, California—and show why "dark laughter" continues to confound us, and how a culture habitually flattered by its own assumptions about the serious and the non-serious manages to protect itself when the laughter rings out too loudly, too darkly.

Notes

1.   Writing in collaboration with Dominique Julia and Jacques Revel, de Certeau claims that the study of popular culture, "presupposes an unavowed operation." That is, the birth of the study of popular culture is tied to the social censorship of popular culture: "The studies devoted to this form of literature were made possible by the act of removing it from the people's reach and reserving it for the use of scholars and amateurs. Therefore it is not at all surprising that street literature is judged by these groups to be 'disappearing,' that they go about preserving ruins, or that they see in it the tranquility of something preceding history, the horizon of nature, or paradise lost. Scientific interest no longer understands that, in searching out *popular* literature or culture, it is repeating its origins, and is thus attempting to elude the *people*" (*Heterologies: Discourse on the Other*, 119–120).

2.   Susanne Langer acknowledges a similar attitude and observes the difficulty with which some critics have tried to hold comedy to ethical and moral standards:

> The amoral character of the comic protagonist goes through the whole range of what may be called the comedy of laughter. Even the most civilized products of this art—plays that George Meredith would honor with the name of 'comedy,' because they provoke "thoughtful laughter"—do not present moral distinctions and issues, but only the ways of wisdom and folly. Aristophanes, Menander,

Molière—practically the only authors this most exacting of critics admitted as truly comic poets—are not moralists, yet they do not flaunt or deprecate morality; they have, literally, "no use" for moral principles—that is, they do not use them. Meredith, like his contemporaries, labored under the belief that poetry must teach society lessons, and that comedy was valuable for what it revealed concerning the social order. He tried hard to hold its expose of foibles and vindication of common sense to an ethical standard, yet his very efforts to justify its amoral personages he only admitted their amoral nature, and their simple relish for life... (346)

3.   I would like to invoke D. A. Miller's claim that what matters is not the contra posing of comedy and the police (in my case), or of the novel and the police (in his case), but "the possibility of a radical *entanglement*" of each (2). Fine, but a true "entanglement" would have to take into equal account the invisible mobilizations of disciplinary power (which act as the "amateur supplement" to the police) *and* other, more comic, ways of making do (which would act as the "amateur supplement" to the lawless and truant tendencies of the novel) (11). Miller's "entanglement" of the novel and the police is not symmetrical in this way. *The Novel and the Police* is a story of "a social order whose totalizing power circulates all the more easily for being pulverized" (xiii). In other words, the radical entanglement of the novel and the police appears to be nothing more than the radical dissemination of the latter. To undertake a project that proposes a "radical entanglement" of comedy and the police is to undertake a project that will be less interested in comedy as such than in the way it supposedly facilitates disciplinary procedures within the social order. A fuller exploration of this idea is addressed in Chapter 2, though I replace the work of D. A. Miller with that of Peter Stallybrass and Allon White, whose approach to cultural and literary forms has much in common with Miller's.

4.   Nomenclature, says Marcel Gutwirth, is a tricky thing. Comedy, humor, laughter, wit, satire, parody, and the grotesque usually either share the same definition or appear mutually defining. These definitions can be, as Gutwirth says of his own definition of "the comic," as elastic as they are tautological (6–7). Though the governing term used throughout this introduction is "the comic vision," or "the world of comedy," other terms will be employed when necessary. This project will proceed with permission from A. Roy Eckardt to use carnival, humor, and laughter interchangeably. This, I trust, will not appear as carelessness on my part. On the contrary, says Eckardt, "[s]uch a procedure affords a certain flexibility to the work of the interpreter, helping him or her to: (a) vary usage depending upon the demands and exigencies of context, and (b) live with the fact that there are infinite usages of 'comedy,' infinite usages of 'humor,' and a whole congeries of analyses of their relation" (23–24).

5.   The 1953 translation of *Poetics* has Aristotle saying comedy "does not include the full range of badness, nevertheless to be ridiculous is a kind of deformity" (from *Aristotle on the Art of Fiction*. Trans. by L. J. Potts. (Cambridge: Cambridge University Press, 1953). Rpt. in *The Comic in Theory and Practice*. ed. by John J. Enck et al. (New York: Appleton-Century-Crofts, Inc., 1960), 5–6. Marcel Gutwirth uses a slightly different translation [*Poetics*. Trans. by S. H. Butcher. (New York: Hill & Wang, 1961)]:

When in the *Poetics* Aristotle gives as the proper object of comedy 'the imitation of characters of a lower type [*phauloteron*],' he specifies that they are not to be taken as 'in the full sense of the word bad [*kakian*],...the Ludicrous being merely a subdivision of the ugly [*tou aischrou*]'...Embedded in a discussion

18   Loopholes: Reading Comically

of tragedy, the few remarks that pertain to comedy partake of the character of antithesis. Tragedy elevates, idealizes its personnel; comedy depreciates or caricatures the human race. The one genre depicts our betters, the other those who we feel able to look down upon, our moral and social inferiors—morally inferior because they *are* socially inferior. (29–30)

6.   Martha Nussbaum, however, sees tragedy as relief from the need for solution. In a sense, her definition of tragedy comes remarkably close to comedy (see Gerald Bruns' "Tragic thoughts at the End of Philosophy; Martha Nussbaum's "Ethics of Particularity").

7.   Georges Bataille, "Hegel, Death, and Sacrifice" in *Yale French Studies*, No. 78, "On Bataille" (1990). Bataille is speaking of what he refers to as "a gay reaction in the face of the work of death" (24–25): "If I envisage death gaily, it is not that I too say, in turning away from what is frightening: 'it is nothing' or 'it is false.' On the contrary, gaiety, connected with the work of death, causes me anguish, is accentuated by my anguish, and in return exacerbates that anguish" (24).

8.   Think, here, of the end of Woody Allen's *Love and Death* (1975) in which the recently executed Boris (Allen) is seen by his wife (Diane Keaton) swirling with the Grim Reaper atop a hill. This shot is not so much a parody of the end of Ingmar Bergman's *The Seventh Seal* (1957) as a comic reinterpretation of it. The Scandinavian attitude is to take the negative seriously. Allen takes it comically. The point, however, is that in both cases, the negative is *taken*. That is, its existence is acknowledged. That Boris looks so *goofy* as he dances with death, so impish and absurd, suggests that he refuses to acknowledge the *negativity* of death, it's serious. But he does not at the expense of failing to acknowledge death. Death is not dissed. This operation is what might be called comic. Derrida, in his reading of Bataille, describes the operation this way:

> it is convulsively to tear apart the negative side [of death], that which makes it the reassuring *other* surface of the positive; and it is to exhibit within the negative, in an instant, that which can no longer be called negative. And can no longer be called negative precisely because it has no reserved underside, because it can no longer permit itself to be converted into positivity, because it can no longer *collaborate* with the continuous linking-up of meaning, concept, time and truth in discourse; because it literally can no longer *labor* and let itself be interrogated as the 'work of the negative.'" (*Writing and Difference,* 259–260)

9.   See *Writing and Difference.* (Chicago: University of Chicago Press, 1978).
10.   For more on comedy, Bataille, and Hegelian philosophy—specifically in relation to silent Hollywood comedies by Buster Keaton and Charlie Chaplin—see Lisa Trahair, *The Comedy of Philosophy: Sense and Nonsense in Early Cinematic Slapstick.* (Albany, NY: State University of New York Press, 2007).
11.   See, in particular, Michel De Certeau, *The Practice of Everyday Life.* (Berkeley: University of California Press, 1984).
12.   Although Rose never states her complaint in this way, her analysis, with its repeated emphasis on the restrictions that modern, late-modern, and post-modern theorists attach to parody, suggests that the rich complexity of comedy is misunderstood. See, especially, her concluding remarks in Chapter 6 (279) and Chapter 7 (284).
13.   The terms I apply here are James R. Kincaid's, who first used them to describe Dickens's anti-comedy, *Little Dorrit*: "the prison is simply a microcosm of the social world, with its snobbery, unreal distinctions, and vicious self-delusions, and that all men really share the same isolation" (193). So appropriate are they to

the society Elia censures that I had to repeat them here.

14.   "The depth, variety, and power of separate grotesque themes can be understood only within the unity of folk and carnival spirit. If examined outside this unity, they become one-sided, flat, and stripped of their rich content" (*Rabelais and His World,* 52); "For the correct understanding of these carnivalesque gestures and images we must take into consideration that all such gesticulations and verbal images are part of the carnival as a whole, infused with one single logic of imagery" (149); "Rabelais scholars usually understand and evaluate the novel's billingsgate and marketplace elements in the spirit of modern interpretation, distinct from the carnival action as a whole. The deep ambivalence of these images is no longer understood" (150).

15.   All of the critics I've cited here refer directly to Bakhtin, "whose work on carnival," says Purdie, "is the principle source of its exploration as a mode of signification" (127).

16.   From *The Novel and the Police*:

> Just as I will argue that the theme of the police is an "alibi" for the station-house that now is everywhere, even or especially in the novel one reads at home, so I will imply the complementary claim that the novel's critical relation to society, much advertised in the novel and its literary criticism, masks the extent to which modern social organization has made even "scandal" a systematic function of its routine self-maintenance. From this perspective, the enterprise of the traditional novel would no longer (or not just) be the doomed attempt to produce a stable subject in a stable world, but would instead (or in addition) be the more *successful* task of forming—by means of that very "failure"—a subject habituated to psychic displacements, evacuations, reinvestments, in a social order whose totalizing power circulates all the more easily for being pulverized. (xii-xiii, emphasis mine)

17.   Carnival laughter is dialogic, not dialectic. Although some have suggested a similarity between the two concepts (see, especially, Frederic Jameson, *The Political Unconscious: Narrative as a Socially Symbolic Act*, 1981), Bakhtin insisted on fundamental differences between the two. Dialogism, simply stated, sees the world as an open-ended symposium that resists ready-made truths summarized by systematic thought, such as dialectics. Late in his life, Bakhtin, distinguished dialogue from dialectics this way, "Take a dialogue and remove the voices (the partitioning of voices), remove the intonations (emotional and individualizing ones), carve out abstract concepts and judgments from living words and responses, cram everything into one abstract consciousness—and that's how you get dialectics" ("From Notes Made in 1970-1971," 147). The last line of this statement is perhaps the most useful: dialectical thought is mono-logical, it is an "all-encompassing system...that can be comprehended and fully contained by a *single* consciousness—in principle, by any consciousness with sufficient intellectual power. Even if a thought has been produced collectively, it is imaged as spoken by a single abstract entity: science, history, or the spirit of an age or people" (Emerson and Morson, 236). On the subject of dialogism and a polyphony of consciousness, Bakhtin adds this: "It is quite possible to imagine and postulate a unified truth that requires a plurality of consciousness, one that in principle cannot be fitted within the bounds of a single consciousness, one that is, so to speak, by its very nature *full of event potential* [*soytiina*] and is born at a point of contact among various consciousnesses. The monologic way of perceiving cognition and truth is only one of the possible ways. It arises only where consciousness is placed above

existence" (*Problems of Dostoevsky's Poetics,* 81). The above passage appears to put great emphasis on the "plurality" of voices, a familiar idea to many who engage in the kind of "systematic thought" Bakhtin criticizes: dialectical materialism, post-structuralism, multiculturalism, and so on. Indeed, the competition of competing discourses brings Bakhtin very close to Foucault. Foucault's model of discourse, however, differs greatly from Bakhtinian dialogue in that the former assumes "total interdependence of power and resistance" (Young, 57). This kind of stratification (for instance, those with power, those without) is alien to dialogism, in which nothing is so antagonistic. "Dialogism," claims Robert J. C. Young, "does not of itself offer any theory of power" (57). As much as Jameson wishes to see the form of Bakhtinian dialogue as "essentially an *antagonistic* one, and that the dialogue of class struggle is one in which two opposing discourses fight it out within the general unity of a shared code," dialogism actually resists general unity and shared codes. What Jameson may be describing is the antagonism of monologic voices that are informed strictly by the "true/false, either/or forms of Western rationalism" (Young, 55). A useful example of a more Jamesonian application of Bakhtinian dialogue as the stratified conflict of discourses can be found in Peter Stallybrass and Allon White's *The Poetics and Politics of Transgression* (1986). Julia Kristeva has come closer than any other scholar has to fully distinguishing dialogue from the antagonism of dialectics. Young notes, in a useful section on dialogism and dialectics (*Torn Halves: Political Conflict in Literary and Cultural Theory,* 33-66) that "[d]ialogism is not finite: it is open, and seeks neither final resolution nor synthesis. Its fundamental structure is one of alterity: poles stay apart...For Kristeva, it was this discovery of a 'logic of distance, relativity, analogy, nonexclusive and transfinite opposition' which constituted the particular significance of [Bakhtin's] work" (55).

18.   Here I use Derrida's words: "Once sovereignty has to attempt to make someone or something subordinate to itself, we know that it would be retaken by dialectics, would be subordinate to the slave, to the thing and to work. It would fail for having wanted to be victorious, and for alleged that it kept the upper hand" ("From Restricted to General Economy: A Hegelianism without Reserve," 265).

19.   More recently, and in very real headlines that strangely echo the events in Cohen's story, a mother of young boy who slammed his single-engine plane into a high-rise office building in Tampa, Florida, brought a lawsuit against the makers of Accuatane, a prescription acne drug her boy was taking. "He was a friendly, social boy" who "loved his country," his mother said ("Teen Pilot Might Have Taken Acne Drug"). The Tampa Police Chief disagreed and claimed that the boy "was very much a loner" and that, from his actions, "he was a very troubled young man" ("Teen Pilot"). As we jostle clumsily for causes and cures, we fail to entertain the very real possibility that there are no causes and cures. Even worse, that the firm belief we have in "causes," and the unshakeable confidence we have in our "cures," may be doing more harm than good. "Why not offer a re-description of the story?" asks James Kincaid. "Maybe we don't need surgery but recess" (*Erotic Innocence,* 280).

2

Laughter, Affect, and Power

Nothing is easier to study, finally, to know, than laughter. We can observe and define the different themes of the laughable precisely enough; it does not at all elude clear and distinct knowledge, methodical consciousness. What's more, once the cause of laughter is revealed in its various aspects, we can reproduce its effects at will. We have veritable recipes handy, we can unleash laughter, through various means, just like all other known effects we have at our disposal. In sum, we can create the laughable. Now, one might say, and we have said, that to understand [connaître] is to know [savoir] how to do. But because we know how to laugh, can we say we truly understand the laughable?

—*George Bataille*, The Unfinished System of Knowledge

Introduction: "You Laugh at That?"

Georges Bataille's claim, that "[n]othing is easier to study, finally to know, than laughter," is a somewhat remarkable one given that nearly every book on the subject begins with the assumption that laughter is a mystery, a phenomenon yet to be sufficiently explored. In one recent study, laughter is said to be a "nicely impossible object" (Critchley, 2). Nevertheless, our exhaustive taxonomies (wit, puns, jokes, humor, satire, irony, nonsense, etc.) seem to have proven Bataille right: laughter is not an insoluble problem. On the contrary, we have mapped the field. What remains beyond our grasp, however, is what he calls "the laughable." And if he is right, then beyond our grasp it shall remain, as "the unknown character of the laughable is not an accident, but essential. We would laugh, not for a reason that we would happen to know, for lack of information, or for want of sufficient penetration, but because the unknown makes us laugh" (Bataille, 135). If, as Bataille suggests, what connects us to the laughable is not knowledge but non-knowledge [non-connaissance], how do we reason with it? Speak to it? In short, how do we think the laughable?

"You laugh at *that*?" is one of the questions to which this chapter seeks an answer. It is the kind of question that raises the awareness of a cultural repression of comedy. One answer, "I have to," completes a brief exchange in the well-known 1993 Steven Spielberg film, *Schindler's List*, an exchange to which we bear witness. If one hears the answer, "I have to," as defeatist in some way ("The Germans have taken everything I own and cast me to the streets only to file me, ultimately, onto the Dachau trains. What can I do?"), then surely the laughter that prompted it could only be imagined as bitter, macabre—the kind of laughter to which we, as an audience, concede in principle but do not share. A sad head shake—in the name of solemnity—is perhaps all we allow ourselves as we witness this brief moment of *Schadenfreude*. After all, it is more difficult to imagine the laughter as optimistic than as a form of psychological resistance to an inevitable fate and the absurdity of one's own resignation to it. The laughter that *does* prompt these words, however, is hardly restrained or solemn; it's downright boisterous, raging, and even joyous. A Jewish man, robbed of his possessions and cast from his home, stands in a street crowded with hundreds of fellow Jews and tells us he is living out a nightmare: to be stripped of all his valuables and forced to live in one room with twelve strangers. He has to laugh.

Do *we* laugh? That is, if we are asked to share solemnity, do we also share laughter? In Bataille's terms, what is so laughable about this scene? Its depiction of ritualistic terror? If so, do we laugh at other similar scenes? Spielberg warns us that we shouldn't, but a small group of high school students felt they had to. For whatever reason, students from Castlemont High School in Oakland, California laughed at a scene from *Schindler's List* in which a Nazi officer casually shoots a young Jewish woman. The projector was abruptly shut off, and the students were asked to leave. As an ambassador of tolerance, Spielberg visited the high school later that year and announced to a full assembly that he believed that "Castlemont High School has received a very bad rap about what had happened" and that he too was once thrown out of a movie theater when he was young—for talking during *Ben Hur*. As an act of closure to an incident that elicited cries of protest throughout the nation, Mr. Spielberg chalked it up to "the privileges of youth." In other words, the students were too immature to appreciate the seriousness of the film's subject matter. Kids will be kids.

The ending to this story seems all too mechanical, too predictable. Here we have yet another instance of the systematic privileging of solemnity over laughter; some things are simply not meant to be laughed at. The point of this chapter is to explore this common attitude—one granted too much explanatory significance in contemporary culture. What I offer is a different set of inquiries into the operations of laughter. Beginning with the philosophical insights of Henri Bergson and Mikhail Bakhtin, the psychoanalytic theories of Sigmund Freud and Silvan Tomkins, and the so-called "anthropology of binary extremism" outlined by Peter Stallybrass and Allon White, I pose several alternative ways of understanding the laughter that occurred that January afternoon of 1994. I then return to the possibility of seeing laughter not as reactive to power, but as altogether different, free from the terms and conditions of power so central to our cultural investigations. I believe the impermissibility of laughter at a screening of *Schindler's List* tells us more than simply which obligatory emotions are mobilized when we confront representations of the Holocaust. It tells us that we often deny the confusion and strangeness associated with laughter in particular and that we continue to be frustrated by the fluid relationship between affect and object in general.

In an introduction to a collection of essays by psychologist Silvan Tomkins, Eve Sedgwick and Adam Frank show how our theoretical currents treat affect "as a unitary category, with a unitary history, and with unitary politics" (17).[1] By choosing not to differentiate between types of affect, claim Sedgwick and Frank, we rely on a binary formula composed merely of "the presence or absence of some reified substance called Affect" (17). In other words, by reducing inquiry to the digital formula of "on/off," our theories minimize the risk attached to essential differences among affects. The strict anti-essentialism of our current theoretical and cultural discourse manifests itself in a variety of ways (Sedgwick and Frank cite the Lacanian calculus of presence or absence as "the most blatant" example of digital thinking) but each manifestation has a common adversary, what Sedgwick and Frank dryly call "that conversation-stopping word, *innate*" (15). The further we are from relying on any biological basis for our theories, the closer we are to doing justice "to difference (individual, historical, and cross-cultural), to contingency, to performative force, and to the possibility of change" (1). There are two points Sedgwick and Frank conclude from these observations, both of which are important for our discussion. First, a bipolar analytic framework leaves "no theoretical room for any difference between, say, being amused, being disgusted, being ashamed, and being enraged" (17) (and, for that matter, any difference between types of amusement, disgust, shame, and rage). Inspired by the work of Tomkins, Sedgwick and Frank suggest that a more analogic model, "a periodic table of the infinitely recombinable elements of the affect system," can replace, or work in combination with, the digital model (20). Second, the choice between theoretical models (analogic or digital) is not a choice between essentialism and anti-essentialism, but a choice between "differently structured residual essentialisms" (20). To understand the digital model as less essentialist than the analogic merely reflects "the habitual privileging of digital models wrongly equated with the machine over analog models wrongly equated with the biological" (18).

Consider the first point: there seems to be, when analyzing the behavior of the Oakland teenagers, no theoretical room for any difference between cruel laughter and reparative laughter. Indeed, the critical responses to the events in Oakland seem to flatter our most powerful notions of affect; all qualitative differences disappear into one category that is then swiftly condemned as *wrong*. These condemnations operate according to the most unshakable habits of procedure: first, one must *respond* to the scene of Nazi terror; second, this response must be *singular* (solemn). In this case of the Oakland high school students, we judge behavior by the presence or absence of an obligatory response (Baum). As we scan the teenagers' response and find a striking absence of solemnity, we reprimand them for their shameful behavior. Obviously, there are many different *kinds* of affect (laughter and solemnity being only two of a whole spectrum of possibilities), but we tend to figure affect as rather like a Scantron form. Instead of setting our protective machinery in motion, why not suggest that laughter is not obliged to appear in the highly moralistic, binary metaphors of solemnity/frivolity, good/bad, right/wrong and that the behavior of the Oakland students can tell other, less-predictable stories?

What of the laughter that appears in the film? The Jewish gentleman's laughter clearly doesn't respect our conventional understanding of affect: it is generated by and enters into a combination with other feelings such as fear, rage, and distress. These other affects are perhaps what prompted the students from Castlemont High School to respond so openly and disturbingly. The students' laughter at the grisly scene of a Jewish woman shot pointblank surely prompted many other audience members to think to themselves, "They laugh at that?" Rather than condemn or condone the students' laughter according to such simple binary formulas as respectful/disrespectful, mature/immature, intolerant/tolerant, we might have allowed the possibility of understanding it in more analogic terms, terms which are many-valued rather than dual-valued. We might have asked, "You laugh *like* that?" (a query which implies many different kinds of laughter are possible) instead of "You laugh *at* that?" (a query which implies a singular substance known as "laughter" that can only be present or absent in any particular context). However, we didn't. Instead, we mobilized the most powerful cultural and political forces—among which was Spielberg's visit to the Oakland high school and his speech before the student assembly, his nationwide campaign to reform Holocaust education pedagogy, and his work with then California Governor Pete Wilson to establish the Schindler's List Project—an education program that combines the teaching of the Holocaust with screenings of Spielberg's film in high schools across America.

Our current routines of theory become routine largely because they adhere too strictly to digital models of thinking. Sedgwick and Frank suggest that bipolar analytical frameworks have "so evacuated the conceptual space between two and infinity" that we boldly advocate the "inertial friction of a biologism to even suggest the possibility of reinhabiting that space" (15). In the case of "dissing" *Schindler's List*, the apparent consensus is that we must not allow abusive racist biologisms to go unchecked. The homology of laughter/solemnity, intolerant/tolerant, immature/mature is held so firmly in place that our responses to the Oakland event are automatic, and the questions we ask are governed entirely by a fear of risk. On the one hand, laughing at the violence in *Schindler's List* suggests anti-Semitism, and in order to evade this suggestion laughter is condemned. In a similar way, we avoid calling young, African American men anti-Semitic by infantilizing laughter and characterizing the young men as too young and ignorant to be truly anti-Semitic. The paranoia quotient in these formulations is staggering, but the harm it guards against simply cannot be risked. That is, by staging the crisis in binary terms, we presumably secure ourselves from any hurt that operates in opposition to (in this case) respect for Semitism. What is lost, however, is the possibility of understanding a whole spectrum of responses that are not aroused by such binaries. Even if we flirt with the possibility that the context within which the laughter occurred might complicate the apparent simplicity of the binary (e.g., the students from Oakland live with terror in their everyday lives), we do so only in order to attach ourselves more firmly to bipolar thinking (i.e., the students "barely have the context to understand their own lives" [Weston]) and, therefore, their laughter still remains *negative* and our explanations knowing and condescending. There's no evidence of any interest in finding something else to say about the affair; there's no evidence of any keen acuity, no interest in determining what exactly occurred that afternoon during the screening of *Schindler's List*. The unthinkable happened; African American teenagers laughed at the sight of Jews being murdered.

The possibility of suggesting that there was something useful or redemptive in the laughter of the teenagers has been so resolutely closed off that it seems perverse to explore other possibilities.² If we were to detach their laughter from these assumptions, we might discover other meanings awaiting us. I'll suggest just a few: first, there is the possibility that what is so comical in the scene from *Schindler's List* is what Henri Bergson would call "elasticity," or the sudden transformation of the body. Bergson wanted us to see laughter as movement, rather than a state or condition. To see the latter would be to attach some "epistemological essence" to the people whose laughter we behold.³ Instead, argues Bergson, laughter erupts not because of some change in *attitude*, but because laughter itself is the very element of change (66). Attach some moral concern and the change becomes even more striking, even more comical: the young Jewish woman approaches a German officer with suggestions on how to construct safer, more efficient encampments. Her excessive enthusiasm to cooperate amounts to a stiff adherence to the compliance-as-freedom ethic—an inflexibility made flexible when her body topples to the ground. The young Jewish woman touts an inverted but equally powerful moralism, an irrational separatist attitude ("hard work and cooperation will save us") that calls attention to her own physicality. As Bergson argues, a sudden shift from soul to body will, as a general rule, induce laughter. "Why do we laugh at a public speaker who sneezes just at the most pathetic moment of his speech?" asks Bergson (93). The answer lies, no doubt, in a moving appeal to pathos failing to divert attention away from the body as thing.

Or perhaps we can find, in this scene, a simple reversal of Bergson's notion of inflexibility. The woman's attitude is that in order to survive, one must be flexible. The compliance-as-freedom work ethic that enabled the work camps to function efficiently demands that all stiff and stubborn opposition be relaxed: "forget our anger and hatred, we must adapt in order to survive." The young woman's energetic cooperation is answered, quite without warning, with a bullet to her head, and she is made stiff. Marcel Gutwirth, summarizing Bergsonian laughter, observes that the body "collapsing like a sack of potatoes could similarly 'crack us up' by turning a live person into some sort of thing" (87). The body's inert matter is dumped down upon the woman's eagerness to rebuild the encampment. "The impression of the comic," Bergson adds, "will be produced as soon as we have a clear apprehension of the putting the one on the other" (92–93). One might assume Bergson had no particular order in mind, because in this graphic scene, a flexible, energetic body is reduced to a rigid, machine-like thing: expendable labor.

Regardless of how one might choose to define the physical dynamics of this scene, it's quite easy to imagine how an audience would have little choice but to be drawn into its comic element—despite the absence of feeling such reasoning would seem to belies (one student who was at Grand Lake Theater described the scene this way: "The woman who got shot fell funny and people just laughed").[4] However, one of the first observations made by Bergson is also, not coincidentally, the most important observation about laughter:

> Here I would point out, as a symptom equally worthy of notice, the *absence of feeling* which usually accompanies laughter. It seems as though the comic would not produce its disturbing effect unless it fell, so to say, on the surface of a soul that is thoroughly calm and unruffled. Indifference is its natural environment, for laughter has no greater foe than emotion. I do not mean that we could not laugh at a person who inspires us with pity, for instance, or even with affection, but in such a case we must, for the moment, put our affection out of court and impose silence upon our pity. (63)

Bergson's human animal can be driven by some puzzling biological motives[5]; and in an effort to sort them all out, he is thwarted somewhat by his own language (Why is emotion a foe to laughter? Isn't laughter simply a different kind of emotive response to stimuli? Can't laughter be a way of expressing affection?). After reading this passage, one might feel a bit cramped—as if the theoretical space into which we are invited is no more roomy than your average doll house (Why is affection put "out of court" to make room for laughter? Why is pity smothered by silence?). We should applaud Bergson for having the wisdom to acknowledge human motives as complex and contradictory, but we should also recognize a confined and confining style to his description of the affect system. Rather than imagine pity as "silenced," why not see it as comfortably co-habiting with laughter? Would this renovation reduce some of the theoretical bumbling that goes in such close quarters?

Perhaps—though it isn't the only way to reduce bumbling. Common to some approaches to the phenomena of human response (laughter in particular) is what some scientifically minded readers would call path analysis—a method by which causal relations are represented diagrammatically in order to show the "paths" along which causal influences travel. In its most reduced form, path analysis visualizes the separateness of each affect along only two end points of a continuum. Consider this variation of the path analysis: in *Comic Effects* (1989), Paul Lewis pauses in his consideration of the politics of comedy and social functions of humor to suggest a few common laws about *laughter*:

> When we laugh with a given character, we must at the moment feel that the subject at hand is a fitting one for amusement; when we laugh at a character, we must feel that his or her qualities are at the moment ridiculous. When a character says something he or she regards as amusing and we fail to share in the humor, our lack of identification with the character is both highlighted and intensified. (35)

Here, the "paths" are so well policed that both complexity and confusion are reduced to absolute zero. Like a traffic cop, path analysis sends us in a single direction whether we like it or not. It's not that path analysis doesn't work; on the contrary, it has enormous explanatory power. In addition, there is great relief to be found in this sort of thinking; one finds comfort in theoretical models that minimize our danger and point the way to clarity. The responses to the Oakland incident moved very quickly and with great confidence. No sooner had the bedlam begun did it quietly disappear.

In all the uproar over the events in Oakland, however short-lived it may have been, no mention was made of the brief exchange between two minor characters in the film—an exchange that takes place in a scene *immediately prior* to the one at which the students from Castlemont High School laughed. The conversation in this scene seems to point, *so plainly*, to the problem at hand: "You laugh at that?" "I have to." As suggested earlier, the laughter of the old gentleman frustrates our conventional understanding of the affect system: the laughter appears to enter into a combination with a whole spectrum of different responses, such as fear, rage, and distress. It is a remarkable moment in the film—precisely because it is so un-momentous, innocuous. Despite its seeming insignificance within an otherwise solemn narrative, I'd like to center this moment of the film and suggest the influence it may have had on the young, African American students in Oakland. The fictional gentleman in the film (who cannot but laugh at his misfortune) and the African American teenagers in Oakland (who cannot but laugh at the misfortunes of the Jews) might have mutual interests. Perhaps the laughter in the film (of the gentleman in the streets) represents a response to the utter absurdity of a situation. We may be wagering too much by suggesting that the irrational premise of ghetto life is the source of the teenagers' laughter as well. If we concede that the conditions of the Oakland ghetto and the historical significance of the day on which the film was shown (Martin Luther King, Jr. Day) both allow for the possibility that the laughter in that theater was not oppositional, but cooperative and coadjutant, as emerging from "within" the suffering witnessed on the screen, do we risk allowing what is "actually" injurious and hateful behavior to go unchecked? Certainly, but this formulation works both ways: by insisting on the latter, do we not risk allowing what is "actually" reparative and compassionate to go uncelebrated?

There is, it should be emphasized, a whole "repertoire of risk" announced by acknowledging the freedom of affects to combine with and overlap each other—not the least of which is the suggestion that the laughter of African American teenagers honors the Holocaust and its dead. I am reminded of the infamous episode of "Seinfeld" in which Jerry and his date are discovered necking during a screening of *Schindler's List*. The scene travesties one of the several prescriptions attached to representations of the Holocaust, the guidelines by which we convey strongly held feelings in "the right way," the most succinct of which were delineated by Terrence Des Pres. First, "the Holocaust shall be represented, in its totality, as a unique event, as a special case and kingdom of its own, above or below or apart from history"; second, that "representations of the Holocaust shall be as accurate and faithful as possible to the facts and conditions of the event, without change or manipulation for any reason—artistic reasons included"; and third, "the Holocaust shall be approached as a solemn or even sacred event, with a seriousness admitting no response that might obscure its enormity or dishonor its dead" (217). That *Schindler's List* could evoke arousal is perhaps no surprise to a television audience familiar with the characters of "Seinfeld" and the comic gambits the show took. That the gag offended so few does not, however, diminish its relevance to our discussion. Our laughter during this scene is directed not so much at the unimaginable overlapping of arousal and pity,[6] but the hawkish displays of outrage from the character Elaine, who happens to witness the ill-mannered, kissy-faced Jerry and his date. One might say that the gag doesn't so much "obscure the enormity of the Holocaust or dishonor its dead" as it does transgress the prescriptions attached to a representation that depends so heavily on them. Yet, these prescriptions would not have such a powerful command of our thinking, I believe, if we granted a measure of complexity to our understanding of affect and laughter in particular. Within the comic frame, where all is fair game, such prescriptions become easy targets; outside the frame, however, they are granted enormous power.

"...But Seriously, Folks!" The Fundamental Turn in Cultural Studies

Cultural forces work very hard to keep laughter in a diacritical relationship with seriousness. Why is this so? Allon White suggests, "seriousness has more to do with power than with content. The authority to designate what is to be taken seriously (and the authority to enforce reverential solemnity in certain contexts) is a way of maintaining power" (182). It doesn't matter that words and things are, *in and of themselves*, neither serious nor frivolous; what matters is that there exist rituals of power that enable us to designate what is and is not to be taken seriously. It doesn't matter that we can't say, with any certainty, that any image on the screen is intrinsically grave. What matters is that there are people who act as if they were. Structuralist theory would have it that these rituals (of deploying seriousness) constitute a sort of collective mobilization of binary codes and that these things *just happen* according to the rules of "structured structures predisposed to function as structuring structures" (Bourdieu, 72).

Scholarship aimed at exploring cultural transformation has, in recent years, eagerly announced a "turn" from structuralism—a significant and favorable shift from simple binary metaphors to their more complex effects. This turn finds its source in the spirit of Foucault's Copernican Revolution: ask not, "Is it true?" ask, "What does it do?" (Easthope, 119). We turn from binary pairings because they seldom, if ever, reveal themselves to be the stable hierarchies we expect them to be; cultural practices transgress them repeatedly. These transgressions are given their own metaphors—"carnivalization" being perhaps the most often used. "Carnival" suggests something of limits and boundaries (it is an organized program that acknowledges the restrictions of a season or the ecclesiastical calendar; it begins and it ends, it has a definable space that it occupies conditionally and temporarily). The term "carnivalesque," however, suggests something less tangible, less manageable. It can be applied to *any* text, to *any* event: James Joyce's Buck Mulligan "carnivalizes" the Catholic Mass; Jerry Lewis's impish characters "carnivalize" masculinity; Angela Carter's "the Fabulous Fevvers" "carnivalize" the female body; Frank Zappa's outrageous performances of "Bogus Pomp" and "While You Were Art" "carnivalize" orchestral music. In each of these cases, it is assumed, a binary (sacred/profane; potent/impotent; beautiful/grotesque, high art/low art) is inverted.

To know the way power functions is to know what is to be taken seriously, when to respond to things and how to respond to them. Power creates a community that sees everything that evades its grasp or threatens to expose its deficiencies in strictly negative terms (Kincaid, 25). In exchange for room and board in this community, those who calculate things according to a power discourse can be reasonably assured that things will be turned to their favor. There is no question: re-inhabiting the space emptied out by binaries risks relinquishing the defenses of such stringent thinking; my point, however, is that these defensive operations are central to the structures that are capable of deploying ritualistic terror. Re-inhabiting the space requires faith, perhaps comic faith. Bakhtin makes this point when he urges that laughter is liberation from fear, a movement from prohibitions that explain and exercise power to understandings that open and un-finalize. Bakhtin would not have us imagine laughter at the spectacle of suffering as an exercise of power that banishes seriousness from the world. Rather, laughter at the spectacle of suffering is a movement toward what he calls "true, open seriousness." Seriousness that is fearful of laughter, however, is incomplete, fanatic, pedantic, easily intimidated, oppositional, didactic, and naïve no less! We should not be attaching this kind of attitude to things we care deeply about. Binaries indeed explain, but they don't understand.

I'm not suggesting that we haven't attempted to turn from the binaries that structure our everyday lives. This "turn," however, has no clear trajectory upon which we can all agree. Whereas some scholars rush enthusiastically toward new horizons (Sedgwick and Frank are among a few), others are less optimistic. Stuart Hall, for instance, is suspicious of any "turn" that seeks to abandon binaries altogether, given that they are so resolutely tied to "real" questions of power. We are more than willing to address the limitations of binary thinking, but are we quite ready to imagine the cultural politics of laughter in any other way? In his introduction to a collection of essays by the late Allon White published posthumously under the title *Carnival, Hysteria, and Writing*, Hall asks: "What alternative metaphors do we have for imagining a cultural politics? Once the simplistic terms of the classic metaphors of transformation have been abandoned, do we also abandon the question of the relationship between the social and the symbolic, the 'play' between power and culture?" (3). Hall implies that there exists a cherished analogy between the social and the symbolic and, what's more, that this relationship should *not* be in question. To suggest that abandoning one (the "classic metaphors of transformation") would necessarily mean abandoning the other ("the social and the symbolic") is to indicate that we must *not* abandon classic metaphors, for to do so would be to disengage ourselves entirely from the only set of questions we can ask about cultural transformation. In posing the problem this way, Hall's introduction works to keep the classic metaphors of transformation outside the reach of critical inquiry altogether. The introduction is at once an epigraph for the work of Allon White and a summary of the "anthropology of binary extremism" that he, along with his colleague Peter Stallybrass, laid out in the *Politics and Poetics of Transgression* (1986); it measures the value of structural approaches to cultural transformation at the same time that it resists alternative approaches that seem "so fashionable in critical theory as almost to have acquired the status of the banal" (Hall, 21). What Hall ends up demonstrating most powerfully, however, is not so much the value of

Allon White's contribution to cultural studies as the arbitrary hold his method has over contemporary scholarship.

Hall wants to assure us that in order to avoid reproducing hierarchies of high and low (a move that he fears may defeat all efforts at repairing the problems in culture) we need only shift our attention from the hierarchies *as such* to the tangible traces of their effects. Such a shift, we are assured, reveals cultural hierarchies as "*necessarily arbitrary*—as an attempt, transcoded from one domain to another, to fix, stabilize, and regulate a 'culture' in hierarchical ascending order, using all the metaphorical force of the 'above' and the 'below'" (Hall, 23). But where does the "necessity" of these arbitrary relations come from? And why is this "necessity" transcoded from culture as such to our own critical inquiries? These questions are never clearly addressed, and it is likely because Hall really believes they needn't be. Examine, in the passage below, how deftly he reassures us of the necessity of his method:

> The classification of cultural domains into the self-sufficient and apparently transcendental distinctions of high and low is revealed, by the operation of the carnivalesque, and by the transgressions of pleasure, play and desire, as an exercise in cultural regulation, designed to make cultural practices into a *formulation* which can then be sustained in a binary form by strategies of cultural power. The fact that the cultural field cannot by stabilized in this way does not prevent the exercise in boundary construction being attempted again, in another place, for another time. *Cultural practices are never outside the play of power.* And one way in which power operates in the apparently decentered sphere of culture is through the struggle to harness it, to superimpose it, to regulate and enclose its diverse and transgressive forms and energies, within the structure and logic of a normative or canonical binary. (23–24; second emphasis added)

Hall begins with a fairly innocent description of the social implications of transgression by suggesting that the "transgressions of pleasure, play and desire" are capable of destabilizing any binary that works to regulate culture. In turn, however, power will always make efforts to restore these regulatory binaries once again. Fair enough. But Hall doesn't stop there: "Cultural practices," he continues, "are never outside the play of power." Although this claim reads much more like a hypothesis than a summary of what comes before, it is expected to play upon us as the latter and, in so doing, command the status of unimpeachable fact. To say that power can always be exercised in response to transgression is one thing; to say that such transgressions are never outside the play of power is quite another. Hall's claim, whether he intends it or not, blurs the line between a discourse *on* power and the discourse *of* power.[7] This blurring occurs, perhaps, because we cannot really *know* power; we cannot, supposes

James Kincaid, "produce explanations of power that hope for anything more than being powerful, that somehow partake of the power they are not explaining but entering into" (17). Our explanations of cultural practice tend to be nothing more than explanations of power—even when the cultural practice we try to clarify is an ostensibly subversive one. Terry Eagleton's explanation of one such practice is so powerful that it doesn't know where to stop: the carnival is "a licensed affair in every sense, a permissible rupture of hegemony, a contained popular blow-off as disturbing and relatively ineffectual as a revolutionary work of art" (148). Hall's explanation functions similarly. At best, the claim that "cultural practices are never outside the play of power" is a *non-sequitur*. At worst, it is a Mickey Finn at the cocktail party: by the time we reach the end of the paragraph, we never knew what hit us.

Though often bracketed as givens, claims such as the ones discussed above are central to current trends in theory, and Stallybrass and White's "anthropology of binary extremism" is but one variation. Theirs is a devastatingly totalizing vision, one that creates a field in which only certain rules apply, rules by which we can distinguish which are the most incisive questions (the serious ones), and which ones are simply banal (the frivolous). Hall is disturbed by scholarship that seeks to abandon hierarchical metaphors altogether, but it is never entirely clear why alternative metaphors of cultural practice should be so abhorred. Our only clue is that they are now "so fashionable in critical theory as almost to have acquired the status of the banal" (21). Such estimations suggest that the academy is susceptible to the same complex of hierarchical binary ordering as those of culture at large. Let's take, for instance, the following hierarchy as it pertains to "academic scholarship":

Table 2.1

Low	High
Fashionable	Un-conforming
Banal	Incisive
Common	Noble
Irresponsible	Responsible
Politically Reckless	Politically Fair

It would appear odd, on the one hand, that these implicit hierarchies should introduce a collection featuring an essay that struggles to examine critically the social reproduction of "seriousness" in the academy. On the other hand, it isn't odd at all, as one reads through White's brief but compelling study of this "fundamental hegemonic maneuver," that we should get trapped so easily in the very workings we are mapping. "Metaphors of Transformation" ask that we take White's work *seriously*, and is quite unable to do so without, simultaneously, minimizing other types of scholarship. What begins as *epigraph* to the life of Allon White quickly becomes *epitaph*—a window onto eternity through which we bear witness to White's "anthropology of binary extremism" in the process of canonization. Whereas the epigraph simply introduces the work of an author, the epitaph locates the power of the author's mind. Even better, it *produces* the power of the author's mind. Better still, it produces the power of the "general movement" to which the author's mind belongs (Hall, 25). In this way, power becomes institutional, rather than authorial.

What is staged as a "fundamental turn" in cultural studies is little more than a powerful consolidation of those essential assumptions central to the very theoretical models from which we have supposedly "turned." As Sedgwick and Frank have suggested:

> the structuralist reliance on symbolization through binary pairings of elements, defined in a diacritical relation to one another and no more arbitrarily associated with the things symbolized, has not only survived the structuralist moment but, if anything, been propagated ever more broadly through varied and unresting critique—critique that reproduces and popularizes the *structure*, even as it may complicate an understanding of [its] *workings*. (1)

The structural approach advanced by White, Hall, and others detaches itself from the binary pairings they critically examine with "commonplaces" that are themselves governed by these pairings. White, echoing Hall's tune, wants us to remember that "the point of interest is not the commonplace idea that the dominant languages dominate, but rather how the difference is inaugurated and maintained in educational institutions of language" (White, 129). White and Hall have made it more than clear they want little to do with what is "common." Nevertheless, this "commonplace idea" becomes the very impetus behind their own rigorous method; its exclusion is necessary to their theoretical operations.

Commonplaces such as "dominating languages dominate" or "cultural practice is never outside the play of power" can be deployed not simply to secure the necessity of "sober realism" (as Eagleton chooses to phrase it), but to squelch the possibility of its opposition: the festive, the comic, the joyous. "Absurdly one-sided though this may be," admits Eagleton, "it is a fact that throughout class history the fate of the great majority of men and women has been one of suffering and fruitless toil. The dominant narrative of history to date has been one of carnage, wretchedness and oppression" (182). This claim doesn't self-evidently justify the analogy between history and its narration; instead, it appeals to our common sense (How else can an appeal to "fact" be "absurdly one-sided?"). Why should we speak only of a history of suffering? The answer is because it is the dominant narrative of history. This mimetic fallacy fashioned as intense moralism, however, only works to silence the joyous, comic, and festive. Why? Precisely because these narratives are not dominant. The only way such narratives can speak themselves is first to acknowledge the dominance of that "other" history and, somehow, emerge on the other side. In other words, the joyous, comic, and festive must always acknowledge their subordinance—must always "show their papers" as they walk the streets, so to speak.

The logic of Eagleton's analogy is remarkably similar to that of N. F. Blake—the subject of Allon White's essay on academic language and the social reproduction of seriousness. In the introduction to his dictionary of non-standard English literature, Blake notes that "non-standard language will...often signal comedy, because the serious matters will be handled by the major characters" (in White, 131). White, however, refuses to let this bit of common sense pass unchallenged, and insists that Blake has his logic reversed: "It is not that non-standard equals comedy *because* the serious matters will be handled by the major characters. What is serious and what is comic, what is 'major' and what is 'minor' is a function of the social reproduction of seriousness, itself achieved through the equation of humour with non-standard English" (131). Eagleton's lament for the political futility of Bakhtin's carnival and its incapacity for the accurate narration of history evades, by way of creaky, reactionary rhetoric, the possibility that festive laughter already pays respect to suffering in its own way and therefore has enormous historical validity.[8]

For the moment, however, laughter appears best suited for the playground. What is reserved for the classroom is the seriousness with which we respect the history of suffering. One wonders just how the Castlemont High School students regarded the dark interior of the movie theater that afternoon of January 17, 1994—as playground or classroom. Perhaps they didn't feel there was a choice to be made. Judging by the responses to the laughter that day, however, it seems clear that most adults thought those few bad apples simply needed to reminded of the difference between the two. The organizer of the field trip (who insisted the students see *Schindler's List* instead of *House Party 3* much to the students' disappointment) responded to the intense media scrutiny by insisting that the incident was simply about "high school students not acting mature." He should have known, suggests Sander L. Gilman, that "anything and everything at a school assembly is understood by high school students as potentially the butt of laughter" (281). The manager of the movie theater, sharing Gilman's wisdom in these matters, said the behavior of the students was no worse than any other example of "bad etiquette" he's witnessed when the lights have gone down ("Laughter"). What we see in these moves (of dividing practices into binaries like bad/good, immature/mature, or even playground/classroom) is "not just that children are socialized into accepting the difference between work and play," suggests White, "it is in the daily reproduction of the play-ground/ classroom division that the category of serious knowledge is actually produced as a social practice, an institutional norm, and a ruling idea" (133). White's playground/classroom distinction can very easily explain the workings of power in the case of dissing *Schindler's List*. It is impossible, however, to explain how this "ruling idea" has attained its commanding position in our discourse. We are asked to consent to a curious notion that it doesn't *matter* that "power" has no relation to thoughts intrinsically or essentially important. What matters is that ritu-als of power have real effects, that their insubstantiality does not destroy the force of their operations—even if it means suppressing the behavior of a certain group of people. In effect, power isn't nearly as powerful as those who believe in it. And those who believe in it take it very seriously. Furthermore, the rewards can be very real indeed: exactly three weeks after the incident that made it famous, Castlemont High School received the "Courage to Care Award" from California Governor Pete Wilson at a ceremony held at the Simon Wiesenthal Center's Museum of Tolerance in Los Angeles. A happy ending for all.

Conclusion: Springtime for Hitler

In the case of dissing *Schindler's List*, I have suggested that we shift to the arguably "imagined" effect of laughter (a liberating vision of the world) at the cost of suppressing particularity. In other words, we should be confident confronting the chance we take in failing to acknowledge satisfactorily that the students from Castlemont High School may *re-ally* have unleashed hateful, anti-Semitic laughter. To ask if the laughter that echoed in the theaters of Oakland in the early winter of 1994 rang entirely "outside" the reach of those mechanisms of power that caused the very real plights depicted in the film is, perhaps, imaginative. It is no less imaginative, however, than other questions. The difference is that we are more *comfortable* with other questions. They're asked more often and with more certainty that they're the *right* questions—perhaps even the *only* questions. Why do we return to the binary metaphors of power even when we admit their ideal status is a figment of our imagination? The answer is that the effects of these metaphors are so very real. The effects of laughter, though indeed quite "real," don't necessarily share the lasting energy of the effects of power (so the story goes).

Understanding that laughter is not subordinate to seriousness is certainly a good start, but it is only half the picture. In his chapter from *Rabelais and His World* entitled "Language in the Marketplace," Bakhtin gives us what is arguably his clearest (and, sadly, most often ignored) description of laughter's difference from power:

> For the correct understanding of these carnivalesque gestures and images we must take into consideration that all such gesticulations and verbal images are part of the carnival as a whole, infused with one single logic of imagery. This is the drama of laughter presenting at the same time the death of the old and the birth of the new world. Each image is subject to the meaning of the whole; each reflects a single concept of a contradictory world of becoming, even though the image may be separately presented. Through its participation in the whole, each of these images are devoid of cynicism and coarseness in our sense of the words. But these images, such as tossing excrement and drenching in urine, become coarse and cynical if they are seen from the point of view of another ideology. If the positive and negative poles of becoming (death-birth) are torn apart and opposed to each other in various diffuse images, they lose their direct relation to the whole and are deprived of their ambivalence. They then retain the merely negative aspect, and that which they represent (defecation, urination) acquires a trivial meaning, our own contemporary meaning of the words. (149–150)

As these words suggest, Bakhtin was well aware of the tendency to locate carnival laughter within a dialectic. But as I suggest in the previous chapter, carnival images do not exist in opposition to official culture, they belong to an innate and singular logic of their own that appears oppositional only from a certain viewpoint. When images of death and birth are held firmly in a dialectic of antagonism, a different world emerges: a world of power. In carnival, however, images of death and birth are not oppositional; like the infinitely re-combinable, but finitely multiple qualitative differences of affect described by Tomkins, the images of Bakhtin's carnival are finite in number, but infinitely re-combinable in their various mutated forms (shit, urine, breath, foul language, laughter, the feast, the wedding, the movie screening). Laughter at the sight of death is not forbidden in Bakhtin's view of the world, because such laughter is understood as emerging from "within" death. Only from another point of view does such laughter take on its coarse and cynical meaning. There is, of course, a powerful bias toward this line of thinking, which is the primary reason why some contemporary readers find Bakhtin's statements about the liberating possibilities of festive laughter to be naive, optimistic, or utopian. This new wave of Bakhtin scholars has sobered up since the initial intoxication with *Rabelais and His World* and has sought to make him more compatible with Foucauldian thought.

Fortunately, alternatives to such skepticism are plentiful and prevail even under the most desperate of conditions. Steve Lipman's marvelous study of Jewish jokes, *Laughter in Hell: The Use of Humor during the Holocaust*, provides an invaluable insight into the subtlety, complexity, and necessity of Jewish humor. The following joke comes from Lipman's book:

> Two Jews had a plan to assassinate Hitler. They learned that he drove by a certain corner at noon each day, and they waited for him there with their guns well hidden. At exactly noon they were ready to shoot, but there was no sign of Hitler. Five minutes later, nothing. Another five minutes went by, but no sign of Hitler. By 12:15 they had started to give up hope. "My goodness," says one of the men. "I hope nothing's happened to him."

Read one way, the punch line ("I hope nothing's happened to him") strikes us like a miscue, or a flubbing of lines, because we expect something else, something that is more fully engaged with the play of power: instead of *Rogue Male* and *Valkyrie* we get *Rosencrantz & Guildenstern are Dead*. The joke's success seems to hinge on its ability to quickly shift our perception from the serious to the frivolous. To be sure, the joke's structure fits Kant's description of the comic as an intense expectation that comes to nothing. The gentlemen's disappointment is anything but grievous; they accept the "nothing" (Hitler's failure to arrive) so gracefully, and with such down-to-earth concern that they seem like oafs. In fact, you would sooner find these two gentlemen in the Pickwick Club than in the Jewish resistance, for only a true Pickwick would transgress the rules (of power, plots, and counter-plots) so nonchalantly, so blindly.

On the other hand, perhaps the joke springs from the same source that produced the lyrics compiled by survivor David McCullough for his "Holocaust Cantata": "Hey! There's no life like life at Auschwitz!" (Clines). These words reveal what Freud, in his 1928 essay "Humor," calls a characteristically humorous attitude toward experience: what appears to be a strange intoxication with one's own doom is actually a form of resistance. The humorist acknowledges suffering, but his relationship to the world is not reducible to it. In other words, he refuses to allow suffering to have the last word, or the only word, about human experience. "There is no doubt" says Freud, "that the essence of humour is that one spares oneself the affects to which the situation would naturally give rise and overrides with a jest the possibility of such an emotional display" (216). Later in the essay, Freud encounters some mild difficulty in preserving the integrity of these "natural" affects (anger, frustration, fear, horror, despair) by slyly acknowledging the alluring possibility that there is nothing unnatural (or abnormal, or pathological) about humor (217–218). In fact, Freud cannot help but find in humor something "fine and elevating" (216) and wonders if there is still much to be learned about the nature of the superego's command over what seems to be a surprisingly complex affect system (220–221). Although there is, in the joke about the two would-be assassins, genuine concern for Hitler's non-appearance, it is a concern that stems from the faith that ours is a world free of danger, free of suffering—an eternal springtime (even for Hitler). Any other attitude would risk giving too much to the force and reach of Nazi terror. Read this way, and the joke differs not just from the "nothing-from-something" structured joke, but also from much of the anti-Nazi humor that emerged at the same time.[9] The two gentlemen lack the hostile spirit of the tendentious jokester who cares only about the gratification afforded by psychic expenditure and who seeks to provide an outlet for his aggressive impulses.

Another remarkable example from Lipman's book that also dodges the tendentious joke structure goes like this:

> During the onset of Nazi terror, an elderly Jew was walking down the streets in Berlin when he was stopped by two storm troopers. "Halt, Jew!" they cried, and proceeded to interrogate him. "Who is responsible for all of Germany's troubles?" they demanded. The Jew looked at them and said, "Why, the bicycle riders and the Jews." "Bicycle riders?" they snorted. "What foolishness. Why the bicycle riders?" "Why the Jews?" replied the man. (206)

Even before it reaches the punch line, the joke is steeped in the topsy-turvy logic of oppressed/oppressor. In this case, the German oppressor assumes the role of the oppressed in order to qualify his oppression of the Jews while simultaneously creating an opportunity for the Jewish man to reverse the roles once again, perhaps with obscenity or hostility. Recognizing a losing game when he sees it, the Jewish man instead chooses to expose the logic of Nazi terror for what it is: absurd; the blame for "Germany's troubles" is directed at bicycle riders and Jews so that the logic of oppressed/oppressor will snuff itself out. Instead of a tendentious joke, we have what Freud calls an "innocent" joke: a nonsensical representation that *appears* to be lacking in substance but is actually of great substance. The substance of the above joke is independent of the joke itself and is, as Freud would say, "the substance of the thought, which is, by means of a special arrangement, expressed as a joke" (*Jokes,* 109). The substance of the thought, in this case, is that the role of "anti-Nazi, pro-victim" is not the only role available to Jewish consciousness—perhaps not even the best. "Pro-victim," after all, is part of the social fantasy upon which German Fascism thrives. "The whole Fascist ideology," argues Slavoj Žižek, "is structured as a struggle against the element which holds the place of an immanent impossibility of the very Fascist project: the 'Jew' is nothing but a fetishistic embodiment of a certain fundamental blockage" (127). Žižek would likely argue that anti-Nazi, pro-victim jokes are politically useless because they fail to articulate the Symbolic in this way. By denying they are a social symptom, Jews only produce evidence of the antagonistic nature of the Symbolic that German Fascism needs. The above joke, however, seems to function differently than the anti-totalitarian joke of which Žižek is so skeptical. The storm troopers do indeed ask, "Who is responsible for Germany's troubles?" not in order to find evidence of some positive cause of social negativity, but to mark the Jew as "a point at which social negativity as such assumes a positive existence" (127). But the Jewish man's response, "the bicycle riders and the Jews," is not at all antagonistic, it willingly provides the storm troopers with exactly what they need. In fact, it does so in excess. German Fascism doesn't need "Jews," it needs the thing that the "Jews" occupy, the thing that virtually *any* object could occupy: its own "immanent impossibility." The Jewish man understands all too well that he is being excluded from the Symbolic. But instead of returning to the Real simply as a paranoid construction of "the Jew," he comes back as a bicycle rider as well. The joke shows that the anti-Semitic idea of "the Jew" has no more to do with Jews than it does with bicycle riders, watchmakers, luggage clerks, or brown mustard. The joke, then, seems less like "part of the game" than a different game altogether. For this reason, Žižek would do well to replenish his definition of "the anti-totalitarian force of laughter." I'm sure he'd be delighted to discover some jokes that are truly fine and elevating, that don't necessarily flatter coarse and cynical visions of the world. We'd be delighted, too, if we did the same. Although the "underlying message" of Jewish jokes that circulated throughout World War II was "decidedly *pro-victim*" (Lipman, 192), it is clear that some jokes signaled very different messages and offered up different ways of organizing and understanding experience.

I have illustrated above how laughter can resist being reified by an antagonistic model of analysis and have suggested the multiple and sometimes conflicting meanings that laughter can take. Our culture's response to a few high school students at a screening of *Schindler's List*, however, gives little evidence that the availability of these possible meanings is even known, much less valued. Many who spoke of the incident were determined to fix the meaning of laughter according to a digital model of right/wrong. The easy part was understanding that no laughter at the sight of a murdered Jew could be "right." Such a move preserves much (a tradition of solemnity regarding the Holocaust; the centrality of power to our current ways of thinking) but risks nothing (the possibility that laughter is reparative, not destructive; the availability of other equally useful theoretical models of culture and affect). However, once we imagine laughter as *different* rather than oppositional and antagonistic, we can begin to consider how laughter "not only coincides with a high value placed on life and with a responsibility to fight to the end for this life—but it is in itself an expression of this high evaluation, an expression of the life force that eternally triumphs over any death" (Bakhtin, 198). This view of laughter, so similar to Freud's definition of humor, poses a risk most contemporary critics have sought to excoriate, correct, and atone for. We'd prefer Bakhtin say something else. The price we pay by making Bakhtin speak within the hermeneutics of suspicion so common to this post-structural moment is that we lose the possibility that "laughter" is qualitatively different from and free to co-exist with anger, frustration, fear, horror, and despair, without being subsumed by them in the spirit of some metaphysical, ordering principle.

But such a risk, argues Sedgwick and Frank, "is far from being obviated by even the most scrupulous practice of digitalization" (18). What these two thinkers mean by "digitalization" is akin to the sort of ordering principle Bakhtin denounces in his writings on the Rabelaisian chronotope. We are speaking, however, of two different historical moments when we speak of the Rabelaisian purge of false hierarchies sanctioned by religious ideology and the "political vision of difference that might resist both binary homogenization and infinitizing trivialization" so characteristic of current theoretical writing (15). There is, however, a certain alliance between the "dialogics" of Bakhtin and the "analogics" of Sedgwick and Frank's "Shame in the Cybernetic Fold: Reading Silvan Tomkins" in that they take aim at the same problem: both are resolutely determined to restore the possibility of inhabiting space emptied out by binary ordering principles. Sedgwick and Frank add to their "politics of difference" a Bakhtinian confidence in taking chances. Remember, Bakhtin never hesitates to promise us the world: "Complete liberty is possible only in the completely fearless world"; "the grotesque liberates man from all the forms of inhuman necessity that direct the prevailing concept of the world"; "laughter purifies the consciousness of men from false seriousness, from dogmatism, from all confusing emotions." This litany of essentialisms from *Rabelais and His World* is something of a nuisance to many critics—so much so that most feel compelled to steer away from Bakhtin altogether.[10] It is perhaps more a habit of criticism than anything else, this fear of risk. Gary Saul Morson and Caryl Emerson have rightly turned our attention to Bakhtin's own thoughts on this matter: a brief response to the editors of the Russian literary journal *Nova Mir*, written in 1970. Bakhtin's concern in this short piece, written just months before his death, is that criticism suffers from what he calls "a certain fear of the investigatory risk"—a condition that leads, inevitably, "to a predominance of truisms and stock phrases" in scholarship (1). What Sedgwick and Frank's own work offers us is confidence to confront the risk—a confidence that begins with the assurance that the "binarized, highly moralistic allegories of the subversive versus the hegemonic, resistance versus power" are no less essentialist than allegories of qualitative difference among these two oppositions (16). In turn, Bakhtin's writings suggest the possibility of giving flesh and bone to that "inertial friction" that opens up the theoretical space so evacuated by binary thinking. Bakhtin would call this inertial friction "festive laughter," and it functions not as something *oppositional* to "official culture"—as many semiotic applications of Bakhtin's work would have it[11]—but as something *different*. Perhaps it is through our presumptions as readers that we detect in Bakhtin's writings on festive laughter a "stiff binary nature" (Emerson, 165). Reading Bakhtin within the metaphysics of power, however, is like adding too much starch to the linen: it leaves scant breathing room and virtually no flexibility.

Several years have passed since laughter erupted in that Oakland movie theater, though I trust it has erupted many times since (at more "appropriate" moments, I'm sure). Since then, not much has been written about the uneasy relationship between laughter and representations of the Holocaust (see Gilman). Roberto Begnini's *Life is Beautiful* (1998)—the story of an Italian Jew who protects his son from the horrors of the death camp with his clownish pranks—gave American audiences a suitable frame for their laughter. It also sparked mild interest in the social function of humor in dealing with the memory of the Holocaust—though much of the discussion about the film reveals, still, how little we understand about laughter. A typical defense of *Life is Beautiful* relied on the conventional oppositional framework of comic/tragic, and the habitual privileging of the latter over the former (e.g., "the first half of the film is funny, then it takes a serious turn," or "in spite of its brilliant comic moments, Begnini's story is really about the horrors of the Holocaust"). Perhaps this response is the most complicated one we can articulate at the moment. But we can do better. There is hope in the fact that our laughter continues to bewilder us from time to time.

Excursus: Frank Zappa versus
the Los Angeles County Museum of Art

In 1986, a small ensemble known as the Ear Unit (two percussion, two keyboards, a flute, and a clarinet) asked to work with composer Frank Zappa. As Zappa recalls, "they commissioned a piece to be performed at the Monday Evening Concerts at the [Los Angeles] County Museum. They specifically requested an arrangement of one of the tunes on the guitar album [*Shut Up and Play Yer Guitar,* originally released in 1981]—a piece called 'While You Were Out.' So I did it. And I did it here on computer" (in Birchall). When the ensemble came by Zappa's home to pick up the parts, he played them the electronic realization on the Synclavier (a portable digital system that is capable of reproducing "real" sounds) so they might have an idea of how the piece should sound. After listening to the piece, the ensemble complained that it would be too difficult to play (the Synclavier's programming capabilities are so advanced that one is able to compose music so complex that only computers would be able to perform it accurately). Zappa insisted that the ensemble either play it correctly or not play it at all. This, of course, was an impossible ultimatum, since the event had already been announced on the program.

The problem was solved in this manner: Zappa simulated the sound of all the instrumental parts with the Synclavier and made a digital recording of the piece. Computer generated music sheets were made so that each musician could see his or her part, and Zappa supplied individual analog cassettes that the musicians could listen to while they practiced feigning the piece. Claimed Zappa, "that frees the performer to do what he really wants to do, which is look good on stage. He doesn't have to worry about a single note, because the machine takes care of that." Zappa assured the ensemble that they need only listen carefully to their own private analog cassettes and master their respective parts: "You guys work on your choreography, and bingo, we have the missing link between electronic music and 'performance art'" (in Birchall). When the time came for the musicians to perform, however, the musicians were unable to play the special digital VHS video tape recording Zappa had made for them on the Sony PCM-F1 digital processor. The musicians, not knowing the difference between VHS and Beta, couldn't use the digital recording and were forced to use one of the analog rehearsal cassettes, which put out a miserable wall of hiss into the recital hall.

Despite these unfortunate acoustics, nobody knew the difference. Nobody realized what was occurring on stage. "Nobody knew that they didn't play a note," recalls Zappa. "Not the man who runs the Monday Evening Concerts, not Morton Subotnick, not either the reviewers for the *Los Angeles Times* or the *Herald Examiner*" (in Birchall). It is no wonder that Zappa had appeared to have pulled a fast one. Those who did find out what actually occurred at the county museum thought it was all a swindle. According to Zappa, "it caused a scandal, to the point where three members of the group actually apologized to the musical community and swore they would never do anything like it again" (Zappa, 1986; 50).

We might be tempted to praise Zappa for letting the computer outwit the humans, just as we might be tempted to feel as angry as those poor, deceived music patrons. The fact that we could feel either during this performance should make us stop and realize how difficult it is to distinguish one level of half of the binary (computer music good) from its pair (real music good). To suggest either one is to be sure of who is aping whom. To suggest both, however, is to suggest something entirely different. The problem is that without the binary of human/machine, we're not sure what happened. The musicians simulated the computer, which simulated the musicians, who in turn simulated themselves. In short, we are tempted to suggest nothing happened during the performance of Zappa's "While You Were Out." It might appear that without some sort of homology, we are left with only one possibility: there was no "there" there.

But surely something was there, and this something is trying to tell us that analytic frameworks predicated strictly on binaries will always come up short. If we were to simply ignore the rigidity of the binary "human/machine" and the values to which these oppositions are locked, we would be able to say that what took place in that marvelously carnivalesque performance at the county museum was a dramatization of the ascent of digital technology. Zappa's remark about his quest for the "missing link" is quite apt here: Homo Sapiens, by "aping" the Syncla-vier, act as a missing link between some ancient analog past—one of quaint chamber music recitals that warm the satisfied patrons—and the dawn of digital technology. But we must remember that the Synclavier, too, is "aping"; computer music "apes" human, ambient, "real" music. As one bounces back and forth between the two oppositional elements ("human"/"machine") they no longer appear oppositional, but dialogic. Remember, what Zappa wished to do was provide the link between electronic music and performance, rather than between "fake music" and "real music." In short, Zappa wished to play with technology in order to carnivalize the seemingly essential binaries we use to think about music. The two ("human"/"machine") elements are no longer policed by a structuring force of "real/fake." Instead, they play freely within a field leveled by a carnivalizing force. As it was suggested in the introduction of this project, the idea of carnival and the festive laughter that pronounces it, is to see oppositions as if they existed in paradoxical rather than diacritical relations.

Notes

1.   I am, for the moment, less interested in Tomkins' own writings than I am in Sedg-wick's and Frank's shameless appropriation of them. Sedgwick and Frank do not, in the opening essay of *Shame and its Sisters: A Silvan Tomkins Reader*, "introduce" Tomkins (1911–1991) to a large, largely literary readership so much as expose "the broad assumptions that shape the heuristic habits and positing procedures" of this same readership. Tomkins's hypothesis regarding human motivational response goes something like this: the affect system is comprised of a finite number of innate responses (interest-excitement; enjoyment-joy; surprise-startle; distress-anguish; fear-terror; shame-humiliation; contempt-disgust; anger-rage) that are infinitely re-combinable. Influenced heavily by systems theory and cybernetics, Tomkins's work relies on both digital and analogic forms of representation—the former characterized by a dual-valued system (such as "on/off" or "1/Ø") and the latter by a many-valued system (such as a color-wheel or a periodic table of elements). Sedgwick and Frank were drawn to Tomkins's "complex phyllo dough of the analog and the digital" because of their own "motivational intuitions" that a range of difference was sadly lacking in current theoretical trends. I share the editors' love of Tomkins's daring work, but for the purposes of this essay I am more interested in sharing Sedgwick and Frank's gut feeling that there is "much to learn first by observing the automatic nervous system of a routinized dismissal of [Tomkin's hypothesis] in the terms of today's Theory" (23).

2.   I am purposely deflecting the issue away from "what really happened" towards a far more interesting but relatively impoverished idea "what might have hap-pened" in the hopes of showing that what is at stake here is *not* the event itself, but our culturally scripted responses to the event (which itself may be culturally scripted). That is, I don't mean to, in Sedgwick's words, "hypostatize, here, 'the way it actually did' happen, or to deny how constructed a thing this 'actually did' may be—within certain constraints. The realm of what *might have happened*

but didn't is, however, ordinarily even wider and less constrained, and it seems conceptually important that two not be collapsed; otherwise entire possibility of things' *happening differently* can be lost" ("Paranoid Reading and Reparative Reading," 37).

3. See Sedgwick who, in her essay on Diderot's *La Religeuse*, claims that we should read the character Suzanne's ignorance not in terms of what "epistemological essence it attaches to her as if allegorically but more simply *what it makes happen*, then there are readier answers to be had" (38).

4. Spolar, Christine. "The Kids who Laughed Till it Hurt; Students' Reactions to *Schindler's List* Fires Racial Tensions." *The Washington Post* 10 (Mar. 1994: final ed.).

5. I remember many years ago my sister breaking the awful news that my best friend had passed away while I was away. She met me at the door as I carried my bags inside and told me that he was dead. Strangely, as she was telling me the news, she broke into a huge grin. Embarrassed by her own emotional response to such a grave situation, she covered her mouth with her hand as she began to giggle and tried to explain, "I'm sorry, I don't know why I'm laughing." A similar episode occurred years later when I told my roommate that my girlfriend had just telephoned to explain that she was breaking up with me. He began to chuckle, but apologized immediately, "Forgive me. I always laugh when I hear news like this." Rather than being furious with either of them, I recall sharing their uneasy laughter.

6. Rather than call this overlapping of affects "unimaginable," one might call it "imaginable but forbidden." Raymond Federman, while watching *Schindler's List*, imagines the similarly (un)imaginable overlapping of hunger and pity: "Interesting, there does not seem to be as much popcorn munching for this movie as with other movies"; and "Has anyone ever studied the semiotic implications of popcorn eating while watching a Holocaust movie?" (201).

7. In the opening pages of her *Solitude and the Sublime*, Frances Ferguson points out a similar issue at stake in the work of Peter de Bolla and Neil Hertz: "This distinction between discourses 'on' and discourses 'of' underwrites de Bolla's interest in effecting the kind of collapse we earlier observed Hertz making in relation to [Thomas] Weiskel; the effort to avoid making statements about any kind of consciousness on the basis of discourse eventuates in the more or less explicit claim that it is impossible to be *about* something without also being *of* it" (18). Stuart Hall's claim about the reach of power illustrates the ease with which one effects the collapse de Bolla points out and upon which Ferguson elaborates. I do not believe, however, in the inevitability of this collapse. The larger purpose of this essay is to suggest ways of speaking about power *without* being of it.

8. Twice, in *Rabelais and His World*, Bakhtin cites the words of Alexander Herzen: "It would be extremely interesting to write the history of laughter" (59; 92). Having once understood these words to mean simply "it would be extremely interesting *to document the appearance of laughter throughout Western history*" (ancient laughter, laughter in the middle ages, Renaissance laughter), I can now find in them another meaning: "it would be extremely interesting *to write history as laughter*." Given his totalizing vision of laughter, Bakhtin was capable of writing such a history. His concept of "reduced laughter" allowed him to follow "the track left by laughter in the structure of represented reality" even though "the laughter itself we do not hear" (*Problems of Dostoevsky's Poetics*, 164). History as laughter is a fuller, richer history since laughter does not exclude suffering. I'm not suggesting that histories *of* laughter or *of* suffering are superficial or uninteresting (see Morris's *The Culture of Pain* for an especially fascinating example of the

latter). Still, what would it mean to reverse the direction of Eagleton's logic? "The dominant narrative of history to date," argues Eagleton, "has been one of carnage, wretchedness and oppression; and any Bakhtinian celebration which has not in some sense gone through this belief and emerged somewhere on the other side is politically futile" (182). One might argue that a simple reversal is impossible, since no Bakhtinian celebration can be torn from the reality of carnage, wretchedness, and oppression.

9.   A characteristic anti-Nazi joke told in the ghetto would look like this:
    What is an Aryan?
    The rear end of a Proletarian. (Lipman, 99)
    The joke is verbal, tendentious, and obscene—hallmarks of the type of joke frequently discussed in Freud's *Jokes and Their Relation to the Unconscious*. The joke's success depends not simply on word play, but on the bawdy allusion to a bit of anatomy as well. The word "Proletarian" is reduced to one of its constituent parts, and this reduction functions also as an act of exposure (when you drop a pair of syllables from the word "Proletarian," you expose the "butt" of the joke). This bit of political "de-pantsing," however, is quite different from the joke I'm interested in examining here.

10.   "There is," some argue, "a possibility that Bakhtin's extremely complex body of work might be reduced to a series of slogans and clichés—a situation suggested by Edward Said's remark in a published dialogue with Raymond Williams that he hates even to use the word 'dialogical' because of its associations with the 'cult of Bakhtin.'" (in Booker and Juraga, 2). Said's comment makes me even more certain that Bakhtinian criticism has been split, more or less, into a devastatingly predictable and persistent couple: it is either a matter of sobering up what would otherwise be an aberration in Bakhtin's *oeuvre* (here we find Terry Eagleton, Peter Stallybrass and Allon White, Michael Gardiner, and others) or a matter of tossing Bakhtinian clichés indiscriminately about (I'm not sure which scholars comprise this latter contingent, but the members of the former camp insist they're out there). Booker and Juraga's reading of Bakhtin defies such a categorization.

11.   See Sebeok, Thomas A., ed. *Carnival!/Umberto Eco; V. V. Ivanov; Monica Rector.* (New York: Mouton, 1984).

3

Comic Perception

In this chapter, I will move away from more our traditional understanding of laughter (as an explosive guttural response to the ridiculous, as Saturnalian excess, as the transgression of culturally prescribed boundaries, or simply an interesting theme) to a less-known conception of laughter formulated by Bakhtin in his book on Dostoevsky, as a "form-shaping ideology." What Bakhtin means by "form-shaping" is not always clear; Gary Saul Morson and Caryl Emerson see it as a kind of "force" or "impulse" that "shapes an image, a scene, or a work" and "imparts a carnival sense of the world and of change" (464). Bakhtin argues that although laughter does not ring out in Dostoevsky's novels (as it does in Menippean satire), it nevertheless leaves its trace. That is, we can find a trace of laughter "performing its work of artistically organizing and illuminating the world. We find such traces in the structure of images, in numerous plot situations, and in certain characteristics of verbal style" (Bakhtin, *Problems of Dostoevky's Poetics,* 165). For Bakthin, laughter is more than a guttural response; it is "a specific aesthetic relationship to reality" (164). Laughter is a condition or predisposition, if you like, to see the world a certain way: as open and incomplete. Laughter can "grasp and comprehend a phenomenon in the process of change and transition, it could fix in a phenomenon both poles of its evolution in their uninterrupted and creative renewing changeability: in death birth is foreseen and in birth death, in victory defeat and in defeat victory, in crowning a de-crowning" (164). Because laughter is best understood as a general attitude (call it a comic attitude), one can find it in what would seem the least likely of places, even *Crime and Punishment.*

Or Henry James? For the critic, the comic in Henry James is a specific difficulty. Nearly four decades ago, Richard Poirier lamented the fact that "[t]he extraordinary amount of published criticism on the works of Henry James does not encourage the idea that the element of comedy in his novels is either strong or pervasive" (7). His book, *The Comic Sense of Henry James: A Study of the Early Novels,* tries to demonstrate how "attention to comic expression in James's early novels can, in fact, lead us through the language to his most vitally personal meanings" (7). As these words from the preface suggest, the "comic expression"—so often ignored in James criticism—is nevertheless subordinated by Poirier to other meanings, including "qualities of style" and the "psychological identity of the author" (7). In other words, the comic expression itself is not an object of study. Recognizing this, Leon Edel complained that Poirier failed "to give us a working definition of the comic sense or to attach James's comedy to a tradition" (87). Though it is true that Poirier gives little evidence to suggest that James's achievements owe *anything* to writers in the comic tradition—the occasional reference to Twain or Shakespeare doesn't help—it is clear that there *is* a definition of comedy at work in his book, one that has worked for us for years. Poirier claims that James's comedy has been ignored because it is "usually on the very surface of the action and language" (9). The assumption is obvious: comedy is superficial, and readers who disregard the superficial in favor of "the supposedly deeper realms of meaning" will necessarily overlook it (10). James's comedy, it seems, is a purloined letter, and Poirier is our Dupin.

As admirable as they are, Poirier's efforts to include the comic in the overall "meaning" of James's writings rely on the trite association of comedy with "the simplest forms of excitement and entertainment" (10), and on the assumption that James's comedy (or comedy in general, for that matter) reveals itself only at the most "obvious" moments—moments where the reader is most amused, excited, or pleased. We are led to think that a great deal of critical effort is required to encounter meaning in James, whereas very little is required to encounter, as in *The Europeans,* "the excitement of overhearing some of the wittiest dialogue in James's fiction" (8). The central problem, of course, is not that one has to be carefully selective when pursuing the comic in James, that one must necessarily exclude the difficult, later writings. Rather, the problem lies with the inadequacy of our definition of comedy. Ronald Wallace suspects as much in the opening pages of his book-length study of comedy in Henry James, *Henry James and the Comic Form.* He argues, as Lionel Trilling does in his study of E. M. Forster, that "[t]he lack of any extended critical discussion of James's comic manner and affinities with a comic tradition arises from a misunderstanding of the comic seriousness" (3). What James teaches us about his own comic sense differs little from what Bakhtin teaches us about folk humor and the carnivalesque. It may include the serious and become what Bakhtin calls "true open seriousness"—a critical philosophy that dates as far back as Socrates (*Rabelais and His World,* 121). "In world literature," claims Bakhtin, "there are certain works in which the two aspects, seriousness and laughter, coexist and reflect each other, and are indeed whole aspects, not separate and comic images as in the usual modern drama" (122). Here Bakhtin briefly quotes Euripides, but he will revise and expand on this idea using the work of Dostoevsky. "True open seriousness" will later be known as "reduced laughter"—a critical feature of Dostoevsky's work. It is also a critical feature of James's work and emblematic of his comic seriousness. It's a deliberately self-critical attitude, highly expressive, and uncompleted.

Borrowing from James's own comments in *The Scenic Art: Notes on Acting and the Drama,* Ronald Wallace proposes that comic seriousness "suggests little connection with high animal spirits. It seems a matter of invention, of reflection and irony" (4). It is the middle term that I'd like to take up as important to our understanding of James's comic sense. The activity of moral reflection—a theme that I find to be thoughtfully worked out by Martha Nussbaum in her writings on James and moral philosophy and, to a greater degree, by Bakhtin in his writings on Dostoevsky and the dialogic principle. To associate comedy with something as sober as philosophy is an admittedly odd and even deceptive critical maneuver, but what this chapter will show is that, when defining James's comic sense, it is also a necessary one. "The Beast in the Jungle" (1903) is a fine starting point for two reasons: first, it has so many elements that we commonly associate with the Jamesian, not the least of which is the story's theme of the unlived life; second, and more important, the plot or action of the story is not only found in the dialogue, the plot *is* the dialogue. One could say that "The Beast in the Jungle" is made up of a series of conversations taking place over the span of some years. To be precise, the story is characterized by dialogue on the threshold—that is, conversation that takes place at "the gates of the other world," of another way of Being (Morson and Emerson, 60). John Marcher, of course, presumes there will come a moment in which he will "have got across" to the other side and discover the real truth about himself (James, "The Beast in the Jungle," 251). That this moment never arrives—or arrives as its own failure to arrive, a missed opportunity—is what makes "The Beast in the Jungle" so typically Jamesian. But it is also what makes the story typically Bakhtinian. In his book on Dostoevsky, Bakhtin describes the threshold moment as "the moment of crisis, the decision that changes a life (or the indecisiveness that fails to change a life, the fear to step over the threshold)" (*The Dialogic Imagination,* 248). John

Marcher and May Bartram seem to live not in biographical time, but in threshold time. Yet, the two are not always in step. Quite the opposite: Marcher and May understand the threshold in very different ways. In the broadest sense, Marcher understands it as tragic, May as carnival. Or, in more precise terms, the one sees the threshold as fate, the other as possibility. That we read James' story (and much of James in general) only from the tragic point of view and not from the carnival point of view is the single most important obstacle to understanding James's comic sense. In this chapter, I will turn an ear to Marcher and May's dialogue in search of reduced laughter, or what Martha Nussbaum calls in her essay on Proust's *Remembrance of Things Past,* "smiling conversation" (280)—a term that signifies both openness and flexibility (in the figure of the smile itself), as well as the absolutely essential Other and the achievement of community (in the activity of conversation). In James, reduced laughter is a means of critical reflection; it is a form-shaping, meaning-bearing attitude, and not (merely) a literalization of an expressive response ("Ha!"). This is not to say laughter is *always* reduced in James (it rings out quite frequently in what James called his "ugly little comedy," *What Maisie Knew*), but this chapter asks that we understand laughter a certain way, because it seldom reaches the level or condition of being *heard.* If we are to understand anything about James's comic sense, it's that it is extremely quiet. So rather than associate laughter with the atmosphere of the carnival or marketplace, we might instead associate it with a certain mode of moral and philosophical reflection, one that understands the world as essentially open and incomplete, and that we, as social beings, must remain open to others.[1]

By doing so, we will be attaching James's comic sense to the unlikely but convenient tradition of the carnivalized novel. Unlikely because critics usually associate the modern carnivalized novel with Joyce or Pynchon, with heteroglossia, excremental imagery, and orgiastic excess. Convenient because when one speaks of carnivalization in the novel, one speaks of "a vision of humanity and culture as they really are: responsible to the core, creative at every moment, and, above all, unfinalizable in their very essence" (Morson and Emerson, 90). Only a genuine appreciation of dialogue permits this vision, and it is in James that one finds this appreciation. But if, in Dostoevsky, Bakhtin finds the dialogic principle idealized, it is in James that one often finds the inverse.[2] The oddness of a story like "The Beast in the Jungle" is that it dramatizes the spectacular failure of dialogue to bring about change in Marcher's consciousness, and for this reason might be misread as a striking example of how *un*-comic James can be. But meaning in James often finds its fullest expression in things not happening, in failures, flaws, finitude, incompleteness, and (particularly in "The Beast in the Jungle") the "tragically necessary blindness" of characters.[3] David Lodge, in his preface to *The Spoils of Poynton,* reminds us that James's style is "much concerned with consciousness, with representing mental acts of perception, speculation and inference" and that the typical Jamesian plot "is conveyed through the consciousness of a single character whose understanding of the actions and motives of others is necessarily limited and often unreliable" (130). For this reason, a close study of James's work means attending to hesitation, fragility, and extravagant but untimely epiphanies as bearers of meaning. That so many Jamesian characters fail to reach the heights of their potential testifies to James's persistent preoccupation with unfinalizability, responsibility, and creativity.

The focus of our attention, then, should not be Marcher's "Beast," but his dialogues with May Bartram. And although we know little about her—Eve Sedgwick concludes that "we are permitted, if we pay attention at all, to *know* that we have learned very little" about her (*Epistemology of the Closet*, 199). I argue that it is possible to know as much about May's consciousness—not just what it understands but *how* it understands—as we know about Marcher's. We should begin by suggesting that May is something much more than a witness to Marcher's secret, a mirror to his thoughts and ideas, complicit with them in every way. Unless we do allow for her expansion, we risk losing sight of the idea that May Bartram's consciousness functions quite differently than Marcher's. May Bartram understands consciousness in terms of its potential, its freedom and openness, and (in Bakhtinian language) its "unfinalizability." She struggles to baffle Marcher's doom by performing what could be called a comic reading of his predicament: there are no "Beasts," only other people. May Bartram, if understood in the terms I set out in this chapter, may be read as an ideal Jamesian agent—one whose "finely aware and richly responsible" character, whose comic distrust of falsifying abstraction, and whose gift for intimate dialogue can shed light on other potentially ideal Jamesian agents who, for now at least, exist only in the margins of our readings. Better still, May Bartram can be our guide to a fuller understanding of what one may call comic perception in Henry James.

I

"The Beast in the Jungle" is a tale that can be summed up with any verbal formula: it is a love story, a mystery, a Freudian case study, a

Hegelian fable, an illustration of Lacanian sublimation, an allegory of homosexual panic, a portrait of the philosopher's compulsion to turn life into a riddle, and so on. It is not unique in this respect. The story is a fine example of James's late style, one marked by a conscious suspension of meaning that demands "a little extra attention" of the reader (Gard, 3). *The Turn of the Screw* (1898) is perhaps James's most popular story in this tradition, and it's in the Preface to the New York edition of 1908 where James defines his motive for this aesthetic experiment: "it is a piece of ingenuity pure and simple, of cold artistic calculation, an *amusette* aimed at catching those not easily caught" (120). That's us James is referring to, by the way, the readers not easily caught. Each of the narrative elements that go into James's piece of "child's play"—all of which, James tells us, were wrought with "pains, as indeed great pains were required"—are nothing more than "blanks" upon which a "created expertness" (us again) might "proceed to read into them more or less fantastic figures" (123). It's no wonder that "The Beast in the Jungle"—which is, along with *The Turn of the Screw* and "The Figure in the Carpet," a successful experiment with this form—has been puzzled over more than any other of his works. So much so that one can't help but imagine, as Sedgwick says in reference to Lionel Croy, that "[t]he interpretive paths by which any sense is to be made...are completely paved" (*Tendencies,* 79).

What I'd like to suggest is that there remains a story to be told about "The Beast in the Jungle"; a path to be paved, marked out, or traced; a different point of departure that might lead us to some fuller understanding of James's comic sense. To begin with, one might assume that there is a comic reading to be made of James's story, a reading only someone as savvy as Eric Solomon could produce.[4] May Bartram is that savvy. For as much as John Marcher is precisely that sort of imaginative mind not easily caught, but unquestionably catchable, May Bartram is the one figure who might baffle Marcher's doom. Not by indulging in the "secret," but by trying to expose it for what it is: not a definitive, incontrovertible truth, but a wide-open and endless text that promises fantastic and ever-changing possibilities. That Marcher fails to register or articulate the precise nature of his moral development, and that May Bartram suffers the most for this failure, is not unique to the Jamesian tradition. On the contrary, this failure is precisely what makes Marcher a Jamesian exemplar: by the story's end, he has learned nothing, or perhaps the wrong thing.[5] It is my hope that by shifting our focus away from the "Beast," Marcher's haunting apprehension, and towards the (failed) dialogic relationship that May Bartram encourages, we may begin to articulate a conception of what the comic means for James.

There is no question that "The Beast in the Jungle" occupies itself most of all with John Marcher's secret expectation—a secret shared with no one but May Bartram, who chooses to dedicate her life as a witness to Marcher's "strange complexion." The two soon form a "goodly bond" that is broken only when May succumbs to a "disorder" in her blood. What May Bartram leaves behind for Marcher is the assurance that his "Beast" had, in fact, leapt; that the *thing* that was to occur, did occur. At last, however, Marcher is faced "with the fact that he was to profit extraordinarily little by the interest May Bartram had taken in him" (253). What Marcher earns, instead, is the knowledge that he is, in James's famous phrase, "*the* man...to whom nothing on earth was to have happened" (261). But why does Marcher profit so little, when so much is to be gained? My aim is to explore the verbal exchanges of John Marcher and May Bartram and the way the two fail to reach true *dialogic* interaction in the Bakhtinian sense. For if it's true that May Bartram does indeed fight to the end for a comic plot, it remains to be explained *why* Marcher is unable to recognize her struggle. The subsidiary purpose of exploring this relationship is twofold: (a) to distinguish Bakhtin's concept of "dialogue" from mere verbal exchanges of two or more people and (b) to demonstrate how the dialogic creates comic loopholes through which we escape laws, systems, "Beasts" of burden.

It's not that John Marcher and May Bartram don't *speak* very well. On the contrary, the two share several wonderful dialogues; in fact, the real commotion of the story is found in the five dialogues James gives us. But these exchanges do not become fully dialogic in the Bakhtinian sense because Marcher never fully interacts with May. For Marcher, May Bartram's role is to be witness to rather than participant in his consciousness, his process of becoming finalized. In fact, the exchanges in the story are entirely capable of proceeding without May Bartram's presence, as is evidenced by this passage:

> "I don't think of it as—when it does come—necessarily violent. I only think of it as natural and as of course above all unmistakable. I think of it simply as *the* thing. *The* thing will of itself appear natural."
> "Then how will it appear strange?"
> Marcher bethought himself. "It won't—to *me*."
> "To whom then?"
> "Well," he replied, smiling at last, "say to you."
> "Oh then I am to be present?"
> "Why you *are* present—since you know." (224)

May Bartram's *actual* presence is incidental to John Marcher, since he is entirely capable of "bethinking himself." May Bartram's response to this curious statement that she's somehow been present without even knowing it is that of one who has been reminded of having neglected a crucial component of a theorem or formula: "I see" (224). But this is precisely what May Bartram is: an essential component in Marcher's aesthetic task. Her place and function within the system is as empathic witness to the "eventness" of Marcher's event. It would be quite wrong to see May Bartram as responsible for the way Marcher sees her. If the above passage is any indication of May Bartram's remoteness from Marcher's view of her, then perhaps it would be best to say that what Marcher calls "May Bartram" is nothing more than a witness to his monologic imagination; she is an ideal, and purely formal, sympathetic listener. From Marcher's perspective, however, it is difficult to see May Bartram as anything but an accomplice. Furthermore, the fact that May Bartram "knows" does not change the basic character of this secret. In other words, if the "real truth" of Marcher is monologic precisely so long as nobody knows about it, it is no less monologic just because May Bartram *does* know. If, indeed, Marcher "had thought himself, so long as nobody knew, the most disinterested person in the world, carrying his concentrated burden, his perpetual suspense, ever so quietly, holding his tongue about it, giving others no glimpse of it nor of its effect upon his life, asking of them no allowance and only making on his side all those were asked" (227)—which is to say, *if* John Marcher is, without May Bartram, nothing short of a monologic hero, the author of his own empty form and lifeless interaction in the world, then we must submit to the fact that he remains so even as May Bartram becomes his confidante. "There was that in his situation, no doubt, that disposed him too much to see her as a mere confidant, taking all her light for him from the fact—the fact only—of her interest in his predicament" (226–27).

This point affords us an excellent opportunity to distinguish Bakhtin's idea of dialogue from mere "interaction." The problem with those definitions that see dialogue as requiring simply some kind of "interaction" between at least two people is that it is entirely possible for more than one person to share a single point of view and for one person to have several. A dialogic environment is a necessarily tension-filled environment. If there is any tension in "The Beast in the Jungle," it stems not from the verbal exchanges of John Marcher and May Bartram—on the contrary, the tension stems from the fear that the two might have *nothing* to talk about. In short, John Marcher does nothing but allow May Bartram to enter into his own monologic field of vision. He has, in May Bartram, an "insider." Caryl Emerson puts it this way: "[a]ny instinctive clustering of like with like threatens to reduce my 'I' and its potential languages to a miserable dot. Those who surround themselves with 'insiders'—in heritage, experience, appearance, tastes, attitudes toward the world—are on a rigidifying and impoverishing road indeed" (223).

John Marcher and May Bartram walk a rigidifying and impoverishing road. Their verbal exchanges only sound the depths of monologic truth in order to finalize it. Marcher's "secret" is, in Bakhtin's words, his alibi for "Being": the thing that absolves him of any responsibility in a base and petty world. "The great rooms caused so much poetry and history to press upon him that he needed some straying apart to feel in proper relation to them" (215–16). Not being inclined to having "proper relations" is, as Sedgwick has demonstrated, precisely what remains secret. Marcher's only relation is with his own immutable law—whatever that may be. As Sedgwick puts it, Marcher's "readiness to organize the whole course of his life around the preparation for it—the defense against it—remakes his life monolithically in the image of *its* monolith of, in his view, the inseparability of homosexual desire, yielding, discovery, scandal, shame, annihilation" (*Epistemology*, 204). I would replace "monolithically" with "monologically," for this is precisely what Marcher is: a hero of monologism. And if Marcher is, indeed, a hero of monologism, then the "Beast in the Jungle" is a powerful tale of the danger of living monologically, the danger of living systematically, the impossibility of *becoming* without the "surplus" of a genuine Other. This is not to say that Marcher is not collaborating with someone, but let's not call that someone May Bartram. Rather, let us call it Marcher-made Law—a formidable partner indeed. Says Marcher, "One's in the hands of one's law—there one is. As to the form the law will take, the way it will operate, that's its own affair" (232). The hero of monologism, as John Marcher so clearly indicates, is a hero of systems—of language, meaning, and power. Madame Merle may be James's finest creation in this regard. To Madame Merle, the self is really just the sum total of one's possessions—"I've a great respect for *things*!" she says (223). "One's house, one's furniture, one's garments," even "company" is looked upon as something one "keeps" (223). She says this to Isabel in the hope of convincing her that the self has no boundaries, that it "overflows into everything" and "flows back again" (223), but one gets the sense that this bold analysis applies to Madame Merle alone. *She* may have no boundaries, but this is because she extends her self so far, and all are subject to her gravitational field.

To *be* is not to communicate but to possess, and because Madame Merle possesses so much (she even says she understands Henrietta Stackpole "as well as if I made her!"), because she is so thoroughly *cultivated* (so much so that Isabel is led to think that Madame Merle "had all of society under contribution"), she has the appearance of being the center of the world "wherever she might be" (212). Madame Merle's Ptolemaic view of things is not entirely lost on Isabel, who decides very early on that the great lady's only real fault, interestingly enough, is that she is "too final" (213).

Madame Merle is perhaps James's supreme example of the power of monologism. She is a wholly finalized being whose expressions, often inaudible, are aimed not at seeing how others see her or seeing how others see themselves, but at bringing everything into her own field of vision so as to eliminate the need of surplus meaning. Whereas Miss Stackpole sees all sides and likes to think she takes great interest in what others have to say for themselves, Madame Merle sees things her way and takes great interest in speaking for others. For instance, when Mrs. Touchett says she never exhibited the smallest preference for anyone else but Mr. Touchett, Madame Merle mentally observes, "For anyone but yourself"; and when Mrs. Touchett adds, "I never sacrificed my husband to another," Madame Merle silently comments, "Oh no...you never did anything for another!" (228). Such "mental observations," which the narrator admits contain a "certain cynicism" worth accounting for (we are told it stems from her having been excluded from the distribution of Mr. Touchett's property), are evidence of a furiously stubborn monologic imagination.

Like Madame Merle, Marcher believes that he himself is the sole expression of himself. In this way, he is an obstacle to genuine dialogue. He regards his *becoming* as answerable only to a single Law, finalized, complete, and wholly contained "event" within his own consciousness. It is something only he will see, something he will face himself, something that will change, perhaps even annihilate, only him. It is something "striking at the root of [his] world and leaving [him] to the consequences" (223). Bakhtin calls this point of view aesthetic seeing "beyond its bounds": "insofar as it pretends to being a philosophical seeing of unitary and once-occurrent Being in its eventness, aesthetic seeing is inevitably doomed to passing off an abstractly isolated past as the actual whole" (*Towards a Philosophy of the Act,* 17). Imagine the verbal exchanges of John Marcher and May Bartram as if they belonged to the solemn services of confession and you will quickly discover that John Marcher is actually faithless. He uses confession as a way of bringing about the unitary event of Being—which, argues Bakhtin, is counter to faith ("Author and Hero," 143–45). In short, the solemn monologues of John Marcher work to defeat possibility in the name of some guaranteed "finalizability." This is why he returns, over and over again, to ambush May Bartram with questions. He is in search of the final word about himself, as if it's his divine right to be finalized. Marcher asks, "You mean it has come as a positive definite occurrence, with a name and a date?" To which May Bartram replies, "Positive. Definite. I don't know about the 'name,' but oh with a date!" (249). In light of these words, it might be easy to see that May Bartram, too, sees Marcher's *becoming* as something singular, unequivocal, and unique. In doing so, however, we would risk suggesting that John Marcher and May Bartram think alike—and clearly they don't. Perhaps it would be better to suggest that May Bartram never confuses Marcher's "Beast" with his genuine *becoming*.

Who, then, is May Bartram? Is she a victim of unrequited love? Is she a sacrifice to Marcher's "Beast" who, like Dorothy Wordsworth in *Tintern Abbey,* must disappear in order to allow the author-hero to establish himself? What, finally, do we *know* about May Bartram? If one were asked to guess, one would find it rather easy to regard her as nothing more than a "consolidation and fortification" of Marcher's Beast (206). We know, however, that only Marcher is capable of such workmanship. We come closest to May Bartram precisely at those moments when the Beast is weakest, when it is on the brink of complete dissolution. When May Bartram asks what Marcher "sees" in her point of view, he senses the terrifying possibility that "it's all a mistake":

"A mistake?" she pityingly echoed. *That* possibility, for her, he saw, would be monstrous; and if she guaranteed him the immunity from pain it would accordingly not be what he had in mind. "Oh no," she declared; "it's nothing of that sort. You've been right."

Yet he couldn't help asking himself if she weren't, thus pressed, speaking but to save him. It seemed to him he should be most in a hole if his story should prove all a platitude. "Are you telling me the truth, so that I shan't have been a bigger idiot than I can bear to know? I *haven't* lived with a vain imagination, in the most besotted illusion? I haven't waited but to see the door shut in my face?"

She shook her head again. "However the case stands *that* isn't the truth. Whatever the reality, it *is* a reality. The door isn't shut. The door's open," said May Bartram. (246)

May's rhetoric of *initiation,* rather than *resolution,* is perhaps what vexes Marcher the most. May spends much of the story (as she does in the above passage) restoring everything to the present tense. The past is of no concern to May Bartram, because "*that* isn't the truth" ("that" being, as Marcher rightly fears, his years of deliberation). In other words, May wants Marcher to step out of his novel of ordeal. Rather than being a "consolidation and fortification" of the Beast, May Bartram is its leading antagonist. It is only when we posit the "Beast," as John Marcher himself does, as the center of all meaning do we see that nothing that passes from May Bartram's lips should ever betray his Law. This is how John Marcher sees things: "the effect on him was of something co-ordinate, in its high character, with the law that ruled him. It was the true voice of the law; so on her lips would the law itself have sounded" (250).

Yet, Marcher is never satisfied by May Bartram's words. They only confound him—perhaps because she never acknowledges the "Beast," never confuses John Marcher's "truth" with some immutable Law; she merely acknowledges something "different," (246) "[s]omething new," (246) "something more," (247) and "something else" (247). Put another way, May Bartram struggles to help John Marcher find his "loophole," his way out. Even as John Marcher presses her to admit to him that the "thing" that was to happen has indeed happened, May Bartram speaks of the "thing" not as a "Beast," but as a "loophole":

> "You've had it," said May Bartram.
> "But had what?"
> "Why what was to have marked you out. The proof of your law. It has acted. I'm too glad," she then bravely added, "to have been able to see what it's not"... On this slowly she turned to him. "Did we ever dream, with all our dreams, that we should sit and talk of it thus?"
> He tried for a little to make out that they had; but it was as if their dreams, numberless enough, were in solution in some thick cold mist through which thought lost itself. "It might have been that we couldn't talk?"
> "Well"—she did her best for him—"not from this side. This, you see," she said, "is the other side."
> "I think," poor Marcher returned, "that all sides are the same to me." Then, however, as she gently shook her head in correction: "We mightn't, as it were, have got across—?"
> "To where we are—no. We're here"—she made her weak emphasis. "And much good does it do us!" was her friend's frank comment. "It does us the good it can. It does us the good that it isn't here. It's past. It's behind," said May Bartram. "Before—" but her voice dropped. (250–51)

These are not the words of a woman who is aiding and abetting John Marcher's "Beast," though much of the story lends itself to the view that May Bartram is, in fact, conspiring with Marcher. Nor are they the blunt, oppositional (or "counter-monologic") words of a lion-tamer. If we see May Bartram as a *foil* to all of this hysteria, then we perhaps might begin reading her as if she were another brave Henrietta Stackpole who "went into cages" and "flourished lashes, like a spangled lion-tamer" (*Portrait of a Lady,* 110). But these are not May Bartram's methods; she is more comic than Miss Stackpole. May Bartram is the soda water in Marcher's face, not the flourished lashes at the feet of the Beast. The extent to which Marcher is rescued is the extent to which he is willing to see and think dialogically and adopt what Sedgwick quite rightly calls May's "different" and "more fluid" ways of understanding the secret (206). What May Bartram reveals to Marcher is *not* the figure in the carpet, but the absolute approval of his desire to find one, and the wisdom to see that his figure could be boundless and limitless. That Marcher never finds a figure in the carpet, never applies the "created expertness" needed to produce the evidence of his own Law, does not undermine in the slightest May Bartram's perspective. Because *he* doesn't understand May Bartram doesn't enjoin a necessary failure on our part to do the same. May would laugh at Eric Solomon's joke, that he had found the figure in the carpet, and cheer its campy claims to precision and fact. Marcher would not.

II

Although Bakhtin tends to criticize the modernization of the novel for "reducing" festive laughter to mere irony, parody, or satire, he also speaks highly of another sort of "reduced" laughter. In a lamentably brief section of the Dostoevsky book, Bakhtin claims that, "[u]nder certain conditions and in certain genres, laughter can be reduced. It continues to determine the structure of the image, but is itself muffled down to the minimum" (164). Reduced laughter gives Dostoevsky's novels a "carnivalistic-fantastic atmosphere" (164). It isn't easy to ignore the fact that the laughter one finds in Dostoevsky's novels is hardly the sort one finds in those of Rabelais, though it is Bakhtin's claim that both function in the same way. Though laughter does not ring out, we nevertheless can see it in the literature of the nineteenth and twentieth centuries and in Dostoevsky in particular: "the track left by laughter in the structure of represented reality" (175). Bakhtin's examples of reduced laughter in *Crime and Punishment* and *The Idiot* tend to be exaggerated instances of carnival's ambivalent logic: Raskolnikov's dream (in which he reenacts his murder of an old woman) is a typical carnival combination of laughter and death. In the latter novel, the element of carnivalization can be seen in the image of Prince Myshkin. "Wherever Prince Myshkin appears," writes Bakhtin, "hierarchical barriers between people suddenly become penetrable, an inner contact is formed between them, a carnival frankness is born" (174).

Bakhtin also notes how Myshkin's ability to "penetrate social barriers" functions justifiably as evidence of the carnivalistic manner, just as his inappropriate speech is evidence of "carnivalistic frankness" (174–75). Such examples link the great Russian novelist to a specific literary tradition: ancient Menippean satire. What one hears in Dostoevsky's novels are faint echoes of a kind of laughter that rings out much more fiercely in the works of Dickens, Hugo, Balzac, Diderot, Voltaire, and Rabelais. Carnivalization in the novels of these authors, says Bakhtin:

> made possible the creation of the *open* structure of the dialogue, and permitted social interaction between people to be carried over into the higher sphere of the spirit and the intellect, which earlier had always been primarily the sphere of a single and unified monologic consciousness, a unified and indivisible spirit unfolding with itself... A single person, remaining alone with himself, cannot make ends meet even in the deepest and most intimate spheres of his own spiritual life, he cannot *manage* without another consciousness. One person can never find complete fullness in himself alone. (177)

What Bakhtin describes here is not simply the novel as carnival, but carnival as a sphere of moral perception and philosophical reflection. Nowhere in the above description passage does Bakhtin stress the invocation of the politics of inversion, the transgressive activities of the lower bodily stratum, or even the parodic hybridization of different literary styles—what many critics see as the "carnivalesque energies" central to the development of the novel.[6] M. Keith Booker, in his *Joyce, Bakhtin, and the Literary Tradition* (1995), sees *Ulysses* as a carnivalized novel largely because of its "various outrageous Rabelaisian motifs" (80). "Joyce parodies the strict Catholic definition of intercourse by having Bloom own an erotic photograph showing the 'anal violation by male religious... of female religious'... an image that links up with the earlier blasphemous (though subtle) suggestion that Joseph and Mary may have had anal intercourse...in order to maintain her technical status as a virgin" (74). Images such as this, argues Booker, help to make Joyce's work function as "a carnivalesque celebration of physicality and marginality" (80). There is no doubt that these images do indeed help. For Bakhtin, however, the carnivalized novel is too rich and complex to be reduced to a set of ritual inversion motifs.[7] To her credit, the critic Margaret Rose acknowledges Bakhtin's rich and complex analyses of carnival forms—but only as a way of distinguishing his ideas from the prejudices of the Russian formalists, and not as a way of re-conceptualizing the carnivalized novel in general (166). In all of Bakhtinian criticism, not enough stress is placed on the repeated claim that carnivalized novels are characterized largely by the open structure of dialogue and the inadmissibility of conclusions.

By broadening the scope of carnivalization in this way, Bakhtin is able to find echoes of Menippean satire not simply in more outrageous novels like *Ulysses,* but in novels where laughter is significantly reduced, like *Crime and Punishment.* Take, as an example, the above passage from *Problems of Dostoevsky's Poetics* in which Bakhtin explains what carnivalization in the novel makes possible.

Carnival, when understood as broadly as Bakhtin understands it here, seems less like a world "of topsy-turvy, of heteroglot exuberance, of ceaseless overrunning and excess where all is mixed, hybrid, ritually degraded and defiled" (Stallybrass and White, 8) and more like a rather sober, though no less comic, realm of human perception and philosophical reflection. Readers of Henry James will recognize that his writings may very well belong to the tradition of the carnivalized novel. But because laughter simply doesn't ring out very fiercely in James, one may really only grasp his comic sense as exceedingly intimate moments of reduced laughter, the hallmark of the modern carnivalized novel.

What, then, does something characterized precisely by its absence from a text *look* like? Tyrus Miller wonders as much in *Late Modernism: Politics, Fiction, and the Arts between the World Wars* when he questions how "physically embodied laughter [can] become virtual in language, 'reduced,' sedimented in textual forms" (55). As unclear as Bakhtin's concept of reduced laughter is, so says Miller, it is nevertheless quite provocative and can even help to identify the loosening of symbolic unity characteristic of late-modernist literature. What sort of utterance, wonders Miller, does a subject denied any stable place in the universe, any firm ground from which to judge the just and the true, *make*? The answer is, though it comes not without some reservations, *laughter*—"the only appropriate response in this nonsensical world from which authenticity has been banished" (61). Not satirical laughter, since the satirist's view of the world depends upon stable positions in both ethical norms and in knowledge, but mirthless, self-reflexive laughter—the sort described by the servant Erskine in Beckett's *Watt* (1953): "the mirthless laugh is the dianoetic laugh, down the snout—Haw!—so. It is the laugh of laugh, the *risus purus,* the laugh laughing at the laugh, the beholding, the saluting of the highest joke, in a word, the laugh that laughs—silence please—at that which is unhappy" (in Miller, 59). This mirthless laughter, says Miller, is "a pure laughter in which all subjectivity has been extinguished" (64).

But what Miller has a hold of is the laugh that rings out. Reduced laughter, however, is laughter that is without any direct expression. Rather than a specific utterance engendering a concrete, bodily response, reduced laughter is a general attitude toward the world, a "form-shaping ideology." Miller's error lies in the conceptualization of reduced laughter as a theme whose function it is to serve as the specific philosophical content of a work. Bakhtin speaks of this general attitude when he refers to Shakespeare's tragedies (*Rabelais,* 122; "Forms of Time," 199). For although it would be easy to multiply examples of visible, sonorous laughter in, say, *Hamlet* and *Macbeth* (from the cheerful gravediggers in the former and from the drunken night porter in the latter), one would be too easily tempted to "reduce" them to minor ingredients in order to diminish their explanatory power.[8] Bakhtin asks us to understand reduced laughter as a form-shaping, meaning-bearing attitude, and not (merely) as a literalization of an expressive response. Reduced laughter is in the quiet fidelity of Cordelia, not the noisy histrionics of the Fool. Reduced laughter is a kind of carnival spirit that struggles to shape the course of things and strives for an ever-expanding consciousness. Meredith speaks of it when he writes about Molière's farces: "The *Misanthrope* and the *Tartuffe* have no audible laughter, but the characters are steeped in the comic spirit" (51). The value of Bakhtin's concept of reduced laughter is that it helps us recognize that a comic hero's relationship to the world is not reducible to his chuckles and gurgles, just as the tragic hero's relationship to the world is not reducible to his howls and sobs. For all his curiosity about reduced laughter, what it looks like and what it means, Tyrus Miller finally declines to pursue it. Instead, he simply isolates examples in late-modern literature of "nonhuman, nonpersonal" laughter, "mirthless laughter," and "self-reflexive laughter" (63). Reduced laughter is unnecessarily reduced to visible content, to an interesting theme.

The simplest way to describe reduced laughter is as an expression of the basic openendedness of things; it is, in Bakhtin's words, the "open structure of dialogue." So it seems, more so in the Dostoevsky book and its revisions than in the Rabelais book, that laughter and dialogism are mutually defining. And one should not assume that the former's influence in texts couldn't be traced in texts that don't ring out with laughter. To do so is to assume that reduced laughter is best understood as the scattered eruptions of literal, guttural snorts made virtual in a text ("Haw!"). It is more useful, perhaps, to suggest that reduced laughter in James's "The Beast in the Jungle" functions, structurally speaking, not unlike the "open secret" of homosexuality. That is, if homosexual content can be understood through the articulations of the unspeakable, or what Sedgwick calls a "thematics of absence" (201), then perhaps the comic element in James can best be understood through the articulations of the laughter that does not laugh. There is no doubt that one can find in a text such as "The Beast in the Jungle" the visible residue of homosexual content,[9] but to read solely for visible residue is to read "straight." When one reads queer, such residue is provocative but superficial. Similarly, one may encounter in James's story the visible residue of the *risible*: "I was of course an ass" (220); "such a feature in one's outlook was really like a hump on one's back" (228); "for there was, always, if nothing else, the hunchback face" (228); "the most harmless of maniacs" (229); "It isn't that I *am* a blockhead?" (246); "I shan't have been a bigger idiot than I can bear to know?" (246); "The creature beneath the sod *knew* of his rare experience, so that, strangely now, the place had lost for him its mere blankness of expression. It met him in mildness—not, as before, in mockery" (257). Such language has an obvious debunking function: to encourage a comic perspective. This perspective is at home in a comic world in which "Beasts" are just paper tigers and "hunchbacks" are king; it is a world of gaiety and laughter. But do we halt, as Poirier would, at the "the very surface of the action and language" in James's story? What the surface language suggests is that yet another story is waiting to be told, one that might be called "The Hunchback of Weatherend." This text enjoys a certain extra-territoriality from the one being told by Marcher's "Beast." Yet, the shadowy appearance of the Hunchback of Weatherend, whose aberrations threaten to identify Marcher as the "funniest of the funny," is not itself a critical end but a means to a different set of possibilities than those afforded by interpretive paths already paved.[10] Perhaps this possibility is close to what Bakhtin means when, in *Rabelais and His World,* he speaks of "the defense of gay truth and the right to laughter" as a liberation from the gloom of seriousness and suffering (174). Imagine that Bakhtin isn't simply describing the Prologue of the Third Book of *Gargantua* but is defining the task of the modern critic as well.

The danger here, as Gary Saul Morson and Caryl Emerson have already predicted, is the "fast and loose application" of this concept—a fault that these authors find even in Bakhtin's own work. The danger, more precisely, is that reduced laughter is defined in such a way that one is perfectly capable of finding it everywhere. Bakhtin takes the absence of laughter as proof of its pervasiveness "much the same way as Freudians take the absence of evidence as proof of repression and therefore as the strongest kind of evidence" (467). But Bakhtin's way of tracing laughter where it does not ring out situates him more comfortably within a rhetorical-heretical tradition than in a paranoid-analytical tradition, for "reduced laughter" is anything *but* a model of deciphering. When one reads for reduced laughter, one's aim is not to unveil hidden meaning the way analysts do, but to keep things unfinished and open-ended the way rhetoricians do. There is no sense in arguing which approach—paranoid-analytical or rhetorical-heretical—is better suited to determining what should and should not be said about a text. There is, however, a great deal of sense in making the distinction between the two. Regardless of whether the former's applications are oftentimes just as "fast and loose" as those of the latter, one can say with a good deal of confidence that the paranoid-analytical model of reading is close to prescriptive these days.[11] The rhetorical-heretical model, however, is far from prescriptive. Besides, when attempting a more rhetorical style of reading, one is perhaps better off playing "fast and loose" as we shall see in this book's epilogue. The phrase seems to fit in so well with the great narrative of comedy. After all, comic narratives are narratives of escape. The basic comic plot is also one of movement, of getting out of tight situations, of freedom, of seeking escape hatches and loopholes. For Bakhtin, being purified by laughter is a bit like finding a loophole through which to escape the grievous conclusion that otherwise awaits you. This is why Bakhtin reads the Socratic dialogues as fine examples of reduced laughter. Though we don't hear laughter ringing out in Plato, "it remains in the structure of the image of the major hero (Socrates), in the methods for carrying on the dialogue" (*Problems of Dostoevsky's Poetics,* 164). Reduced laughter, for Bakhtin, is "in dialogicality itself, immersing thought itself in the joyful relativity of evolving existence and not permitting it to congeal in abstractly dogmatic (monologic) ossification" (164). In this sense, reduced laughter can be found in the image of May Bartram, who tells Marcher: "The door isn't shut. The door's open" (James, 246).[12]

But Morson and Emerson's criticism that reduced laughter could, by definition, be heard echoing in *any* text is certainly fair—not simply because the evidence comes so cheaply, but because this evidence can then be used to determine a general pattern that can differ from, or be inclusive of, patterns whose evidence rings out far more clearly or conventionally. The logic of festive laughter, with its view of the world as free, open, and incomplete, may indeed permeate certain scenes in Dostoevsky's novels, but, as Morson and Emerson argue, "it hardly determines their larger structure or ideology" (467). Put another way, not only do we risk exaggerating significantly what is *in* the text, "[w]e may even," to use Millicent Bell's words, "by a process that resembles the midrash of Hebraic commentators on sacred text, supply what is not in the text at all but which we now imagine to have been there, in order to make a particular pattern" (7). Yet Bell, who has to admit that "[t]here is some midrash in every reading," also admits that the compulsion to find in a text "what is really never seen all at once" is what confirms our adventure as readers (7). Furthermore, claims Bell, it is Henry James who, perhaps more than any other author in his time, deliberately encourages us to set out on precisely this adventure.

III

It may seem counterintuitive to read "The Beast of the Jungle" as a carnivalized text. After all, the proper place for the language of hunchbacks is the marketplace, not the petrified forest of Weathered. Still, "The Beast of the Jungle" is about the marketplace, or it is about free and familiar intercourse, frankness, and openness. Though the presence of *billingsgate* elements are reduced, I'd like to suggest that it does appear in the text as ever-present precisely in its nonappearance—the tangible traces of *possibility*. Recall the dialogue in the garden (where "privacy reigns supreme") from the opening chapter of *The Portrait of a Lady,* and you will find plenty of examples of free and open discourse that characterizes festive, laughing dialogue. Note how Lord Warburton and his guests mull over the very ideas that haunt Marcher:

"Daddy's very fond of pleasure—of other people's."
The old man shook his head. "I don't pretend to have contributed anything to the amusement of my contemporaries."
"My dear father, you're too modest!"
"That's a kind of joke, sir," said Lord Warburton.
"The young men have too many jokes. When there are no jokes you've nothing left."
"Fortunately there are always more jokes," the ugly young man remarked.
"I don't believe it—I believe things are getting more serious. You young men will find that out."
"The increasing seriousness of things, then—that's the great opportunity of jokes."
"They'll have to be grim jokes," said the old man. "I'm convinced there will be great changes; and not all for the better."
"I quite agree with you, sit," Lord Warburton declared. "I'm very sure there will be great changes, and that all sorts of queer things will happen. That's why I find so much difficulty in applying your advice; you know you told me the other day that I ought to 'take hold' of something. One hesitates to take hold of a thing that may the next moment be knocked sky high."
"You ought to take hold of a pretty woman," said his companion.
"He's trying hard to fall in love," he added, by way of explanation to his father.
"The pretty women themselves may be sent flying!" Lord Warburton exclaimed. (25–26)

James's festive language hardly resembles the shit-flinging one finds in *Gargantua* or *Pantagruel,* but it appears to function in a similar way. The scene of afternoon tea that opens the novel is made up of characters who have a sense of what Richard Poirier calls "the hovering ridiculousness" of things—of ugliness, of Warburton's politics, of boredom, of seriousness itself (194). Even Ralph Touchett's fatal illness is a comic target. He is "the humorous invalid—the invalid for whom even his own disabilities are part of the general joke" (James, 364). He is past finding out the reasons for "his own continued presence," and for this reason, is one of James's great comic characters. Unlike Ralph Touchett, John Marcher has no "want of seriousness" in his view of the world. Rather, he has a want of laughter. Had Marcher been invited to join the young gentlemen in their comic tea taking, he surely would have been fair game. In fact, one gets the feeling that Marcher's condition is the intertextual butt of the joke at afternoon tea, and not just because he, too, anticipates that something "queer" is to happen to him and never hesitates to "take hold" of something, even as it sends him "sky-high."

Can "The Beast of the Jungle" be read as a parable of the dangers of imagination? Of taking things too seriously? Of turning away from the festive, laughing, dialogic word and the "gay truth"? If Marcher's life is the anticipation of the roar of his "Beast," it is also a turning away from the laughter of a buffoon: "What he had asked of her had been simply not to laugh at him" (222). A turning away from the carnivalesque existence awaits Marcher if he chooses to ignore his "Beast." Carnival, claims Bakhtin, rescues us from "the prevailing point of view of the world, from conventions and established truths, from clichés, from all that is humdrum and universally accepted" (*Rabelais,* 34). It is indeed an alibi for Being, but not the sort to which the early Bakhtin, the Bakhtin of "Towards a Philosophy of the Act," objected.[13] As she endeavors to open up dialogue with Marcher, May endeavors to destroy Marcher's individuality, his "real truth." May is not after any "real truth" as Marcher imagines it; what May Bartram has in mind is *truth as unfinalizability*: "However the case stands," she insists, "*that* isn't the truth. Whatever the reality, it *is* a reality. The door isn't shut. The door's open" (James, 246). This insistence on unfinalizability is why May Bartram is a heroine of the festive, carnival spirit. Her utterances and expressions are lively and impressive; take, for instance, this striking passage (which I quote at length):

> It had become suddenly, from her movement and attitude, beautiful and vivid to him that she had something more to give him; her wasted face delicately shone with it—it glittered almost as with the white lustre of silver in her expression. She was

right, incontestably, for what he saw in her face was the truth, and strangely, without consequence, while their talk of it as dreadful was still in the air, she appeared to present it as inordinately soft. This, prompting bewilderment, made him but gape the more gratefully for her revelation, so that they continued for some minutes silent, her face shining at him, her contact imponderably pressing, and his stare all kind but expectant. The end, none the less, was that what he had expected failed to come to him. Something else took place instead, which seemed to consist at first in the mere closing of her eyes. She gave way at the same instant to a slow fine shudder, and though he remained staring—though he stared in fact but the harder— turned off and regained her chair. It was the end of what she had been intending, but it left him thinking only of that. (247)

Though the above passage could be read (and indeed has been read) as May Bartram's expression of desire for Marcher—a desire to which Marcher is simply blind or numb—I argue that if anything is expressed, it is the possibility of openness.[14] What we read into it hardly matters. The promise of heterosexual coupling is only one of any number of things one could see in May's expression, one of several figures one can see in the carpet. This scene is yet another of James's great "blanks," and the point is *not* that Marcher has no "created expertness" with which to work, it is that he is incapable of imagining something that might fill the blank. He is, after all, about as much of an artist as one can possibly be without actually being one. Marcher's discomfort in the society of Weatherend is quite evident early on in the story when he mingles with persons absorbed in the "dream of acquisition." There are "persons to be observed" making their way to "objects in out-of-the-way corners." They bend, with their hands on their knees, mingling "their sounds of ecstasy" or melting "into silences of even deeper import." They have what Marcher calls "the air of the 'look round'...that excites or quenches as may be, the dream of acquisition." He finds himself surrounded by this palpable and oppressive climate and is disconcerted "almost equally by the presences of those who knew too much and by that of those who knew nothing" (215). Marcher's problem is not that he is indifferent to "the fine things" of Weatherend, its "intrinsic features, pictures, heirlooms" and "treasures of all the arts" (215). Quite the opposite: Marcher is a man of feeling. Yet he is not suited for the conditioned poses of aesthetic discrimination served either too poorly or too skillfully by those well-bred pupils of a more sensual education. He is, nonetheless, impressed by the finer things—perhaps too much. One might say he is precisely the sort of person James refers to in his Preface to *The Turn of the Screw,* the sort of person "not easily caught": Marcher is "the jaded, the disillusioned, the fastidious" (120). So why does he not find what he's looking for in

May's expression? Perhaps it is because Marcher doesn't realize that he is, after all, not living a James novel. May knows as well as we do that Marcher is, in fact, living a James *amusette*—which is not a particularly bad thing when you think about it. And this is what May is "imponderably pressing": not marriage but creativity.

Although Sedgwick speaks of May Bartram's "desire" for Marcher, James himself never uses the word. Sedgwick's own "created expertness" is the suggestion that, by the end of the story, James must restore some "orthodox of ethical enforcements" to Marcher's secret: "To point rhetorically to the emptiness of the secret, 'the nothing that is,' is, in fact, oddly, *the same gesture* as the attribution to it of a compulsory content about heterosexuality—of the content specifically, 'He should have desired her'" (201). Yet, the passage Sedgwick quotes as evidence of this crucial claim makes no reference to Marcher's obligation to "desire" May Bartram. James merely gives us the admittedly ambiguous line: "The escape would have been to love her; then, *then* he would have lived" ("The Beast in the Jungle," 261). So we are left wondering, finally, what kind of love this *is,* if it is not, strictly speaking, a reference to heterosexual coupling.

Here, we might turn to those writings of Bakhtin that could be catalogued in the "Self-Help" section of your average bookstore. In "Author and Hero," Bakhtin speaks of aesthetic love as "the consciousness of oneself, the seeing of oneself, the forming of oneself in the possible living consciousness of another, the striving to turn the longed-for love of another into a force that impels and organizes my life" (157). Without this kind of love, claims Bakhtin, we risk living as "pretenders," beings who refuse to have any relationship with the world. This is precisely how Marcher lives, even as he pursues a relationship with May Bartram. He believes that by conspiring with May Bartram, he might be able to legitimize his alibi for Being. As if like a criminal, Marcher uses her to cover his tracks. Strangely, it appears that this is *precisely* the role she wants to play: "I'm your dull woman, a part of the daily bread for which you pray at church. That covers your tracks more than anything else" (238). However, what May Bartram has in mind for an alibi is something else besides Marcher's monologic truth. She has in mind "the gay truth"; the loophole offered by the festive, laughing dialogic word, the answer to Marcher's suffering and solipsism. In her essay, "Love's Knowledge," Martha Nussbaum reminds us that laughter:

> is something social and relational, something involving a context of trust, in a way that suffering is not. It requires exchange and conversation; it requires a real live other

person. ...To imagine love as a form of mourning is already to court solipsism; to imagine it as a form of laughter (smiling conversation) is to insist that it presupposes, or is, a transcendence of solipsism, the achievement of community. (280)

Marcher tries to arrive at the truth about himself not through creativity, or through smiling conversation, but through the theoretical transcription of his own Being ("Marcher-as-Law"). Yet, as Bakhtin puts it, any attempt "to force one's way from inside the theoretical world and into actual Being-as-event [is] quite hopeless. The theoretically cognized world cannot be unclosed from within cognition itself to the point of becoming open to the actual once-occurrent world" ("Toward a Philosophy of the Act," 12). May Bartram, however, has quite a different perspective in the story: a dialogic field of vision. In order to describe what this field of vision is, it would be useful to see how much Isabel Archer and Ralph Touchett resemble John Marcher and May Bartram. Miss Archer and John Marcher both enact an indifferent refusal of all "proper relations" of society in favor of some unnamed greatness—though Isabel sees her unnamed greatness as a quest, a going out. Her greatness, she assumes, will come to her in the form of some creative expertness, not through the workings of fate. And, unlike Marcher, Miss Archer finds herself struggling to maintain her openness when those around her seek to close her in and close her down. The men in the novel reduce Isabel's openness to a closed systematicity: Lord Warburton speaks of Isabel's "vast designs" (99). Even Ralph approaches Isabel as if she were a theory, as if he might find in her some "logic...that dictated so remarkable an act" as rejecting a marriage proposal (169). He calls her "the most charming of polygons" (171).

But Ralph Touchett's role is far more complex than that of mere spectator, a mere witness to some impersonal, systematic "idea":

> "Of course you mean that I'm meddling in what doesn't concern me. But why shouldn't I speak to you of this matter without annoying you or embarrassing myself? What's the use of being your cousin if I can't have a few privileges? What's the use of adoring you without hope of a reward if I can't have a few compensations? What's the use of being ill and disabled and restricted to mere spectatorship at the game of life if I really can't see the show when I've paid so much for my ticket? Tell me this," Ralph went on while she listened to him with quickened attention. "What had you in mind when you refused Lord Warburton?" (169)

The demands of Ralph Touchett are the demands of dialogue, and one cannot help but see each of James's characters in danger of withering away for lack of its nourishment (Is May Bartram not ill and disabled by her being "restricted to mere spectatorship"?). Isabel Archer is the referential (and reverential) object of discourse, but Ralph refuses to allow this discourse to be reducible to this object. Ralph insists on conditions, "compensations," and "reward." He demands what Morson and Emerson, using Bakhtin's idiom, call "addressive surplus"—knowledge that can only be ascertained in a more participatory verbal exchange. In other words, Isabel just has to have a *good listen*.[15] Isabel, delightful creature that she is, grants Ralph what he requests. Ralph, too, is delightful in that he never ambushes Isabel, never attacks her from behind:[16] "She rose from her place, but Ralph only sat still and looked at her. As he remained there she stopped, and they exchanged a gaze that was full on either side, but especially on Ralph's, of utterances too vague for words" (172). This gaze, "full on either side," is as clear an illustration of dialogue as in any of the James novels—albeit staged, as it is, with one subject still in need of some surplus from the other.

May Bartram is in need of something similar—something Marcher can ponder over, but never deliver. He is "careful to remember that she had also a life of her own, with things that might happen to *her,* things that in friendship one should likewise take account of" (227). As Marcher ponders this possibility, something "fairly remarkable" happens to him—"a certain passage of his consciousness, in the suddenest way, from one extreme to another" (227). What is "fairly remarkable," however, is also sadly neglected. Marcher never listens to May Bartram; he, instead, ambushes her with questions in an attempt to get her to reaffirm who he is. But the Other should surprise us, not reaffirm who we are.[17] As Bakhtin puts it in the appendix to his Dostoevsky book, "the surplus of the Other is a kind of love; it is also confession and forgiveness. Most of all, it is simply an active (not a duplicating) understanding, a willingness to listen" (299). One must use one's "outsideness" and experience not to ambush and attack, as Madame Merle frequently does, but "to ask the right sort of questions. Recognizing the other's capacity for change, one provokes or invites him to reveal and outgrow himself" (Morson and Emerson, 242). It is fair enough for us to say that Marcher fails to *love* May Bartram—if we understand that the love of which we speak is the love that is indissociable from true dialogue. As Caryl Emerson puts it, "Dialogue and aesthetic love are connected in Bakhtin's thought—but not, it could be argued, because we are necessarily made happier or more secure by their interconnection. Bakhtin was simply of the opinion that life's energy, its drive toward ever more precise articulation and differentiation, can be released solely in this way" (262). In other words, genuine dialogue comes only when there is shared aesthetic love between two or more people. *This* is the love that would help Marcher escape; *this* is the love that would help Marcher live, that would offer him the chance to see his "hunchback" existence as a perfect alibi by which he could "baffle his doom" (261)—a "loophole" in his immutable Law through which he could escape. Learning this lesson, of course, means returning to the social (to London, to Weatherend, and the "stupid world") even if as "a hunchback." As Morson and Emerson suggest:

> [festive language] is described not as a dialogue that generates new and valuable truths, but as the joyful destruction of all truths. And individual responsibility entirely disappears from view when the individual is merged into the great body of the feasting people. There is no longer a self, there is only the carnival mask; other people can accomplish what "I" can if they adopt my festive clothes. Carnival as a whole appears to offer a perfect "alibi for Being." (95)

Marcher cannot have his truth destroyed. That his life should be forever open *is* the truth about John Marcher. And for an individual satisfied only with definitive answers and incontestable fact, this prospect is unfathomable. John Marcher fears the mockery of that other, potential meaning of his life: that he is a hunchback, a fool. He finally remains blind to the loophole consciousness May Bartram struggles to bring into being. And, as the narrator suggests, he cherishes his blindness all too well (260). We may cherish it too. We wish, as Marcher does, to imagine the "Beast" as the center of all the story's meaning. After all, one doesn't expect to find festive laughter in a James novel. James is no Rabelais, to be sure. Yet, James's narrative of a man's hysterical monologism is at the same time a narrative of the dialogic ambitions of the Other. Those who are determined to give Marcher's "Beast" some content will have to do so by centering it at the risk of not seeing (in May Bartram's words) "something else." As it is for Ralph Touchett, May's "unerring touch" is her tender resolve to invite John Marcher to behave, in a sense, like Isabel Archer, to affront his destiny rather than confront it.[18] In a comic world, there is no fate, only other people. The other person in "The Beast in the Jungle" is that hunchback, that "funniest of the funny" pretender, that repulsive creature who had the gall to thumb his nose at the "Beast."

Notes

1.   See Brian Poole: "Stressing the philosophical approach to laughter allows us to avoid the inflationary application of the tiresome epithet 'carnival.' Bakhtin often uses such alternatives as prazdnik (festival) and pir (symposium) in conjunction

with his descriptive approach to the temporal and spatial contingencies of laughter." "Bakhtin and Cassier: The Philosophical Origins of Bakhtin's Carnival Messianism," *South Atlantic Quarterly* 97.3–4 (1998): 539.

2.   For an interesting use of Bakhtin in the study of James's early novels, see Lisa Eckstrom's "Moral Perception and the Chronotope: The Case of Henry James," *Bakhtin in Contexts: Across the Disciplines,* ed. Amy Mandelker. (Evanston, IL: Northwestern University Press, 1995), 99–116. What Eckstrom shows us is that both *The Portrait of a Lady* (1881) and *The Golden Bowl* (1906) portray central characters that are unable to complete their moral development, despite their extraordinary capacities for perception. Although moments of morally charged insight—what Bakhtin describes as chronotopes of the threshold—are central to the novels of both Dostoevsky and James, one finds in the latter an undeniable failure to achieve "self-knowledge and the lucid responsibility it brings with it" (116). Eckstrom claims that Martha Nussbaum, in her essay "James's *The Golden Bowl*: Literature as Moral Philosophy," overestimates the ability of the ideal Jamesian agent to "cross the threshold" and gain the kind of insight of which Bakhtin speaks. In fact, says Eckstrom, one finds in James "almost the direct inverse of the chronotope of the threshold" (105).

3.   I borrow this phrase from Martha Nussbaum who, in the chapter from *Love's Knowledge* on James's *The Golden Bowl*, argues that to experience James's novels is to experience not simply the flawed natures of a character's consciousness (say, Fanny Assingham's), but the flawed nature of James's consciousness too, as well as our own. The "ideal" Jamesian character is not, as Nussbaum puts it, "the work's entire story about human practical wisdom. We know that where there is great love in one direction there may also be, in another direction, a tragically necessary blindness." It is my feeling that May Bartram's ambitions are what is at stake in James's story, not her success or failure at undoing Marcher's blindness. For further elaboration on failure in James, see Lisa Eckstrom, "Moral Perception and the Chronotope: The Case of Henry James," as well as Stanley Cavell, "Postscript: To Whom it May Concern" in *Contesting Tears: The Hollywood Melodrama of the Unknown Woman.* (Chicago: University of Chicago Press, 1996), 151–96, and Martha Nussbaum, "'Finely Aware and Richly Responsible': Literature and the Moral Imagination" in *Love's Knowledge.* (London and New York: Oxford University Press, 1990), 148–67.

4.   See Eric Solomon, "The Return of the Screw," rpt. in *The Turn of the Screw: An Authoritative Text, Backgrounds and Sources, Essays in Criticism.* (New York: Norton, 1966), 237–45. Readers who suspect that James might be having a bit of fun at our expense with these tales, who would rather not see in the young narrator of "The Figure in the Carpet" a little too much of themselves, might proceed the way Eric Solomon does in his interpretation. Proceed, that is, with full-frontal irony. Solomon claims to give us the "definitive" interpretation of the story, a reading that "provides the one, incontrovertible explanation for the strange happenings at Bly. Never again need there be another explication of *The Turn of the Screw*" (238). Solomon knows, of course, that he's being played upon. His line of thinking, that Mrs. Grose has deliberately filled the Governess's head with notions of ghosts in order to drive her away, is a pointed parody of the "created expertness" James expects of those "not easily caught." Solomon's essay, by trying to close the book, in effect, does the opposite by pretending to close the book and suggests there's no closing and maybe no book to close, thus he leaves things more open than he found them, which is doubtless his aim.

5.   For a fuller discussion of this failure, see Lisa Eckstrom, "Moral Perception and the Chronotope: The Case of Henry James."

6. For useful studies of the carnivalized novel that follow this line of thought, see M. Keith Booker. *Joyce, Bakhtin, and the Literary Tradition* (Ann Arbor: University of Michigan Press, 1995); R. B. Kershner, Jr. *Joyce, Bakhtin, and Popular Literature: Chronicles of Disorder.* (Chapel Hill: University of North Carolina Press, 1989); David Lodge. *After Bakhtin: Essays on Fiction and Criticism.* (London: Routledge, 1990); and Allon White. *Carnival, Hysteria, Writing.* (New York: Oxford University Press, 1993).

7. See William Paul. "Charles Chaplin and the Annals of Anality," *Comedy/Cinema/ Theory*, ed. Andrew S. Horton. (Berkeley: University of California Press, 1991), 109–30. I should point out that by posing this way the problem of how critics treat the carnivalized novel, I risk nourishing a rather puritan attitude towards carnival in general, which is not my aim. In his essay on low burlesque forms in the films of Chaplin, Paul makes a good case for getting things as dirty as possible, because "when low culture is embraced by high critics, something inevitably gets repressed" (113). Paul's complaint is that "no one has ever thought to praise [Chaplin] for the anality of his humor"—that Chaplin's critics tend to acknowledge his obscene humor only to point out how much he transcends it (115). I do not refer to Joyce's carnivalized novel for the purposes of showing how it transcends its own bawdiness, and I do not criticize Booker for failing to do just that. I do fear, however, that an over-zealous preoccupation with the "low" aspects of the carnivalized novel gives the lasting (and only half-true) impression that they are its defining features. I understand the carnivalized novel, as Emerson and Morson do, as playing "the same role in literature that carnival is alleged to play in the real life of cultures" (442). This is to say, it is infused with one single logic of imagery, in which the lower bodily stratum plays only a part. To stress only the "low" aspects of a carnivalized novel is to deny its ambivalence and reproduce the reactionary ideology of symbolic inversion that dominates our culture.

8. See Phyllis Gorfain. "Play and the Carnivalesque in *Hamlet*," *Shakespeare and Carnival: After Bakhtin,* ed. Ronald Knowles. (New York: St. Martin's, 1998), 152–76. Gorfain assumes that Bakhtin "implicitly invites us to develop further his theory of the carnivalesque in dramatic tragedy" (153). To do so, one must "discuss more fully how the carnivalesque is more than an ingredient, digression or relief, but is a kind of attitude, a history of languages and practices, which functions as a structural and ideological method" (154). Gorfain implies a distinction between carnival ingredients and "carnivalesque terms and structures" that is particularly useful and which reminds me of both C. L. Barber and, perhaps less obviously, Rick Altman. The reference to laughter as a term for structure is clearly derived from Barber's *Shakespeare's Festive Comedy: A Study of Dramatic Form and Its Relation to Social Custom.* (Princeton, NJ: Princeton University Press, 1959), which has influenced much of the collection to which Gorfain's essay belongs. The distinction between "ingredients" and "terms and structures" also parallels Rick Altman's famous distinction between the semantic and syntactic elements of the Hollywood Western. See "A Semantic/Syntactic Approach to Film Genre," *Cinema Journal* 23.3 (1984): 6–18, rpt. in *Film Genre Reader*, ed. Barry Keith Grant (Austin: University of Texas Press, 1986), 26–40. The semantic approach to genre criticism emphasizes the general atmosphere and the basic elements of the film, such as a Western's use of earth, dust, water, leather, and so on. The syntactic approach, however, emphasizes "relationships linking lexical elements" such as garden versus desert, city versus frontier, future versus past, and so on. I would argue that the study of the carnivalized novel has emphasized, far too much, a version of the semantic approach.

9. For example, Sedgwick turns our attention to a rather healthy inventory of residual meaning (Marcher's "secret," "his singularity," "his queer consciousness," "the great vagueness," "the secret of the gods," "dreadful things...I couldn't name"), yet, she admits that these are only "lexical pointers" and have only "an odd centrality" in the story (*Epistemology of the Closet*, 203–4). As drawn as we may be to these clues, they only animate and perpetuate "the mechanism of homophobic male self-ignorance and violence and manipulability" (204). Additionally, if we agree that to read for homosexual content means to acknowledge the centrality of these "lexical pointers," then we deny the possibility of a plurality of homosexual meanings.

10. See Ellen Douglass Leyburn. *Strange Alloy: The Relation of Comedy to Tragedy in the Fiction of Henry James.* (Chapel Hill: University of North Carolina Press, 1969). Leyburn has shown how James's use of the word "funny" in the late novels involves a "curious stylistic imaging of the fusion of tragedy and comedy," and that the term often retains the element of laughter even as it intensifies the tragic force of suffering (137).

11. See Eve Kosofsky Sedgwick. "Paranoid Reading and Reparative Reading; or, You're So Paranoid, You Probably Think This Introduction Is about You," *Novel Gazing: Queer Readings in Fiction,* ed. Eve Kosofsky Sedgwick. (Durham, NC: Duke University Press, 1997), 1–37.

12. Indeed, May Bartram seems to frustrate Marcher in precisely the way Socrates frustrates his young, philosophically minded students. As William Covino has argued, "[t]he Phaedrus of Plato's dialogue...craves unambiguous advice about discourse. He is confused by Socrates' two speeches (critiques of Lysias' speech on love) that extend and complicate the nature of both love and rhetoric" (63). See "Defining Advanced Composition: Contributions from the History of Rhetoric," rpt. in *Landmark Essays on Advanced Composition,* ed. Gary A. Olson and Julie Drew. (Mahwah, NJ: Hermagoras, 1996), 61–70. Marcher, then, is very much like Phaedrus, who reveals a strong desire for logic and systematic thought, as well as "impatience with being 'led astray' from quick understanding by the intellectual play of Socrates, who knows that truth is broad and complex and can only be pursued through continual, irresolute dialogue" (63). Gerald Bruns also addresses this point when he says, "[a]sk Socrates what justice is and he will require you to give him a definition, and soon the issue will be whether you know what you are talking about" (99). See *Inventions: Writing, Textuality, and Understanding in Literary History.* (New Haven, CT: Yale University Press, 1989). Following Gadamer's extremely rhetorical claim that ambiguity and metaphor is the basis of language, Bruns adds: "It is never possible to say what anything is all at once or once for all; rather, one must say it again and again, each time a little differently as each occasion requires, thus to speak the thing in all its versions, that is, in all its turnings. Thus the saying of anything requires the saying of a great deal" (101). The relationship of May and John, then, is the relationship of Socrates and Phaedrus, of rhetoric and philosophy, of dialogue and monologue, of tongues and systems.

13. During his early period, Bakhtin had claimed, "there is no alibi for Being" (*Toward a Philosophy of the Act*, 112). To live without an alibi—that is, to live without an identity, without a project of selfhood—is to be a "pretender." The early Bakhtin appears to be describing Marcher's life when he describes a life "washed from all sides by the waves of an endless, empty potentiality" (120). Morson and Emerson have shown that the Bakhtin of a later period revised his views of "pretenders": "It will be recalled that in ["Toward a Philosophy of the Act"] Bakhtin insists that

moral responsibility pertains to every moment of life and that there is no legitimate escape from it. But there are legitimate escapes; one may live as if there were an 'alibi for being'; one may live as a 'pretender'...By contrast, in [a later period] Bakhtin experimented with his global concepts by taking one of them, unfinalizability, to an extreme, and by suspending the others. Living by pure unfinalizability makes life a single 'loophole,' a view of life he had previously regarded as irresponsible and futile. In [the later period], pure unfinalizability is treated positively" (351–52). I argue that we read May Bartram as if she were speaking to Marcher the way Bakhtin was speaking to his earlier, more Kantian self. And though the early Bakhtin could hardly be described as a "hero of monologism," as Marcher is in this reading, there is, in the former's claim that "there is no alibi for being," a certain degree of ignorance, skepticism, or outright fear of the Other that characterizes monologic thought.

14.   By "openness," I mean a kind of exposure that is both terrifying and liberating. Gerald Bruns, following the thought of Gadamer, gives us a good account of what this sort of openness means: "Gadamer thinks of it in terms of insight, and less an illumination of transcendence than an 'escape from something that had deceived us and held us captive'...a releasement, say, from some prior certainty or ground, some vocabulary or framework or settled self-understanding" (184). See *Hermeneutics Ancient and Modern.* (New Haven, CT: Yale University Press, 1992). What May Bartram expresses is the possibility of this sort of escape for Marcher. It matters not to her what exactly he is escaping from, what Marcher's deepest fear may be. Perhaps what he needs to escape is self-understanding. What matters is that it is over, that they are, somehow, on the other side. Exposed, but free. Though this idea of openness and release pertains largely to *tragedy* (think of Lear and Oedipus), it pertains only to the degree that tragedy must, in the end, acknowledge something that comedy has always and already acknowledged: that the presentnesss of the world, says Stanley Cavell, "cannot be a function of knowing. The world is to be *accepted;* as the presentness of other minds is not to be known, but acknowledged" (95). See *Disowning Knowledge in Six Plays of Shakespeare.* (Cambridge, MA: Cambridge University Press, 1987).

15.   A more frightening example of the threat of monologism can be found in *Barton Fink.* Several scenes in this film involve verbal exchanges between Barton and his neighbor, Charlie. Barton, the New York playwright, is determined to speak *for* the common man, never *with* him. Alas, whenever Charlie says, "Boy, do I have some stories to tell..." Barton interrupts: "And that's just the point!!!" In reprisal, Charlie unleashes the fury of his *own* monologism ("I'll show you the life of the mind!!!" he shouts)—something that might have been transformed into reparative dialogue had Barton only taken the time to have a *good listen* ("That's your problem, Barton" says Charlie, "you just...don't...LISTEN!!!"). *Barton Fink,* dir. Joel Cohen, screenplay by Ethan Cohen and Joel Cohen. (Rank/Circle, 1991).

16.   From *Problems of Dostoevsky's Poetics,* Appendix II: "Toward A Re-Working of the Dostoevsky Book" (1961): "The most important aspect of this surplus is love (one cannot love oneself, love is a coordinate relationship), and then, confession, forgiveness (Stavrogin's conversation with Tikhon), finally, simply an active (not a duplicating) understanding, a willingness to listen. This surplus is never used as an ambush, as a chance to sneak up and attack from behind. This is open, honest surplus, dialogically revealed to the other person, a surplus expressed by the addressed and not by the secondhand word. Everything essential is dissolved in dialogue, positioned face to face" (299).

17.   For one of the more instructive and engaging discussions of consciousness in the novels of Henry James, see Sharon Cameron. *Thinking in Henry James.* (Chicago:

University of Chicago Press, 1989). Though she employs Husserl's *Cartesian Meditations,* Cameron's perspective is not far from Bakhtin's in both *The Dialogic Imagination* and *Problems of Dostoevsky's Poetics.* Her readings of both James's Preface to *The Portrait of a Lady* and the novel itself suggest that meaning is best understood as *between* persons (61). In Bakhtinian terms, meaning is dialogic. It should be noted, however, that Husserl and Bakhtin share fundamental differences regarding the ontological status of the Other who complements the subject's grasp of meaning. Whereas Bakhtin would stress the need for a real other to supply the surplus necessary for meaning, Husserl would not. Writes Cameron: "For Husserl, who internalizes otherness in the name of consciousness, there is no tension between the mind and the world because in the phenomenological reduction the self is always connected to the otherness which it, in fact, constitutes. In addition, its own existence is inconceivable except with reference to that otherness which... is imagined as its own 'other side.' The 'other' side in Husserl's typology is therefore a side you can see...Thus for Husserl, proof of otherness does not require real others; only in consciousness does the phantom become the real thing" (27). Yet, Cameron doesn't hesitate to point out that, in James's novels, "consciousness and its object are never permitted to be the same *thing*" (31). Bakhtin, however, might say that James is not denying *permission,* but acknowledging *impossibility*—or, more specifically, acknowledging the *dangers* of imagining such a possibility and organizing experience accordingly.

18.   In the Preface to *The Portrait of a Lady,* James says that the "small cornerstone" of this novel was "the conception of a certain young woman affronting her destiny" (10).

4

The Mind of Stanley Cavell: A Comedy

It has been said that not everyone is quite comfortable with Stanley Cavell as a philosopher. As Gerald Bruns puts it, "Cavell is an analytical philosopher for whom the priority of responsiveness and acceptance of others displaces the sovereignty of the cognitive subject...Yet Cavell remains a moral perfectionist who affirms in Emerson's name 'the absolute responsibility of the self to itself.'"[1] Furthermore, Bruns says, "his philosophy is not made up of arguments; instead it is composed of descriptions, readings, musings, fantasies, puzzles about words, imaginary conversations, improvisatory flights" and so on.[2] Anyhow, there is no coherence in Cavell's philosophy. Nothing is necessary and nothing is essential.

It has also been said that not everyone is comfortable with Cavell as a feminist thinker. He participates in what Tania Modleski calls a "feminism without women"—what is properly understood to mean the male appropriation or exploitation of feminist discourse. The charge of speaking for, and therefore silencing, women, and the response to this charge, was played out famously in the pages of *Critical Inquiry* some years ago. It is not entirely clear whether Cavell has responded adequately to the charge. Some may still have it, as Modleski rightly does, that Cavell has not answered a question he was "canny enough" to ask—that is, "Does this idea of the feminine philosophical demand serve to prefigure, or does it serve once more to eradicate, the feminine difference?—to articulate or to blur the difference between the denial to the woman of political expression and a man's melancholy sense of his own inexpresseiveness?" (in Modleski, 9).

And, funnily enough, it has been said that not everyone is comfortable with Cavell as a film scholar. His 1971 text, *The World Viewed,* was written, as Dudley Andrew notes, in theoretical isolation.[3] The experience of watching films, so central to Cavell's investigations, was (and in many ways still is) foreign to film scholars. Cavell's follow-ups, *Pursuits of Happiness: the Hollywood Comedy of Remarriage* and *Contesting Tears:*

the Hollywood Melodrama of the Unknown Woman, did little to help his reputation among film scholars. Philosophers have little patience for a man who thinks film watching and philosophizing are not different things. Film scholars have even less patience. And why take on "the woman's film"? What made Cavell think that women would respond with friendliness to his assertion that a feminist reading of *Stella Dallas* should also be an Emersonian reading of *Stella Dallas*?

It's as if Cavell deliberately eludes greatness at every turn.

And yet, this is precisely why Cavell is still very much with us. He is, if you will, something like a comic hero: he survives. And unlike the tragic hero who blindly, fatally strives to master the world, lay it bare, and bring it under conceptual control, the comic hero survives because he chooses instead to accept the world for what it is. His desire is not to master the world, but to inhabit it. Greatness is not his aim. Like the comic hero, Cavell prefers the everyday, the commonplace, the ordinary. Consider his reading of Beckett's *Endgame*, a text long admired for what Cavell calls its "bizarrerie." We are led to think that the play must be submitted to a philosophical point of view; Cavell wants to convince us otherwise: "the ground of the play's quality is the *ordinariness* of its events" (*Must We Mean what We Say?*, 118). Rather than treat Beckett's play, as most do, as evidence of our "meaningless universe" and the "breakdown, the disintegration of language," Cavell treats it as farce: "[t]he medium of Beckett's dialogue is repartée, adjoining the genres of Restoration comedy, Shakespearean clowning, and the vaudeville gag" (127). Like Kubrick's *Dr Strangelove*, *Endgame* is "a collage whose bits are as common as sand" (134).

Comedy, I'd like to suggest, is everywhere in Cavell. It can be found even in his writings on skepticism. Cavell's skeptic, who longs for "genuine connection," seems less at home in Thebes than in Dingley Dell. Though he has no desire to *know* the world or to master it, he is no knave, no fool. He does not abandon reason as a means of disengaging, but of re-engaging with the world. He desires to be *in* the world, to be *present*: "Our problem is that society can no longer hear its own screams. Our problem, in getting back to beginnings, will not be to find the thing we have always cared about, but to discover whether we have it in us always to care about something" (*Disowning Knowledge,* 120). This is Cavell's assessment of the philosophical problem of skepticism, or the moral he draws from it. It is openness and acceptance even, and perhaps most of all, in a black world. This is, it so happens, Cavell's take on *His Girl Friday* (dir. Hawks, 1940). Mollie Malloy, sickened by heartless newspapermen, reminds us all too well that we are deaf to our own screams. And it is Walter, no stranger to these screams, who dispatches Hildy to find what it is that she has had all along, "knowledge of herself." But such knowledge is grasped only after one emerges from the illusions in which one lives. Says Cavell, Hildy "requires the experience of the forces arrayed against the knowledge, the force of her struggle against giving up on what I called her counterfeit happiness, the panic in intending to divorce herself from her divorce of Walter" (174). Hildy, like Oedipus, must acknowledge herself and the world, herself *in* the world. Her return to Walter instances "a new beginning" (*Pursuits of Happiness,* 174).

One might protest, here, that there is nothing comic in any of this. Cavell's *His Girl Friday* is a tragedy, not a comedy. But this is not at all what Cavell means. The issue is not that *His Girl Friday* resembles tragedy. The issue, as I will attempt to show, is that Cavell reads the tragic comically. The issue of romantic comedies, such as *His Girl Friday,* "is how we are given to understand the relation of the pair we predominantly care about to this surrounding world, how it is that they escape its evils sufficiently to find happiness in it" (183). Here, "escape" does not mean flight to a better, more promising world. Rather, "escape" means finding oneself at home in the black world, finding happiness even. Happiness may come in the form of "reprieve," but only a temporary one. This may sound tragic, but for Cavell, nothing could be more comic. Tragedy is a willing refusal to acknowledge others, or to accept the presentness of the world and everything in it. Clearer still, figures like Lear, Othello, and Macbeth are tragic because they lack openness and responsiveness to the world's finitude and ordinariness. Hildy and Walter are comic not because they escape tragedy, but because they acknowledge it.

In Cavell's work, comedy is mostly, though not always, implicit; it is, at any rate, always there, lingering (if only as a possibility), adjacent to whatever the matter at hand may be—including the Hollywood film genre Cavell calls the Hollywood melodrama of the unknown woman. As William Rothman points out, "it is a claim central to *Contesting Tears* that the genre therein called the melodrama of the unknown woman is derived from the remarriage comedy by the mechanism of negation,"[4] that the genres of remarriage and the unknown woman are companions. But Cavell never gives a straightforward account of the internal relation of the Hollywood melodrama of the unknown woman to remarriage comedy. One might say that the internal relation is Cavell himself, that is, his own preoccupation with the human.[5] "Human beings," *The Claim of Reason* reminds us, "do not naturally desire isolation and incomprehension, but union or reunion, call it community." And what could be more comic? Hence, Cavell's reading of *Stella Dallas*—a reading that is no one else's in more ways than one. Stella doesn't desire isolation and incomprehension (or doesn't bring these things on herself, as so many film scholars believe), but the community seems to offer no alternative. So? When the community is too full of un-comic people (which is what the woman's film seems to suggest to Cavell), then to hell with the community. Leave. Find a different place. *Make out another way.* This is, I think, what is meant when it is said that the melodrama of the unknown woman is derived from the remarriage comedy by the mechanism of negation.

I'd like to suggest that few other philosophers (in our time, anyway) have given us as full an account of what might be called comic thinking as Cavell has. And yet comedy in Cavell has yet to be fully and extensively *indexed*. If you look for "comedy" in Cavell's writings, you will be directed to his work on Hollywood romantic comedies of the 30s and 40s, or perhaps to a few notes on Buster Keaton, or a discussion of the scripts of various Marx Brothers' films. But the indexes fall far short of the importance of comedy in Cavell's thought. I argue that comedy is not simply an occasional topic of interest for Cavell (or, one might say, an occasional subtopic within a more than occasional topic of interest: film), but a way of thinking that influences much if not all of his work. Cavell lovingly, comically, asks philosophy to open itself up to what it is not (literature, film); he lovingly, comically, asks himself (and all male thinkers of the Anglo-American grain) to open up to feminine difference; he lovingly, comically, asks Shakespeare's Lear to risk everything he thought he knew in order to inhabit the world once more (and isn't it true that to read Cavell is to run the same risks?).

And it is with his well-known reading of *King Lear* that I'd like to begin our search for the comic in Cavell. But I should first stop here and explain why it's worth the effort to turn to Cavell's reading of Shakespeare's greatest tragedy in order to uncover what is already bare in Cavell's reading of, say, *His Girl Friday* or *The Philadelphia Story.* Cavell has shown little or no interest in Shakespeare's comedies. Richard Halpern sees this as a symptom of a more general, historical privileging of tragedy over comedy. By focusing on Shakespearean tragedy, Cavell "associates skepticism with the 'higher' of the dramatic modes. (He investigates comedy only in the context of popular film, a mass-cultural form). Tragedy, in Cavell's book," continues Halpern, "not only serves as a privileged point of origin for philosophical skepticism but invests it (and crucially, the response to its challenge) with the grandeur of tragic heroism" (107). There is to be found, in Halpern's words, a well-intentioned (if indirect and oblique) defense of comedy as an unnecessarily underprivileged literary form. But Halpern seems to miss the point of Cavell's version of skepticism when he claims that, by focusing on the tragedies of Shakespeare, Cavell insulates it from "cynical debasement." It is perhaps worth stating, here, what Cavell's moral of skepticism is:

> How do we learn that what we need is not more knowledge but the willingness to forgo knowing? For this sounds to us as though we are being asked to abandon reason for irrationality…or to trade knowledge for superstition…This is why we think skepticism must mean that we cannot know the world exists, and hence that perhaps there isn't one…Whereas what skepticism suggests is that since we cannot know the world exists, its presentness to us cannot be a function of knowing. The world is to be *accepted* as the presentness of other minds is not to be known, but acknowledged. (*Must We Mean what We Say?*, 324)

Shakespeare's play dramatizes the lengths to which humans will go in order to avoid being revealed. Lear's motivation for punishing Cordelia is to avoid acknowledgement, "to avoid recognition, the shame of exposure, the threat of self-revelation," to avoid her love (286). But, says Cavell, to love is all Cordelia knows how to do, "[t]hat is her problem, and at the cause of the tragedy of King Lear" (292). Lear's spectacular failure, even by the play's end, to acknowledge Cordelia and be acknowledged by her, "to put himself aside long enough to see through to her, and be seen through," is what makes the play unbearable (301). What makes the play bearable, Cavell argues, is the capacity of Cordeila.

But who is Cordelia, and what is her capacity? One possible reading is that she is comic, that her capacity to accept Lear—that this acceptance never "caves in at a doubt," as it were—makes her something of a comic hero. Following Cavell's reading, we say that Cordelia acknowledges what Lear himself cannot acknowledge—namely, that he cannot love or be loved. She plays May Bartram to Lear's John Marcher. And whereas the Fool chooses to expose Lear's shame with ridicule, with "cynical debasement," as it were, Cordelia chooses instead to conceal Lear's shame. This is how Cordelia becomes fully human: "by knowing her separateness, by knowing the deafness of miracles, by accepting the unacceptability of her love, and by nevertheless maintaining her love and the whole knowledge it brings…she is the only character whose attention is wholly on earth, on the person nearest her. It is during the storm that Lear's mind clouds most and floods with philosophy; when it clears, Cordelia is present" (302). So the true comic hero of *King Lear* is not the Fool, but Cordelia. And for Cavell, this heroism places Cordelia on the other side of the abyss—one which Lear is unable to cross; one which, if we are fully engaged with the play, we are asked to cross. But how do we? How do we become like Cordelia? "How," asks Cavell, "do we learn that what we need is not more knowledge but the willingness to forgo knowledge?" (324). I take this to mean: How do we give up conceptual control of the world? How do we become responsive? or, How do we become comic?

Let's try to answer that question using another well-known tragedy. We become comic the moment we stop trying to flee Corinth. Oedipus would do well to accept the notion that, after all, nobody's perfect. And let's add to this answer a few words from a well-known comedy: Billy Wilder's 1959 film *Some Like It Hot*. One of the sub-plots involves the love affair between Daphne (Jack Lemmon) and Osgood (Joe E. Brown). By the film's end, Osgood has unwittingly rescued Daphne and Joe (Tony Curtis) from a Chicago gangster known as Spats (George Raft). Tagging along in the getaway boat is Sugar (Marilyn Monroe), who has fallen in love with Joe in spite of the charades he has been playing with her. He repents and reveals his true identity. Daphne, following Joe's lead, decides it's high time he gave Osgood full disclosure and put an end to a rather strange and forbidden would-be romance:

> Daphne: Osgood, I'm gonna level with you. We can't get married at all.
> Osgood: Why not?
> Daphne: Well, in the first place I'm not a natural blonde.
> Osgood: Doesn't matter.
> Daphne: I smoke, I smoke all the time!
> Osgood: I don't care.
> Daphne: I have a terrible past. For the past three years I've been living with a saxophone player.
> Osgood: I forgive you.
> Daphne: I can never have children.
> Osgood: We can adopt some.
> Daphne: You don't understand Osgood! Aww, for...[removing his wig] I'm a *man*!
> Osgood: Well, nobody's perfect.

In spite of being assailed with false histories and deceptions, Osgood accepts and embraces Daphne to the end—which isn't really an end but an opening up of new possibilities, an initiation. Again and again Daphne tries to bring things to a close ("We can't get married," "I'm not a natural blonde," "I can never have children," etc.) only to be frustrated by Osgood's success at opening them up once more, no matter how irrational the outcome may be. After all, nobody's perfect. But acceptance is what the world of comedy is all about. In *The Dialogic*

Imagination, Bakhtin claims that comic figures like fools, clowns, and rogues compel us to experience life as inconclusive, perpetual, open, and indeterminate: "They grant the right *not* to understand, the right to confuse, to tease, to hyperbolize life...the right to act life as a comedy and to treat others as actors...the right to betray to the public a personal life, down to its most private and prurient little secrets" (163). Osgood defends these rights so disarmingly that, at times, Daphne cannot help but be intoxicated by him.

Nor can we. Yet we are not always so willing to climb in the boat. When we try to define what we mean being comic, we often speak as if we were in a prisoner's dock. Though it is widely understood that the problematic of philosophic skepticism lies at the heart of Cavell's work, it is important to recall that Cavell imagines the world is made up principally of other people, such that the problematic of skepticism is often cast as the problem of other people's minds (rather than, say, other things). Not to be known, understood, finalized, completed, or accounted for, but to be acknowledged, accepted—this, Cavell tells us, is the claim other people make on us. With this in mind, it becomes easier to see how important comedy is to Cavell's philosophy—it is not a diversion, as Halpern implies, not a temporary retreat from other serious matters (say, Wittgenstein's puzzles, Shakespeare's tragedies, or Emerson's essay on self-reliance). An old insult is this: comedy is temporary. It is, recalling the words of Charles Lamb, a "passing pageant." A safety valve, the cultural critic might say. It is a licensed blow-off. Recess. Yet Cavell, comic thinker that he is, reminds us in *Pursuits of Happiness* that "the temporary might be as good as the permanent if it lasts long enough or recurs reliably enough" (183). Which it does. Such is the life rhythm, says Susanne Langer—who, if we recall, has given us one of the best definitions of comedy:

> The human-life-feeling is the essence of comedy. It is at once religious and ribald, knowing and defiant, social and freakishly individual. The illusion of life the comic poet creates is the oncoming future fraught with dangers and opportunities, that is, with physical or social events occurring by chance and building up the coincidences with which individuals cope according to their lights. This ineluctable future—ineluctable because its countless factors are beyond human knowledge and control—is Fortune. Whatever the theme...the immediate sense of life is the underlying feeling of comedy. (331)

The risk-fraught future terrifies the tragic hero, but it compels the comic hero to *make another way*. Cavell, thinking like a comic poet, is compelled to take the final sequence of *Stella Dallas* and find within it something potentially comic. Of concern to him is one of the film's most famous sequences:

...one of the most famous, or unforgettable, I dare say, in the history of American cinema—in which Stella's excessive costume at a fancy resort hotel makes her an object of ridicule to refined society and—so the accepted view goes, unchallenged so far as I know—precipitates her plan to separate from her daughter, the act all but universally understood as Stella's "self-sacrifice." This understanding is based on the assumption...that Stella is "as oblivious as ever to the shocking effect of her appearance" when at the hotel she makes "a Christmas tree spectacle of herself." (*Contesting Tears*, 200–201)

Sensing an unacknowledged tension between wanting to see Stella as active or passive, or as triumphant or pathetic, Cavell turns to what he calls massive evidence that Stella is fully aware of what she is doing when she makes her public appearance at the resort hotel. The cause of this ambivalence, argues Cavell, is ours; as in the essay on *King Lear*, Cavell wishes to call attention to our unwillingness to be receptive, and to our willful, complicitous, refusal to see (*Must We Mean what We Say?*, 314). There are several occasions early in the film that demonstrate Stella's "massively authenticated knowledge of clothes," that show Stella to be "an expert at their construction and, if you like, deconstruction" (*Contesting Tears*, 201). Stella's plan to give up Laurel is borne not from a catastrophic misunderstanding; it is much more calculated than this (one might say here that Stella is, in Langer's words, "at once religious and ribald, knowing and defiant, social and freakishly individual").

The source of our fixation on Stella's self-oblivion is no doubt the same source of our failure to engage with Shakespeare's tragedies, our unwillingness to forego our position as detached observer, transcendental spectator. "This may account generally for the sense of Stella's obliviousness and pathos; and it specifically registers a sense of substitution or transformation. But is this surely to be turned in a negative key, taking the substitution to be a denial of something; and not in a positive, taking the transformation to be an affirmation of something? Can we have this both ways?" (207). Borrowing Thoreau's pun on mo(u)rning, Cavell gives us the view that the world Laurel desires is not to Stella's taste, and that she turns her back on the scene of her daughter's initiation into that world and walks toward us, away from "mourning as grief" toward "morning as dawning and ecstasy." (212). That one can make another way for *Stella Dallas* and see in Stella's face glimpses of the future she imagines for herself (a future of anguish, yes, but of ecstasy as well) would seem to suggest that the melodrama of the unknown woman is derived from the remarriage comedy in more than one way—not merely by the mechanism of negation. That is, Stella's—triumphant, in Cavell's view—turn away from the scene of Laurel's wedding may be understood *as* comic.

Let us deal with the bracketed claim first: Stella is triumphant. It is not Cavell alone who senses this. In her marvelous reading of the film, Linda Williams puts the matter plainly before us: "Stella does not simply 'drift away' but marches triumphantly towards the camera and into close-up that reveals a fiercely proud and happy mother clenching a handkerchief between her teeth" (300). Williams understands, however, that this feeling of "triumph" is naive. The task of the narrative is to give us a happy ending, so as to mask the fact that Stella has been unmasked. "Significantly," says Williams, "Stella appears in this scene for the first time stripped of the exaggerated marks of femininity—the excessive make-up, furs, feathers, clanking jewelry, and ruffled dresses—that have been the weapons of her defiant assertions that a woman *can* be 'something else besides a mother'" (314). Yet the ending of the film, that is, its concluding image, has no more power over the beginning of the film, the middle of the film, or any of its 108 minutes than society has over Stella. Williams concludes, "For the film's ending to be perceived as entirely without problem, we would have to identify with this least sensitive and, therefore, least sympathetic point of view" (315). But the female spectator is able to identify with multiple points of view; she may see the image of Stella's eradication, but she may not believe it because the film has also given her glimpses of resistance to the same social forces that brought it about. This disavowal of the film's final meaning, says Williams, "is both a *knowing* recognition of the limitations of woman's representation in patriarchal language and a contrary *belief* in the illusion of a pre-Oedipal space between women free of the mastery and control of the male look" (318). As definitive as the ending is, it defines nothing for the female spectator. The image of Stella at the end of the film cannot contain the ambivalences and contradictions embedded within the film. Stella may acquiesce, but the female spectator may not.

What distinguishes Cavell's reading from Williams's, I think, is that Cavell is convinced that Stella does not acquiesce. I said above that William understands the belief in Stella's triumph is naïve. But for Cavell, Stella's triumph *is* real, but her triumph is not the audience's triumph. That is, Stella eludes us. For to consent to one's own eradication, one would have to see in that final image *another* mother: Mrs. Martin. She appears in one of the film's most striking (and overlooked) sequences. Stella is standing behind the fence that surrounds the front yard of her house as the workers leaving the mill house parade past her. As Stephen Dallas approaches, she feigns interest in a book, *India's Love Lyrics*. Her eyes shift from the book upward and toward Stephen, who appears

Figure 4.1   **Figure 4.2**

to return her glance. But Stephen is not looking at Stella (or perhaps has turned his glance away from her) and he walks past her without acknowledgment. Stella's brother, Charlie, arrives and finds his sister gazing, in the distance, and teasingly sings, "Stella's got a fella!" He then mocks her for "dolling up" every day for the benefit of a man who doesn't even know (or feigns not knowing) that she exists. As Charlie grabs Stella by both shoulders, demanding a kiss, Stella fights him off and cries, "take your dirty hands offa me!" Charlie then tells Stella she is "just like all the rest"—that is, just like all the other female millhands vying for Stephen's attention. "But he don't look at none of 'em," Charile tells her, to which she responds, "Why should he? Millhands." Charlie takes offense and the two begin shouting at each other. Their father arrives and demands that they stop. It is then revealed that Stella has been taking a business course "to improve herself." At just this moment there is an insert, a cut-in, of a full shot of Mrs. Martin, who stands before the

Figure 4.3   **Figure 4.4**

open door of the house. It is one of the most striking shots in the film. She is in a plain housedress, her hair is loosely tied in the back, and she is pale and without make-up, somewhat slouched, weathered and worn by years of motherly sacrifice (see Figure 4.1). She is, it would seem, the very image of Stella at the end of the film (see Figure 4.2).

Though certainly not inconsequential, this little family romance may seem forgettable (even though the striking shot of Mrs. Martin is so *un*forgettable). To be sure, the film's opening scene suffers from some serious critical neglect. But if we indulge in Cavell's comic reading of the film, we might take note that this scene places special emphasis on the true nature of Stella's desire, which is to be something else besides *her* mother. One might say that this desire is built into the very design of the image.[6] As we behold the figure of Mrs. Martin, we hear Charlie say of Stella, "She ain't satisfied with none of us anymore." The next shot is again from in front of the fence, and we catch a glimpse, over Stella's shoulder, of Mrs. Martin disappearing back into the house (see Figure 4.3). We find the father looking at Stella, the son looking at mother, the mother looking back at all three. But Stella short circuits this family network of looks. *Her look is awry.* Her back is turned away from the house, her mother, and the call for supper; Stella appears ready to jump the fence. When the father and son answer the call for supper, Stella remains behind. She turns her head to her left and searches the path she knows she must follow. This shot dissolves into the next (see Figure 4.4), and we see Stella lying in bed reading (this time not feigning an interest in) the book of love lyrics. *And she laughs at it.*

I must stop here so as to take full measure of what has just occurred and its importance to our understanding of Cavell's reading of the film's final image. Cavell takes as the principal issue of the melodrama of the unknown woman the woman's demand for education. As it is for the remarriage comedies, this means that the woman must be transformed and transfigured. But in *Stella Dallas*, as in all melodramas of the unknown woman, she must acknowledge that she is alone and isolated. Her desires and those of her husband are, finally, not at all mutual. What Stella expresses in this, the film's first scene, is that she wishes to make out another way for herself. One might say she finds a path—one that, it so happens, is paved by Stephen Dallas. It is a path that leads her away from home, a path perpendicular to the one that leads her back to nothing else besides her mother.

This scene is invoked by the remarriage comedy *His Girl Friday*, which also opens with a woman in need of escape, in search of a path. In the

Hawks film, Hildy, recently remarried and fresh from her honeymoon, has returned to her former employer, *The Morning Star*, to pay a final farewell. She is viewed making her way through the room in a tracking shot, left to right (see Figure 4.5). "The tracking motion," says Cavell, is:

> heightened, by being back and forth, in a shot-reverse shot between Hildy's gaze and the successive gazes of those with whom she exchanges greetings. These exchanges affirm a special attentiveness the camera pays to Hildy, both in the lyrical impulse to follow her and return to her and in the knowledge it registers of the anxiety in walking back into the familiar room and greeting inquiring faces after an absence of the four months in Reno and then Bermuda. (168)

What's more, argues Cavell, is that the camera movement actually *anticipates* Hildy's arrival and prepares the way for her (168). The shot-reverse-shots between Hildy and the employees reveal that Hildy is actually a step behind the camera, as if some unseen force was towing her. This is tracking shot-as-tractor beam, and it is in the direction of Walter Burns, her former boss and first husband, that she is pulled.

Figure 4.5   Figure 4.6

In *Stella Dallas*, we have a strikingly similar sequence. That the woman is stationary, rather than gliding left to right, is of some significance, but I will return to that in a moment. Here, as in *His Girl Friday*, the woman exchanges greetings with the same people with whom she feels she must disassociate herself (see Figure 4.6). Like Hildy, this woman is drawn irresistibly down a path prepared for her by a man, a path that leads first to his office, then to an impromptu lunch—call it a picnic of sorts—at which the woman and man are joined by another. And in *His Girl Friday*, the picnic takes place in a setting that, of all the film's settings, comes closest to resembling a home. Though the two, Walter and Hildy, had had no home, it is perhaps as right to say this setting, among all of the film's settings, comes closest to resembling a green world

Figure 4.7   **Figure 4.8**

(see Figure 4.7). In *Stella Dallas*, lunch takes place in Stephen's office. And although this is hardly the proper place for a picnic, the three make it one, and make it a happy one—the three being Stella, in sundress and bonnet, Stephen, and a beaming Mr. Beamer (see Figure 4.8).

This is enough to suggest that these two films are, in a sense, re-lated—enough perhaps, even to suggest that the melodrama of the un-known woman is more than "derived" from the comedy of remarriage. The formal and structural similarities are far too striking. But the films are in need of some proper alignment. The position that Stella occupies at the beginning of the sequence (Figure 4.6), immobile and in the center of the frame, suggests an essential difference between the two genres. Stella must ultimately strike out on her own (it is not insignificant that Stella schemes her way into Stephen's office, whereas Hildy, although not against her will but certainly against her better conscience, is drawn to Walter's). In the comedy of remarriage, the woman undergoes some kind of transformation that begins at her behest and with the aid of the man with whom she knows her desires are mutual. But in the Hollywood melodrama of the unknown woman, the woman refutes what is to be learned from the man with whom she discovers her desires are not mutual. Returning to figures 4.7 and 4.8, I do not see how one can align Stephen Dallas with Walter Burns. The logical match for Stephen would be Bruce Baldwin. Like Bruce, Stephen is decent, kind, sensible, concerned about the future. He too suffers, is also easily disappointed, and, most signifi-cantly, is incapable of reading between the lines. Stephen, with whom conversation is impossible, is no Walter, with whom conversation is not only essential, but is something of a honeymoon.[7]

There is no doubt that Stella learns from knowing Stephen. But as in the comedy of remarriage, what she learns is to accept that knowledge of herself she has possessed all along. This is why I take Stella's laughing smile at the book of love lyrics (a book, you will recall, that she feigns interest in from the outset) to be of such importance. And it is the task of the film to show how Stella re-discovers her distaste for the very thing she bestows upon her daughter at the film's end. That is, to borrow Cavell's description of Hildy, what Stella wants is "an escape not from happiness—what [Stephen] offers her is something she genuinely wants—but from counterfeit happiness, anyway from something decisively less for her than something else. There is pain in this decision, whichever way she turns" (165). Perhaps, like the young Hildy, the young Stella (another "doll-faced hick") is in possession of important knowledge: that "the world is not fashioned according to the heart's desire" and, perhaps more important, "knowing the real value of things" means, at the same time, "knowing the falseness of the face of the world" (177). If we grant that Stella is in possession of this knowledge, then we can read Stella's laughing smile at the book of love lyrics in the following way: "Can you beat that?" Given that what Stella keeps in between the book's pitiful little lines—the newspaper clipping describing why Stephen has broken off his engagement to Helen Morrison—it renders all the more suggestive to me her laughing smile later in the film, when she returns from the River Club to find Laurel has been lying in bed awake "and not a squawk out of her!" Stella's laughter here ("Can you beat that?"), as well as earlier in the film, expresses, says Cavell, "an imperative in herself to learn about happiness" (*Contesting Tears,* 211). Unlike Hildy, Stella is finally alone in her adventure. She has no Walter, with whom she may re-discover and share the understanding that to be at home in the black world is to be happy. Stella achieves happiness in utter isolation.

Up until this point, I have been trying to follow Cavell's line of thought on the matter of comedy. But here I must ask an essential question: can comedy thrive in solitude? Recall that Falstaff dies of a broken heart (so too, one suspects, does Ed Munn, with whom Stella shared adventures). One wonders if the moment Cavell asserts that Stella experiences ecstasy in her mo(u)rning is the very moment that he chooses philosophical solitude once and for all. This is the essential tension within Cavell's thought. He is both comic, in that he is responsive to and accepting of others, and he is an Emersonian philosopher, in that he chooses solitude. Like Marcello in Federico Fellini's *La Dolce Vita* (1960), Cavell glances across the tide to find his own Paola. And whereas Marcello turns his back on her and returns, with his fellow revelers, to a life of despair, Cavell lingers on the shore, forever holding Paola's smile within his view, but incapable of surrendering his solitude. It is as if Cavell has reached the absolute limit of philosophy, where it can behold whatever is not itself and nevertheless remain itself.[8]

But following the philosopher who thinks comically can be an extraordinary journey. Consider the implications of Cavell's reading of *Stella Dallas*. To accept his central claim, that the Hollywood melodrama of the unknown woman is derived from the remarriage comedy, is to question Peter Brooks's well-known assertion that the function of melodrama is to provide an adequate response to the loss of tragedy[9] and to ponder, further, the possibility that the function of melodrama is to contribute to comedy's struggle for survival by clearing some space for it. Contrary to Brooks's argument, comedy doesn't disappear with tragedy because tragedy's successor—melodrama—accommodates comedy rather than opposes it.[10]

To feel surprise, or incredulity, that we have reached this conclusion is to join a league of many.[11] Cavell had, between the years of 1989 and 1991, presented to incredulous university audiences his views of *Stella Dallas*. As Cavell recalled later, many in the audience wished "to go over what is quite straightforward evidence for my counteraccount of Stella's behavior and her power of consciousness in the film" and did so with much suspicion. How can Cavell take the archetypal film of self-effacing sacrifice and make it over "as a story—or as the cover for a story—of self-liberation and self empowering?" (36). Cavell defended himself and his counter-reading, which I have been attempting to extend, in the following way: "I find that the pain in imagining in Stella's stage of isolation on that reading is intenser than the pain of the received reading of sacrifice, intenser enough to account for the all but universal wish not to recognize the possibility of that counterreading" (37).

Can you beat that?

Notes

1. Bruns, Gerald. "The Last Romantic: Stanley Cavell and the Writing of Philosophy." *Tragic Thoughts at the End of Philosophy*. (Evanston, IL: Northwestern University Press, 1999), 200.
2. Ibid.
3. *The Major Film Theories: An Introduction*. (New York: Oxford University Press, 1976), 182–183.
4. "Cavell on Film, Television, and Opera." *Stanley Cavell*. Ed. Richard Eldridge. (New York: Cambridge University Press), 222.
5. "My project," says Cavell in *Contesting Tears*, "is through its origin in an effort to bring into play, and relate, a small number of comedies and a smaller number of melodramas, is shaped by a set of preoccupations of mine with intersections

between cinema and philosophical skepticism, between skepticism and tragedy and melodrama, hence (it turned out) between skepticism and gender, and between the two main traditions and institutional formations of Western philosophy, and between each of these traditions and psychoanalysis" (199).

6.   I borrow this language from André Bazin's "The Evolution of the Language of Cinema" in which he analyzes the use of deep focus photography in *Citizen Kane*. [*What is Cinema?* Vol. 1. Trans, Hugh Gray, 23–40. (Berkeley: University of California Press, 1967), 36.]

7.   What remains is the question of Mr. Beamer's place within this formal triangle. Visually, he occupies the position of Bruce Baldwin. But in terms of the film's narrative structure, this position is already occupied by Stephen Dallas. This structural asymmetry can be accounted for by the essential difference between the comedy of remarriage and the Hollywood melodrama of the unknown woman. In the latter, the choice for the woman is not between her man and his rival. For Stella, there is no rivalry, so there is no choice. One may think, then, of Mr. Beamer as a formal placeholder. He stands in for the rival Stella is not allowed to choose: Laurel. Or he stands in for any number of possible female associations, including Helen. I am indebted to Ned Schantz for our conversations about this particular question.

8.   See Gerald L. Bruns, "Tragic Thoughts at the end of Philosophy: Martha Nussbaum's Ethics of Particularity" in *Tragic Thoughts at the end of Philosophy: Language, Literature, and Ethical Theory*. Bruns writes, "At the end of *The Claim of Reason*, Cavell asks whether philosophy could turn into literature 'and still know itself' (CR496). Cavell himself has left this question unanswered; he may never take it up. I take it that the question is asking about what philosophy is willing to risk in opening itself up to whatever is not itself" (125).

9.   See Peter Brooks, *The Melodramatic Imagination: Balzac, Henry James, and the Mode of Excess*. (New Haven, CT: Yale University Press, 1976). Brooks's argument is that the modern melodrama (our melodrama) emerges at the beginning of nineteenth century, in the context of the French Revolution and its aftermath. The function of the melodrama is to fill the void left by "the traditional Sacred and its representative institutions (Church and Monarch)" (15). Contrary to the dominant literary sentiment, melodrama is not "vulgar and degraded near-tragedy" (24). Rather, melodrama is tragedy's successor. In a post-Sacred world, where the tragic vision is impossible, melodrama takes up the task of forcing us to "endure intense pain and anguish" so that we might better judge what is good and what is evil. Unlike tragedy, however, the melodrama strives toward excess, toward what Brooks calls the "too much" (35). Two objections emerge here which, taken together, return us to the profound implications of Cavell's reading of *Stella Dallas*. First, comedy, as an imaginative mode, neither denies nor turns away from pain and anguish. It simply refuses to accept the premise that pain and anguish are the only (or the last) modes of experience. Second, comedy is quite comfortable with excess. It, too, strives toward the "too much." By allowing these two objections, we may understand better why we often respond to melodramatic excess with laughter (think of Chekov and the bemused contempt he has for the lachrymose), why we often treat melodrama as camp, and even why one might read *Stella Dallas* comically.

10.   I am indebted to Ned Schantz for offering this as a possible way of rethinking the relationship between melodrama and comedy.

11.   A credulous take on Cavell's reading of the film is Angel Curran's "Stella at the Movies: Class, Critical Spectatorship, and Melodrama in *Stella Dallas*" in *The Philosophy of Film: Introductory Texts and Readings* (Malden, MA: Blackwell, 2005), 235–245. Curran agrees with Cavell's claim that "Stella learns the futility

of appealing to the taste of those who have no taste for her," but believes that he grants this knowledge to Stella prematurely (in Curran, 243–244). According to Curran, "Stella's recognition that social ascent is not what she wants for herself occurs much later in the film"—specifically, at the very end of the film when Stella watches Laurel's wedding from outside the window. Yet Cavell, who agrees with Linda Williams more more than he can, and should, admit, believes that the knowledge in question—that it is futile to appeal to the taste of others who have no taste for her—stems from Stella's "massively authenticated knowledge of clothes, that she is an expert at their construction and, if you like, deconstruction" (201). Or, if you like, she is expert at "the masquerade of femininity" (Williams, 312). Consider three striking images from the film: the dog, which Stephen proudly presents to Laurel when she arrives in the Morrison home. The dog stands erect on its hind legs directly in front of Stephen, doubling for us and for Laurel the image of the phallic father. The second image follows shortly after the film is of Ed Munn who, with goose under arm, has unexpectedly dropped by Stella's apartment on Christmas Day. As Ed Munn accosts Laurel, the goose neck, cold and limp, flops grotesquely to and fro. Laurel is as repulsed with this second image as she was delighted with the first. It is no surprise, then, that Stella—determined, as Cavell argues, to disgrace herself publicly at the hotel and before her daughter's eyes at the soda shop—chooses to add one final touch to her outfit before she leaves her hotel room, which is the third image I have in mind: a fox stole that flops to and fro across the hotel grounds like Ed Munn's pickled penis. If Stella plans to secure a place for Laurel within upper-class society by ensuring, once and for all, that Stephen becomes Laurel's primary object choice, surely the plan is hatched here. I am grateful to Richard Nunan for bringing Angela Curran's essay to my attention.

5

Get out of Gaol Free, or:
How to Read a Comic Plot

G.K. Chesterton said of Dickens's second book, "*Pickwick*, indeed, is not a good novel; but it is not a bad novel, for it is not a novel at all" (109). This is not, appearances aside, a pure expression of admiration for a work whose power and success continues to survive in spite of its readers' demands for cause and effect, unity, continuity, and resolution. Chesterton is telling us just how difficult it is to avoid using the word *novel*. The problem is this: If *Pickwick Papers* is not a novel at all, then what is it? Just that, not a novel at all. Most critics avoid this problem altogether and simply call *Pickwick Papers* a failed novel, even as they acknowledge that it might never be more than it claims to be: a series of papers. Like his first outing, *Sketches By Boz*, Dickens gives us less a novel than what Victor Shlovsky called *nanizyvanie*, or "a stringing together" of episodes and short stories. This phrase comes from Shlovsky's discussion of the novel in general, whose origins he found in collections of short stories. The earliest literary works (like *Don Quixote*) gave us strange, paradoxical characters not because of a need on the author's part "to illustrate philosophical or psychological insight, but as the purely accidental result of stringing inconsistent adventures together" (Morson and Emerson, 274). Dickens, then, might be considered a master of this "stringing together." His characters are held firmly and consistently *within* character—despite the loose and voluminous chapters in which they are housed. George Orwell, echoing Chesterton's sentiments, says that, unlike our modern novelists, Dickens gives us characters that are "finished and perfect" like "pieces of furniture" (166).[1] A Dickens character has no more mental life than a chest of drawers.[2] In other words, it's impossible to carry on an imaginary conversation with Samuel Pickwick. We don't want to take issue with his choices, his actions, or his motives. We simply watch him go. The idea of episodic movement, coupled with the idea of distanced spectatorship, does much more than inform the way we understand character in Dickens,[3] it nudges us toward how we might read a comic plot. The least novelistic of Dickens's books has paradoxically made us anxious to find ever more shrewd and creative ways of reading it as if it *was* a novel. Just why this is—just why *Pickwick* has been called upon to satisfy the need to read novelistically, rather than to inspire in readers other equally shrewd and creative fictional devices—is the subject of this chapter. *Pickwick* is a book that teaches us to read comically, not novelistically.

From a Formalist perspective, one might say "reading novelistically" means recognizing in any given story a host of literary devices that deform everyday narrative in a special way (Morson and Emerson, 19). Bakhtin preferred the novel to other literary forms because, so he claimed, it had its own unique language. He broke with the Formalists precisely because the uniqueness of this language was not stressed enough by those who chose to judge the novel according to theories derived from poetry. There was, really, no theory of prose available until Bakhtin worked one out. To him, understanding the novel meant understanding how it "reflects more deeply, more essentially, more sensitively and rapidly, reality itself in the process of its unfolding" ("Epic and Novel," 7). When one reads Bakhtin, one comes away with an awareness of the extraordinary complexities of everyday experience and the manners in which we speak of them. At its best, the novel captures, better than any other literary form, the essential open-endedness of being, of existence. In Dostoevsky, Bakhtin found an author who took the language of the novel "beyond the realm of pragmatic plot considerations" (*Problems of Dostoevky's Poetics,* 20). Characters could speak without being held to their word, and events could unfold without being read as mere consequences or causes.

Another way to understand the term "reading novelistically," however, owes less to Bakhtin's appreciation of open-endedness and more to the reader's appreciation of a good plot—the need for what Frank Kermode calls "grand beginnings and ends" (35). The novel is designed to make us analyzers of action, circumstance, events, and causes; it is designed to give us, in Kermode's words, a sense of an ending. Bakhtin, however, had little regard for endings and chose instead to champion the novel's open-endedness (from a certain point of view, claims Bakhtin, Dostoevsky never completed *The Brothers Karamazov*). To him, the novelistic plot was simply a "service function" (*Problems of Dostoevsky's Poetics,* 100), a way of enabling characters to engage in lively dialogues to which the reader can then respond. According to Caryl Emerson and Gary Saul Morson, "readers who understand ideas in terms of their origins and consequences find they are left hanging on too many critical issues. One must read not for the plot, but for the dialogues, and to read for the dialogues is to participate in them" (249). This idea, of course, seems counterintuitive. "What happens to Isabel Archer at the end of *Portrait of a Lady*?" is, for modern readers at any rate, a question of considerably more importance than, say, "How do Isabel Archer and Ralph Touchett speak to each other?" The novelistic plot demands that we, as readers, must always be moving "*end*ward," in a rectilinear fashion, towards resolution, closure, and understanding.[4]

The comic plot, however, has no demands save one: that the reader must always be moving somewhere, anywhere. In the comic plot, characters need not be *understood*—their movement alone can be the object of the reader's desire. As Thomas McFarland has put it, one of the features of the comic plot is that it:

> not only depends on types rather than individuals, but also finds these types adequate in themselves, or at the very least, not dependent upon any particular comic plot... This freedom of the comic character type from plot results in a playful, gamelike organization of the plot itself. Tragic plot or mythos is burdened with the large task of revealing tragic character. Comic plot, questions of character settled beforehand in the comic typology, becomes frolicsome and restive, complex and mazelike. Such plot veers toward the nature of dance, and has as its hallmark the repetitions, formalities, and artificialities of dance. (7–8)

Comic types, like Falstaff, Don Quixote, or Mr. Pickwick, seem to exist as comic entities outside the pages of their respective works. That is, Falstaff has no single plot that defines him; he can walk the Earth wherever he pleases (and through any given plot, be it *1 Henry IV* or *The Merry Wives of Windsor*). This freedom of movement, as McFarland suggests, changes the way we read. We are less interested in what happens to Falstaff in the end than in how he manages to get out of this present situation, and into the next one.[5] The reader of the novel joins the march towards resolution; the reader of the comedy joins the endless dance. With this in mind, one could say that we, as readers of *Pickwick*, have it all wrong—that if we only realized that what we have before us is really a series of comic episodes, we would stop complaining about its sudden shift midway from one kind of story to another.[6]

Because *Pickwick* is a comic story, it stands to reason that it can be read comically, and our failure to read it comically stems, in part, from our inability (or unwillingness) to recognize and understand comic plots.

Part of the problem, no doubt, is that our conception of plot is Aristotelian, and the Aristotelian conception of plot comes from tragedy, not comedy. Aristotle, in the *Poetics*, famously singled out "the end" as everywhere the chief thing in tragedy, but it is not unfair to say that we single out "the end" as everywhere the chief thing in making sense of our own lives, of the world, and of virtually any text we identify as narrative. This is not to say that the world and everything in it is essentially tragic; rather, our ability to create meaning, our ability to make sense of ourselves and the world around us, is tragic. It is not surprising, therefore, to find in any suggestive analysis of narrative an unyielding devotion to ends. In his essay "The Storyteller," Walter Benjamin goes so far as to claim that death, the ultimate "end," is "the stuff stories are made of":

> Just as a sequence of images is set in motion inside a man as his life comes to an end—unfolding the views of himself under which he has encountered himself without being aware of it—suddenly in his expressions and looks the un-forgettable emerges and imparts to everything that concerned him that authority which even the poorest wretch in dying possess for the living around him. This authority is at the very source of the story. (94)

Even as our attitudes towards stories and storytelling become more and more sophisticated and our confidence in the authority of "ends"—literary or otherwise—diminishes, we seldom wander very far from the basic Aristotelian script. Frank Kermode points out that "in 'making sense' of the world we still feel a need, harder than ever to satisfy because of an accumulated skepticism, to experience that concordance of beginning, middle and end which is the essence of our explanatory fictions" (35–36). Peter Brooks' *Reading for Plot*, one of the most original and interesting studies of narrative in recent years, argues that plot is best understood not as a thing but an activity. What carries us forward, onward through the text is the desire for meaning developed through temporal succession. As we read a novel, says Brooks, "we realize the action progressively, segment by segment, as a kind of present in terms of our experience of it" and, more important, "we do so precisely in anticipation of its larger hermeneutic structuring by conclusions" (22–23). In a novel, the action is always moving forward, toward some conclusion that, paradoxically, is already in place, already realized. We push on all the same, confident that "what remains to be read will restructure the provisional meanings of the already read" (23). To read for plot, then, is to accept the idea that what follows is always going to be more important than what precedes, and that what precedes must necessarily be reread or rewritten in light of what follows.

In order to begin some kind of comprehensive resignification of *Pick-wick*, we might first assume that there is no shift, no action that propels the characters towards a destination, no movement towards structural coherence[7]—all hallmarks of the Aristotelian plot. For the reader of the comic plot, *Pickwick* is a discontinuous series of romantic adventures. If we assume that *Pickwick* is not a conventional novel, not even an unconventional book that bumbles its way through several hundred pages before finally establishing "a coherent narrative structure"[8] for itself, we might begin to appreciate its comic episodes differently. More than this, we might begin to appreciate its *un*comic or "bleak" moments differently—that is, to say, comically. *Pickwick* is a length cut from the great comic pattern. The action neither begins nor moves anywhere; it merely grows and proliferates in every direction. Movement is the only rule. Dickens makes it clear, through the moon-like spectacles of Samuel Pickwick, that ladies are rescued as sure as apple pie beds and that tyrants are defied precisely by revealing them to be no more terrible than horse ponds.

You Can't Get Something from Nothing: Reading the Comic "Plot"

Of course, we *can* get something from nothing, and it is the appeal of Dickens's book that we always do. Nevertheless, part of reason we feel the book "shifts" midway stems from our assumption that the early episodes really come to nothing at all, whereas Pickwick's comic snubbing of Mrs. Bardell comes to a great deal. In other words, the early misadventures of Pickwick and company are trifles, and it is only when Pickwick trifles his way into the great expectations of Mrs. Bardell that the book discovers a plot for itself, that something significant occurs. The scales are tipped and the events of Dickens's book begin to take on the weight of importance. J. Hillis Miller puts it this way: when Pickwick becomes involved in the case of Bardell versus Pickwick, his life "begins to have a cohesive duration, and the novel a real plot. Pickwick can no longer reenact in a kind of eternal childhood the rhythm of his innocent adventures. He must now extricate himself from his situation or be destroyed by it" (29). In the fortieth chapter, Mr. Pickwick lands in the Fleet, thus "beginning a term," writes Garrett Stewart, "which probably no reader has ever failed to recognize as the turning point of the book" (47). While we may view the first half of the book with a measure of respect, we seem uninterested in the possibility that it is nearly as important as anything that follows it. Even the great Chesterton is guided by the assumption that the book necessarily darkens after the Fleet episode and that this darkening somehow illuminates "the main story" of suffering and dismay. He must admit, and mildly lament, a sudden and inadvertent *change* in the book. Dickens divides the book in two—the first half being comic (before the Fleet), the second half being epic (after the Fleet). It's as if the first forty chapters of *Pickwick* are nothing more than misfirings. In this section I will discuss the innocent adventures of these chapters in order to illustrate the "artificial, complex, and game-like" nature of comic plots. The purpose of this present discussion is to reveal how comic plots have, in McFarland's words, "no problems about either their point of departure or their destination" (10). I would like to argue that reading a text comically means indulging in this carelessness, this disregard for beginnings and endings, with every new episode. It seems clear enough that we have been producing good readings of *Pickwick,* the failed novel, but we have been inattentive to finding a good reading of *Pickwick,* the comic plot.

Our discussion will begin with the hunting episode from Chapter 7 in which Pickwick and company await the "devastating barrel" of Mr. Winkle as he takes aim at his game: "There was a solemn pause—a shout—a flapping of wings—a faint click" (111). These are the most benevolent misfirings of all. Mr. Winkle's exclamation of "Bless my soul!" signals the failed arrival of something greatly anticipated (devastating barrels and easy targets), a comic trope if ever there was one. Marcel Gutwirth, in *Laughing Matter: An Essay on the Comic* (1993), refers to both Kant and Pascal as the early harbingers of this idea, what he calls an "intellectualist theory" of laughter: "Pascal speaks of disproportion. Kant implies disappointment: we were all set to apprehend 'something' and find ourselves holding 'nothing.' The mind is fooled, the wind taken out of us, painlessly—for the 'disappointment' is far from grievous. The contrast, at all events, is a descending one: *some*thing makes way for *no*thing" (85). This generalization satisfies those readers who choose *not* to see that something does *not* make way for nothing, but instead gives way to something *more,* something *better.* To put it more precisely, the misfirings of Mr. Winkle bring about a great deal. Apart from Mr. Tupman's end of the bargain ("a portion of charge in his left arm" resulting from a hurried re-adjustment on Mr. Winkle's behalf), the whole of Pickwick and company are treated to, perhaps, what they've desired all along: dear Miss Rachael's sympathetic affections, a readied breakfast parlor, and boundless good cheer (113).

Several chapters later, Pickwick and company set out once more with

anticipations that an over-flowing abundance shall take the place of emptiness. When asked if they should be expected to fill two enormous game
bags after the day's hunt is through, old Wardle replies, "Fill them!...
Bless you, yes! You shall fill one, and I the other; and when we've done
with them, the pockets of our shooting-jackets will hold as much more"
(282). This desire to fill bags (only to empty them and fill them once
again) is hilariously careless and unrestrained—Mr. Winkle becomes
wildly entangled in his own gun and threatens to make Sam Weller (and
later a pair of hounds) the bag's first occupant; and Mr. Pickwick, in a
"gross violation of all established rules and precedents" joins the hunt
in a wheelbarrow (284). The misfirings once more commence, sending
portions of charge whizzing by heads and affecting disapproving remarks
and reproachful glances. But there's an almost magical quality to the
misfirings, as if the boldness and enthusiasm of Pickwick and company
were capable of bringing game from the sky. Mr. Tupman knows well
that the best course of action for a man to improve his shooting skill is
to close one's eyes and fire, innocently, into the sky. "On one occasion
after performing this feat," we are told, "Mr. Tupman, on opening his
eyes, beheld a plump partridge in the act of falling to the ground" (287).
If only poor Winkle could have such good fortune! The hunt, however,
is only a pretense for Pickwick and company to simply *go*. To go and
talk at great length of meal pie, knuckle of ham, cold meat in slices, and
all "them noble animals." In short, they went to picnic. We may have a
laugh at poor Winkle's expense, but the reader is assured that all will
be rewarded. The hunt provides everyone nothing more, really, than an
opportunity to swell and ripen: "'This is delightful—thoroughly delightful!' said Mr. Pickwick, the skin of whose expressive countenance was
rapidly peeling off with exposure to the sun" (290).

Pickwick, of course, will awaken from what James Kincaid has called
his "vision from the wheelbarrow"[9] to find himself in the Pound, having
been wheeled away "like a drunken plebeian" by Wilkins and Captain
Boldwig. Our dear Pickwick soon finds himself accosted by the roars of
a crowd that has gathered around him in great anticipation of his com-
ing-to. "What's the matter?" asks Pickwick feebly, to which the crowd
replies, in unison, "Here's a game!" Indeed, Pickwick has fallen, almost
magically, from the skies and onto the floor of the Pound—much to the
glee of the anonymous crowd. Each cry for mercy elicits only hostile
laughter: "'Let me out,' cried Mr. Pickwick. 'Where's my servant? Where
are my friends?' 'You ain't got no friends. Hurrah!' Then there came a
turnip, then a potato, and then an egg—with a few other little tokens of

the playful disposition of the many headed" (295). Things take a turn for the worse, we are often told, in a brilliantly quick succession of events. There's a seeming edginess to revelry, an implicit danger to intoxication and frivolity that always signals the impossibility of limitless peace. We may be granting a bit too much hostility to this scene, however, when we say that it signals "the final inadequacy of escape" for Mr. Pickwick (Kincaid, *Dickens,* 21). Morson and Emerson, following Bakhtin's lead, remind us, "[u]nder noncarnival conditions, such de-basement might signify humiliation and power. In the carnival symbolic, however, a casting-down is always a positive gesture as well, a bringing-down-to-earth and thus a renewal and refertilization" (443). The rotten vegetables are hurled, the narrator assures us, with the kindest of intentions. Each juicy *blap!* to the face is a big, wet kiss. Pickwick's countenance, sunburned and peeling like an overripe tomato, is greeted head-on by some of its earthly counterparts. This is carnival debasement at its most elemental; the tossing of rotten (vegetable) flesh can signal the ritual of rebirth. "You ain't got no friends, Hurrah!" can also be a hearty, festive welcome, a celebration of the humorist's regenerative spirit; it may also signal the mob's recognition of the comic society to which Pickwick belongs. Seen from a different point of view, the hostile mockery Mr. Pickwick is subject to can take on a coarse and cynical meaning, but this is not our hero's view of things. The punishment is lost on him we'll soon see. One might say the hostile mockery is not punishment at all, really. To be sure, the deadened silence of an unresponsive and dispassionate group of in-mates would be far more oppressive, and would likely provide Pickwick with a far more grim experience than the grotesque banquet given in his honor—which is perhaps why his good cheer returns so swiftly. Instead of suffering, Lear-like, the torments and indignities of the Pound, Pickwick becomes part of a triumphal celebration that offers "the potentiality of a new beginning instead of the abstract and bare ending" (Bakhtin, *Rabelais,* 283). Sam and Bardle arrive, Pickwick is released and announces he will prepare a legal suit of false-imprisonment against Captain Bodwig. Bardle then reminds Pickwick of the cold punch he had taken, arguably in excess, only a few hours before: "Do what he would, a smile would come into Mr. Pickwick's face; the smile extended into a laugh; the laugh into a roar; the roar became general" (296). Pickwick's response seems counter-intuitive; it reverses Baudelaire's famous line "The wise man laughs only with fear and trembling" (141). Here, and throughout the entirety of Dickens's book, our foolhardy heroes fear and tremble only with laughter. This attitude, says Susanne Langer, suggests that although the oncoming future is indeed fraught with danger, it is full of opportunities as well, "that is, with physical or social events occurring by chance and building up coincidences with which individuals cope according to their lights" (331). The tragic events in the Pound—Pickwick's exposure to the humiliating taunts of strangers, coupled with the shock of his sudden and complete abandonment—only *seem* to signal to us the emergence of a very dangerous world, the end of horseplay, and the need to take things more seriously. And although readers generally don't hesitate to respond to these signals and shape *Pickwick Papers* into a moral tale with a unified and coherent structure (a beginning, middle, and an end) it is also possible to ignore these signals and produce, instead, a comic pattern (an indeterminate, game-making sense of time) in which complications come and go and come again and go once more. To those who read comically, tragedy is not fate but simply another game. And to those who read Dickens's book comically, the quick succession of events in this chapter doesn't *end* with Pickwick's imprisonment. Rather, it simply endures.

What innocent adventures like this do is help us see comedy as something that opens up endlessly into a something else, a perpetual springing-up of somethings. Meanings don't develop or cohere, they merely accumulate. This is less an intellectual and more a mythic understanding of the comic plot, but it serves us well since Gutwirth's intellectual formula of "something/nothing" tends to put an end to the game before play is done, and this is not how comedy organizes experience. The ability to say that the innocent adventures of the early chapters amount to nothing comes from our willingness to say that the case of Bardell versus Pickwick is a very important "something" indeed—a something among nothings, a something that threatens the comic view of the world that Pickwick's "innocent" adventures have nurtured. Take, for example, the legal business that brings Mr. Pickwick before the magistrate, Mr. Nupkins. We are lead to believe, for all sorts of reasons, that it is not very serious business at all. For starters, Nupkins simply refuses to admit anything as serious as a duel could possibly take place in the town of Ipswich ("I don't think—I do *not* think—"). After all, here's a man who, at the risk of suffering "the angry passions of an infuriated multitude," suspended the contest between the Middlesex Dumpling and the Suffolk Bantam. Here's a man whose idea of a town rebellion involves the pelting of a constabulary ("an elderly gentleman," we are told, "who had been a peace officer, man and boy, for half a century at least") who had been called out to repress a day-school conspiracy to pester an obnoxious apple seller.

Here's a man who is in a perpetual "state of the utmost excitement and irritation" over nothings (366). And though we might say he inflates the nothings so as to mask his own nothingness, so as to protect the mask of power always in danger of deflating, another reading is available here: for the majestic and impartial Mr. Nupkins, nothings are somethings and somethings are nothings. He is, one might say, even if by accident, a good reader of comic plots.

Good readers of novelistic plots, however, will show how the legal business in this chapter prepares us for the trial of *Bardell v. Pickwick*; and although such readings may reach somewhat different ends, they all begin with the very same premise: that the legal business of Mr. Nupkins is nothing and the legal business of Dodson and Fogg is something. Not only do we buy into this premise, we manage to convince ourselves that the nothingness of one scene makes a something out of the other, and vice versa. Referring to Philip Collins's observation that the scene in Ipswich seems "stock," Jonathan Gross says this is precisely Dickens's point: "Dickens is exposing the difference between depicting a stock, traditional, rural trial held by a justice of the peace in his chambers and the urban, lawyered trial of the London courtroom that he has just introduced into his story (177–178). The scene is a digression—a "detour" back to the Pickwickian plot with which we have been primed—meant only to inform us that "there is a new order of trial and a new order of representation at work" (178). In other words, Dodson and Fogg do, indeed, win more than just the trial. They win our faith in the proper attitudes and responses to legal business. Their legalistic attitude ("You'll think better of that before next term, Mr. Pickwick") becomes our novelistic attitude: things get postponed, anticipated, connected. The comic Pickwickian plot no longer guides our readerly responses to the book's unfolding events except as that which must now be retold according to the inflexible principles of the law.

But how is it that, for both us and Dickens, the absence of lawyers in Ipswich "reveals their import" (178)? Where does this readerly presumption come from? Never mind the unsporting charge that something absent from a text couldn't possibly buttress the significance of what is present. There is no flaw in Gross's logic, to be sure. On the contrary, he is simply doing what we all do, and do so very well, which is assume that a comic episode cannot be sustained, that it must displace itself in order to allow for the novelistic plot to unfold. This process resembles what Frank Kermode describes as the "tick-tock" of fiction. In order to sustain a reader's interest, says Kermode, "a thousand-page novel must "maintain within that interval between *tick* a lively expectation of *tock*, and a sense that however remote *tock* may be, all that happens as if *tock* were certainly following" (46). This idea is dry and precise, not as deliciously greasy as Dickens's own bacon metaphor, but it is enormously convincing.[10] The scene in Ipswich (*tick*) is inconsequential without the trial in London (*tock*). But what if we assumed differently? What if we assumed that there is nothing more or less substantial to a *tock*, since what we anticipate is not only the arrival of *tock*, but the promise of another *tick* as well? The presence of the lawyers is significant not because they are absent elsewhere, not because they have no place in a comic plot, but because they are *part* of the comic plot. The "stock" scene in Ipswich has no other effect than to keep the coach moving, so to speak; and it moves to London as surely as *tick* follows *tock*. And although its opposite, *tock-tick*, can be, as Kermode notes, "humanly uninteresting successiveness" (46), it is especially so (and perhaps only so) to the mind that chooses to organize time linearly, according to beginnings and ends, to the beat of *tick-tock*. Time, of course, does not proceed like this in any natural or necessary way. It is simply a common organization, one that insists that no event is inconsequential. Pickwick is acutely aware of people who organize time this way, and he does not hesitate to express how preposterous and dangerous they are: "Gentlemen of your profession," says Pickwick to Serjeant Snubbin:

> see the worst side of human nature. All its disputes, all its ill will and bad blood, rise up before you. You know them from your experience of juries (I mean no disparagement to you or them) how much depends upon *effect;* and you are apt to attribute to others a desire to use, for purposes of deception and self-interest, the very instruments which you, in pure honesty and honour of purpose, and with a laudable desire to do your utmost for your client, know the temper and worth of so well from constantly employing them yourselves." (474)

Pickwick, in this burst of eloquence, is right on target. Not only does he take aim at Snubbin and other gentlemen of his profession; he takes aim at us and our habits of reading. As much as Mr. Pickwick acknowledges its "inestimable value," he would rather be deprived the aid of Snubbin's legal (and our readerly) talents than have the advantage of them (474). Here is a telling scene: the Pickwickian plot needs retelling. Whereas the novel-minded reader will think better of Pickwick's attitude before next term and impose a new order of representation, the comic-minded reader will think better of putting so much stock in *effect* and instead play the "get out of gaol free" card. By playing it, of course, one may never find the answer to what sort of novel *Pickwick* might be—which is, Mr. Pickwick would say, a very philosophical view, but breakfast is waiting (360).

The Education of Sam

It should be noted first that one need not treat the trial of *Bardell v. Pickwick* as *un*important, as if the demands of the Pickwickian plot are such that we treat the trial of *Bardell v. Pickwick* as nothing at all. Rather, the Pickwickian (or comic) plot asks that we treat it as another romantic adventure. Put another way, if we see the comic episodes in *Pickwick* as endlessly unfolding into one another and include the Fleet episode in this great tumbling, then the Fleet will appear to be a *nothing* that will, as sure as eggs is eggs, turn into another in a series of wonderful *somethings*. Of course, one could argue that the transformation of *Pickwick* from comic plot to legalistic novel does not depend at all on whether or not we, as readers, are seduced by the attitudes of Dodson and Fogg. Who is seduced, whether present or conspicuously absent, by a lawyer? It is the duty of the lawyer to intimidate, bully, put down, manipulate, bait and switch, and so on. As lawyer-land threatens to spread into Dingley Dell and elsewhere, we call on Sam Weller to be the interpreter of legal fiction. In short, our responses to the events in the book are orchestrated not so much by lawyers but by Sam, whose rebuttals give Pickwick (and us) the comfort of evasion. He is our "alleybi." We tell ourselves, time and again, the simplicity and benevolence of Pickwick must not be set loose. The real world refuses to be nourished by his benevolence unless it is tempered and tamed. This somewhat cynical view of Pickwick's comic spirit is pasted firmly around *Pickwick* like a bullying book flap: "in the nonrealistic world of *Pickwick* the psychic pattern is so rearranged that the hero can be safely vaccinated against all fancy, forced to give up dreams of any sort, without danger, in order to insure against nightmare" (Stewart, 37); "As the narrative develops, Dickens portrays Mr. Pickwick as a less naïve man who shows positive qualities of integrity" (Hawes, 180); "Mr. Pickwick has moved from the illusory world of the Bagman's Uncle into the black world we all recognize" (Kincaid, 49); the world of Pickwick is a charming but imaginary Eden which must give way, finally, to "the real and fallen world" (Auden, 78). The fellowship Mr. Pickwick forges with Sam Weller does not help this Eden blossom more fully, but instead forces it to both oppose and collaborate with the "real" world. Of course, these scholars are giving us not much more than an apology for the ways in which we, as readers of *Pickwick*, feel compelled to hierarchically arrange the people and plot of Dickens's book.

Here's a pair of people and a plot: Sam Weller leads Mr. Pickwick on a journey from innocence to experience. The latter fellow is the great, benevolent patriarch who surrounds himself with the filial affections of his company: Snodgrass, Winkle, Tupman. The former is the ever-loyal servant, inferior in class and manners to his master. We quickly discover, however, that there is a grandiose humor about Mr. Pickwick; he is as much a patriarch as Snodgrass is a poet, as Winkle is a sportsman, as Tupman is a lover. Alfred Jingle is our first spoiler, and in one remarkable chapter, he single-handedly mocks every lofty aspiration of Pickwick and company. First in line is Snodgrass: "'My friend Mr. Snodgrass has a strong poetic turn,' said Mr. Pickwick. 'So have I,' said the stranger. 'Epic poem—ten thousand lines—revolution of July—composed it on the spot—Mars by day, Apollo by night—bang the field-piece—twang the lyre.'" Next is Mr. Winkle: "'Sportsman sir?' abruptly turning to Mr. Winkle. 'A little, sir,' replied the gentleman. 'Fine pursuit, sir—fine pursuit. Dogs, sir?' 'Not just now,' said Mr. Winkle. [Not just now!] 'Ah! You should keep dogs—fine animals—sagacious creatures—dog of my own once—pointer—surprising instinct'" and so on. Lastly is Tupman: "'You have been to Spain, sir?' said Mr. Tracy Tupman. 'Lived there—ages.' 'Many conquests, sir?' inquired Mr. Tupman. 'Conquests! Thousands'" (34). Just as quickly as he comes, Jingle goes—leaving every man with his pants down.

In a similar although more affectionate exposing of posing, Sam Weller reveals he is best understood as Mr. Pickwick's guardian, not his servant. This comic switch comes early in the book, Chapter 13 to be precise. Here, Sam Weller explains to his master the game of "pumping over independent voters" in which voters are bought for a shilling a head. Pickwick's astonishment at this underhandedness customarily elicits Sam's now famous reply: "Why, where was you half baptized? That's nothin', that ain't" (197). And so it begins—the education of Mr. Pickwick. As Garrett Stewart has suggested, this scene, and others like it, force us to ask our hero: "When will you have learned enough of the world and its suffering to deserve the Pickwickian title in its genuine personal sense?" (57). Stewart's answer echoes our own. The final baptism occurs only after the Fleet episode, only after Pickwick surrenders his naïveté and submits to Sam's views of things. In other words, as we read *Pickwick*, we witness the comic inversion of roles: Mr. Pickwick goes from king to child and Sam Weller from footman to headmaster. Until then, Pickwick's ties to the reality principle are threadbare, as demonstrated by the scene in the Fleet when Sam is told that the debtor's prison is no place for a young man, and that he should leave immediately: "I have felt from the first, Sam," said Mr. Pickwick with much solemnity, "that this is not the place to bring a young man to." Although Sam acts as if he doesn't understand these feelings, we know that Sam understands them all too well: "Vell, sir," rejoined Sam after a short pause, "I think I see your drift; and if I do see your drift, it's my 'pinion that you're a-comin' it a great deal too strong, as the mail-coachman said to the snow-storm ven it overtook him" (651). Sam's fear, that Pickwick is coming at it "a great deal too strong," stems from the parental impulse of a stern master whose duty is to check the tender, yet dangerously naïve notions of the child—such is the super-ego's charge over the ego. The "snowstorm" that threatens to overtake Pickwick is, of course, the world of the law.

I import these explicitly Freudian terms deliberately, for I feel that Freud's insight into the strange world of the humorist may be of some use to us here. In an essay published well after *Jokes and their Relation to the Unconscious*, Freud grapples with what is perhaps the most mysterious category of the comic: humor. The process at work in humor involves the repudiation of reality in service of an illusion. The humorist defies the reality principle and asserts the invincibility of his own ego. Freud uses a bit of gallows humor to make his point: "To take a very crude example: when a criminal who is being led to the gallows on a Monday observes, 'Well, this is a good beginning to the week,' he himself is creating the humour; the process works itself out in relation to himself and evidently it affords him a certain satisfaction." Yet, Freud seems confident enough to insist that there is something "fine and elevating" about humor. Humor is far more dignified than wit. The jokester only cares about the gratification afforded by psychic expenditure. Worse yet, the jokester often seeks merely to provide an outlet for his aggressive impulses. The humorist, on the other hand, "insists that it is impervious to wounds dealt by the outside world, in fact, that these are merely occasions for affording it pleasure" (217). This is not to say the humorist seeks out pleasure, but rather that he is capable of surviving—even enjoying—the most abysmal of conditions. "Humour," writes Freud, "is not resigned; it is rebellious. It signifies the triumph not only of the ego, but also of the pleasure principle, which is strong enough to assert itself here in the face of the adverse real circumstances" (217). In short, humor is a form of resistance. But what, exactly, makes this form of resistance so fine and elevating? Isn't heroic resignation ("I regret that I have but one life to give," "it is a far, far better thing," etc.) fine and elevating? Is Freud really saying that humor is a superior form of comedy precisely because it opposes the reality principle? Because the super-ego, ordinarily the stern master, can say to the ego: "you're *right*, this *is* bullshit"? If we think about it, Freud is taking a great risk here. After all, he is placing humor in a series of *other* methods of repudiating reality, such as neurosis, delusion, intoxication, and other self-induced states of abstraction and ecstasy (217). These methods, of course, are far from "fine and elevating"—perhaps because when we indulge in them we are quitting the ground of mental sanity (217). Without quite knowing why, we nonetheless find in humor something liberating, even as we admit that it functions like a pathology.

Rather than pathologize the humorist, Freud instead casts the humorist in familial terms: the humorist is the adult, and the seemingly dangerous world is mere child's play. This explanation doesn't completely satisfy Freud, however, because a simple inversion of roles only accounts for part of what the humorist's game is. In other words, the humorist doesn't simply view the world as child's play. Something else occurs: "Here we must recall the other, perhaps the original and more important, situation in humor, in which a man adopts a humorous attitude towards himself in order to ward off possible suffering. Is there any sense in saying that someone is treating himself like a child and is at the same time playing the part of the superior adult in relation to this child?" (3–4). This dynamic explanation of the humorist attitude is informed by Freud's own concept of the *ego* and the *super-ego*. It is the super-ego that, in humor, protects and comforts the intimidated ego. This formula works well to explain the relationship of Mr. Pickwick and Sam Weller. Think not of the two as separate individuals. Instead, try seeing the pair, taken together as a unit, as the embodiment of humor. The first few numbers of *Pickwick* function as a prologue. It is often noted that sales of *Pickwick* shot up dramatically when Sam Weller is introduced; "Chapman and Hall," writes Peter Ackroyd, "had printed approximately four hundred copies of the first monthly number. By the end, they were selling some forty thousand" (196). This bit of information has long functioned as evidence of the centrality of Sam Weller, but surely this is only a half-truth. What I'd like to suggest is the possibility that Sam is nothing without Mr. Pickwick's influence. There is something of the obvious in this claim, that Mr. Pickwick and Sam Weller complement and complete each other, that the pair forms a "steady and reciprocal attachment." At the same time, however, there is little talk about precisely what Mr. Pickwick brings to Sam Weller, what the child teaches the parent. And even if we admit that Sam Weller and Mr. Pickwick belong in the humorous marriage of reckless child and indulgent parent, a powerful hierarchy is still secure. That is, even if we have done away with the house rule that Sam is the "unifying imagination" of the book by suggesting his imagination is incomplete without Pickwick's, that theirs is a humorous marriage of ego and super-ego, we end up preserving the familial paradigm of parent/child, with connectedness, with something still on top. In short, we end up with novels and readers.

Yet the curious thing, for Freud at any rate, is that when the super-ego and ego reach agreement in the name of humor, there's a very real risk that the familial paradigm no longer applies and that a completely new paradigm takes over. The super-ego participates in the repudiation of reality, and there is a leveling of the psychic hierarchy. The ego is no longer the child, the super-ego is no longer the parent, and there is only humorous energy. Freud's insights into humor have unlocked an irresistibly powerful set of ideas, perhaps so powerful that Freud doesn't seem entirely ready to throw away the key. Freud ends his lecture with a reassuring disclaimer: "Finally, if the super-ego does try to comfort the ego by humor and to protect it from suffering, this does not conflict with its derivation from the parental institution" (6). I'm not suggesting, of course, that Freud added this point simply as a gesture of appeasement for anyone in his audience who might disturbed by the thought of a parental power magically disappearing. One has to admit, however, that the lecture ends on an awkward note. Freud's final word simply does not follow.

However, we needn't concern ourselves with questions of Freudian intent in order to play with the idea that Mr. Pickwick has a thing or two to teach Sam. I'm not suggesting that what Mr. Pickwick teaches Sam is the joy of innocence or the depths of naïveté, for these lessons do nothing to destabilize the homology of Pickwick : child :: Sam : parent—and I believe it is precisely this homology that governs novelistic readings of the book. And the episode in *Pickwick* that lends itself so well to these satiric readings is the Fleet episode. Pickwick asks Sam to submit to his humorous dignity, his insufferable view of things. Sam, whether we are expected to believe he is aware of it or not, makes a striking allusion to the very metaphor used by Buzfuz during the trial of *Bardell v. Pickwick*. If you will recall, Buzfuz offered as evidence of Pickwick's breach of promise a series of letters addressed to Mrs. Bardell in Pickwick's name. Buzfuz's argument is a hilarious example of loose interpretation, such that letters as seemingly innocent (all the more sly and underhanded!) as

"Dear Mrs. B, I shall not be at home till tomorrow. Slow coach," become "a mere substitute for some endearing word or promise" (519–520). Buzfuz, fearing his point is too soon taken, adds, "[a]nd what does this allusion to the slow coach mean? For aught I know, it may be a reference to Pickwick himself, who has most unquestionably been a criminally slow coach during the whole of this transaction, but whose speed will now be very unexpectedly accelerated and whose wheels, gentlemen, as he will find to his cost, will soon be greased by you!" (520).

The one thing that will speed this coach is the payment of heavy damages—damages that Pickwick refuses to pay. This stubbornness will land Pickwick a room in the Fleet and will occasion Sam to make his curious allusion to the creeping vehicle under scrutiny here. It's easy enough to have Sam wondering if the slow coach, whose drift he sees as being much too reposed, is doomed to be overtaken by the storm. Garret Stewart suggests that although Sam's asides are meant to allow his "more shadowed, realistic picture of the world" to emerge, the prison Wellerisms are "used unexpectedly to soften the blow of sudden understanding" (73). The blow Pickwick refuses to take is that of the storm, which threatens to consume him totally.

Yet, we also presume that Pickwick and company are impervious to such storms. The coach can take its time, creep along if necessary; for the cold that surrounds them is no match for their high spirits. We're concerned with one particular coach here, Mr. Pickwick. Although the book is filled with coaches, fast and faster, roundabout and unexpected, empty and full, Pickwick's coach is often described as especially slow. But what makes Pickwick's coach *dangerously* slow? After all, Pickwick's coach is never in danger, even at its slowest. The Muggleton coach to Dingley Dell is a defining example of the progress of Pickwick. Even the narrator joins in on the slackening pace; his perambulations on the joys of Christmas go on for so long that he must interrupt himself and remind everyone that "we are so taken up and occupied with the good qualities of this saint Christmas that we are keeping Mr. Pickwick and his friends waiting in the cold on the outside of Muggleton coach, which they have just attained, well wrapped up in the great-coats, shawls, and comforters" (415). The narrator's concern is misplaced, however, since the coach isn't ready to leave anyway. There's brandy to be had. When the coach does get on its merry way, it speeds exhilaratingly down the slope, never in danger of collapsing: the coachman, with four horses in hand, can "very leisurely" wipe his forehead, a gesture that virtually guarantees everybody's cozy safety.

The coach stops, more spirits are taken, and all are delayed as the bitter cold begins to bite down once more. Those who wait "shout for the missing gentlemen as loud as they can bawl. A distant response is heard from the yard, and Mr. Pickwick and Mr. Tupman come running down it, quite out of breath, for they have been having a glass of ale apiece, and Mr. Pickwick's fingers are so cold that he has been full five minutes before he could find a sixpence to pay for it" (418). Five minutes at an alehouse or three months in the Fleet, it doesn't matter. The comic plot promises that debts will be paid and forward progress will resume. And once more, there is no danger:

> Such was the progress of Mr. Pickwick and his friends by the Muggleton telegraph on their way to Dingley Dell; and at three o'clock that afternoon they all stood, high and dry, safe and sound, hale and hearty, upon the steps of the Blue Lion, having taken on the road quite enough of ale and brandy to enable them to bid defiance to the frost that was binding up the earth in its iron fetters and weaving its beautiful network upon the trees and hedges (418).

Even Sam, the character upon whom we depend for sober, sensible, but gracious guidance through moments such as this, belongs wholeheartedly to the fearless world of good cheer. The spirit of Sam Weller is every bit as humorous as Pickwick's in several moments in the book, both "before" and "after" the Fleet episode. We are furthest from the bleakness of the Fleet on a particularly chilly Christmas morning in the opening line of Chapter 40. Yet, when Pickwick observes the severity of the weather, it is Sam who beams brightly, "Fine time for them as is well wropped up, as the polar bear said to himself ven he was practicing skating" (448). This may not be Sam at his finest, but it is Sam at his most cheerful. In fact, it is Sam at his most Pickwickian. Odd, too, since we expect, at moments such as these, a darker, more satiric Wellerism: "Severe indeed, sir. And you best not look down upon it, as the polar bear said to himself ven he was skating on thin ice." Or something like that (I'm no Boz). Fearless and cozy is the world Sam is announcing, not cold and threatening. This is no simple cheery assurance, either. It's perhaps because of Sam's ability to say something far bleaker that we rest easy in our coziness. Things *are* okay. Sam not only reminds Pickwick of his cozy world, he brings us into it as well, even gives us (and Pickwick) the authority to bring him back into its warm embrace should he begin to stray.

What we see during the Christmas episode is a charming affiliation that reverses itself throughout the book—here Pickwick is in the role of the super-ego. His duty is to call attention to the severity of the real world. It's Sam's turn to be the humorist; "nothin' to be feared, sir" he seems to say. Later these roles will be switched again and *Sam* will be the one to remind Pickwick of the severity of the storm. We know, however, that the gloom of the Fleet is only a temporary condition. Dickens devotes absolutely no narrative to the three months Mr. Pickwick spends shut up, alone, in his cell. Nothing is happening, and nothing worth repeating is being said. We need not freeze things in the Fleet, as if its gloomy nothingness is of significance. We need not say the game is over. We need not say that Sam and Pickwick have, at last, found their natural strides; they are, at last, in step. No, they will tumble over each other once more. Particularly when it is most needed, as when Tupman, Winkle, and Snodgrass visit Pickwick in his cell: "The triumvirate were much affected. Mr. Tupman shook his head deploringly; Mr. Snodgrass drew forth his handkerchief with undisguised emotion; and Mr. Winkle retired to the window and sniffed aloud. 'Mornin' gen'lm'n,' said Sam, entering at the moment with the shoes and gaiters, 'Avay with melincholy, as the little boy said ven his schoolmissis died. Velcome to the college, gen'lm'n'" (675). This is a very different Sam Weller than the sober and serious one we encounter when he is dismissed from the Fleet. It's as if he has learned his lesson—a lesson he flunked when he sat upon the witness stand during the trial of *Bardell v. Pickwick*. The way to beat the law is not to play by its rules, not to have "a alleybi," but to be obstinate, to refuse. To adhere to a completely different set of rules, as Mr. Pickwick does; to be the irrational humorist, to put faith in the idea that the world is, after all, only a game. This tactic lands Pickwick in the Fleet, certainly, but the first forty chapters have demonstrated well enough that there is nothing to fear. Sam's transformation and education is not complete until he returns to the Fleet, faces the storm, and remarks, "Here's a game!" After all, as Dodson and Fogg have shown, the storm is nothing but swirling air and jumbled letters.

Ways of Reading: Literally, Heretically, Comically

In *Reading for Plot*, Peter Brooks argues that plot is "best conceived as an activity, a structuring operation elicited in the reader trying to make sense of those meanings that develop only through textual and temporal succession" (37). Traditional narratology, with its emphasis on paradigmatic structures, fails to take into consideration the dynamics of reading. For Brooks, psychoanalysis forces us "beyond pure formalism" into an active reengagement with narrative desire. Brooks's insights are useful here because, in our attempt to go beyond conventional (and formalist) readings of Dickens's book that give absolute authority to some locatable shift mid-way, we need to turn an eye toward "our compulsions to read," to our own "competence," and how in our performances, good and bad, we animate "the sense-making process...that carries us forward, onward, through the text" (36–37). From this point of view, one might say that the comic plot is not a particular type of narrative; it is an activity. The comic plot of *Pickwick Papers* is not to be found, it is to be made; it is, like any other plot, to be "actualized in the reading process" (36). What follows may be understood as an attempt to make sense of our sense-making processes, and to show that the differences between reading for a novelistic, legalistic plot and reading for a comic plot are not differences of value, but of kind. In other words, the idea is not to discover new ways of producing heretical readings, transgressive readings, or misreadings. Such critical posturing would belie the extent to which we are dependent on the stability of meaning, the coherence of plot, and the Aristotelian constraints of logical form. Rather, the idea is to simply call attention to the differences between various types of plotting. Whereas novelistic, legalistic plots are animated by what Brooks calls the "suspense of final prediction" (19), comic plots are animated by a desire for what might be called Shandyesque, anarchic, non-linear accumulation.[11]

We might begin by recognizing the conviction that, midway, *Pickwick* becomes a novel and owes nothing to the text itself, but to our keen awareness of what belongs on top, and to an even keener awareness that what belongs on top is really nothing more than a reconfiguration of what goes on underneath. John Glavin has great fun with this idea, but uses the lewdly suggestive (and endlessly fun) metaphor of "the wrong side of the door" instead. For Pickwick and company, heterosexuality constitutes a threat (represented by the shameful act of being caught on the wrong side of the door), and the movement from serialization to novel is precisely the movement from the wrong side (the anxious erotics of homosocial horseplay) to the right side (the demands of the heterosexual bond). And yet, what we find on the right side of the door is *not* the pairing of Mr. Pickwick with Mrs. Bardell, but the far more ideal pairing of Mr. Pickwick with Sam Weller. Arguably, such a pairing is threatened by the prospect of marriage between Sam and Mrs. Winkle's maid, Mary. By the composition of his feelings, however, Sam evidently has nothing more in mind than remaining bound to Mr. Pickwick: "'I do consider the young 'ooman sir,' said Sam. 'I have considered the young 'ooman. I've spoke to her. I've told her how I'm sitivated; she's ready to vait until I'm ready and I believe she vill. If she don't, she's not the young 'ooman I take her for, and I give her up vith readiness, You've knowed me afore, sir. My mind's made up, and nothin' can ever alter it'" (851–852). Sam, we are told, is not going to ask for any more leave; he is firmly "sitivated." And so the anxious erotics of homosocial horseplay are not excluded at all, they are simply repackaged as, in Glavin's words, "cozy and safe" (7). After all, no reading of *Pickwick* can preserve the framework of *x* leading to *y* so easily.

But a special kind of misreading *can* preserve it, which is what Glavin is after. Along the way, he spins some very special misreadings indeed, one of which is the rather wonderfully losing argument that the homosocial erotics in *Pickwick* are far from cozy and safe—they are, from start to finish, "anxious, anxious, anxious" (9). This is a *good* misreading, I think, because it is entirely inconclusive—there's no way of carrying on with this line of thinking, one can only stop writing. Does *Pickwick* resolve the dilemma of fear and shame before the prospect of heterosexual union? It doesn't appear to. And if we needed some dubious evidence to suggest otherwise, there is a host of telling scenes at our disposal. At book's end, for example, Weller the elder is presented, quite undisguised, with the true hope of some marital bliss courtesy of a buxom female cook who bestows "many smirks of recognition upon Sam." After a moment's quiet contemplation regarding the passing of Susan Weller, Sam breaks into "violent perspiration" and turns his thoughts to the intentions of the buxom female: "Sammy, if I wos to stop here alone vun veek—only vun veek, my boy—that 'ere 'ooman 'ud marry me by force and wiolence afore it was over" (794). Sam is better off "on the box," where one can steer clear of the ferociousness and hysterics of females and, more importantly, the shame that nuptial neediness instills. And isn't that where the members of the Pickwick Club are coziest, in the coach that steers them through what Glavin calls "the heterosexual labyrinth" of the book's plot? Oddly, Glavin doesn't run out the clock here but instead pushes on. In doing so, he gives us what he calls the worst misreading yet; "in *Pickwick*, yielding to sex makes men either mad, as in the Madman's Manuscript, or bad, like the perfidious Jingle, or unspeakable, like Messrs. Potts, Raddle, and Hunter. The admirable man, in contrast, finds a way to behave like a child. And so the novel heaps praise on Pickwick for remaining 'juvenile,' a male with a penis but not a phallus" (11). Suddenly, the dilemma of fear and shame before the prospect of heterosexual union appears to be nearing some plausible resolution, and *Pickwick* appears to be turning into a novel. Perhaps these are twin syndromes, misreading badly and reading novelistically.

Glavin himself admits that his worst misreading comes "uncomfortably close" to a good reading, and that he has drifted considerably from his Pickwickian aim (12). To square himself once more, he escapes through a very welcome loophole of comic irresolution by swiftly posing questions that are somewhat unfriendly to the novelistic reader.

What Glavin's essay inadvertently dramatizes is the double paradox of reading novelistically: first of all, to read novelistically is to prevent a novel from saying what it wants to say. For example, *Pickwick* urges us to take as its "literal" sense the story of a man who must emerge from adolescence into full manhood, from innocence into experience, from Eden into the New Jerusalem. This "literal" sense is, of course, merely the index and the result of a specific, socio-historical temperament in Dickens criticism. It is G. K. Chesterton, W. H. Auden, Edmund Wilson, Steven Marcus, and J. Hillis Miller. In our current critical scene, however, we produce "heretical" readings that establish antagonistic relationships with the novel's "literal" sense. Anny Sadrin gives us an example of this sort of critical positioning when she succinctly notes in an essay on *Pickwick* that, in fact, "Dickens' best-plotted stories paradoxically aim at no less than the destruction, or, to use a more fashionable word, at the deconstruction of plot, especially the deconstruction of the hero's plot" (25). Sadrin refers obliquely, here, to her own hermeneutical situation—that of a "fashionable" brand of cynical deconstructionism—in which what the novel *wants to say* must give way to what the novel *really means*.[12]

Here we might turn to the second paradox of reading novelistically, which is that the most heretical "misreadings" are, as Glavin dramatizes quite amusingly, native companions of good readings. One could say that both types of readings, legitimate and heretical, are after the same thing—to produce a text in which x leads to y. Both are informed by that which has come down to us from the past, though they differ in terms of how they stand in respect to this past. That is, although both deposit an enormous amount of faith in "what belongs on top," heretical readings tend to regard what belongs on top with a great deal of suspicion. They monitor the ways in which "what belongs on top" is systematically informed by the symbolic displacement of "what belongs underneath." Our example text, *Pickwick*, portends to trace the narrative progression, among the members of the Pickwick Club, from homosocial horseplay to heterosexual union. However, no reader (no modern reader) of *Pickwick* will be entirely satisfied with this simplistic x-leads-to-y formula. The heterosexual unions at the book's end are ambiguous, at best. For instance, although it appears Mr. Pickwick has put his frivolous pursuits behind him in favor of a permanent house in Dulwich, wherein he will "witness the [marital] happiness of those friends who are dearest to me," skeptical readers will note that there remains, in the end, "an erotically charged dyadic relation" between Mr. Pickwick and Sam (Glavin, 12). The heterosexual union of Sam Weller and Mary Winkle cannot do without the homosocial union of Mr. Pickwick and Sam Weller (in fact, Sam dodges marriage for two whole years in favor of his singular devotion to Mr. Pickwick); rather than the former negating the latter, we see the two enacting a dynamic rearrangement and reconfiguration of domain and hierarchy. Glavin shows that:

> [i]n effect, Sam makes it possible for neither and both [he and Mr. Pickwick] simultaneously to "possess" the phallus. From the heterosexuality that threatens to engulf them, Sam delivers himself and Pickwick by reinventing himself as the eternal son to Pickwick's pre-Oedipal father...Sam lets Pickwick and the novel keep all his many faults [i.e. always being on the wrong side of the door] without ever having to confront their consequences. He thus produces Pickwick as a heroic male text, rather than himself enact the experience of that text. Pickwick: master of the house. Sam: father of the family. We can think about their relation along the lines some psychologists call "phallic narcissism"—a son who has identified himself early on with a weak father repairs the "shame of being weak" through a fantasied union with an idealized male parent...Sam metamorphoses Pickwick from the butt of Jingle's satire to—not merely a good man—but an angel, that is a male with no conceivable use for a penis. (13)

Glavin's winning prose is convincing to say the least, and it is difficult to say, without even the slightest bit of irony, that what we're reading here is, in fact, heretical. It is easier (and perhaps more appropriate) to say that Glavin, in attempting to produce his worst misreading of *Pickwick* yet, has given us a perfectly legitimate reading. More than this, he has given *Pickwick* a resolution; he has made it a novel. Whether or not he knows how easily misreadings give way to legitimate readings (it is very likely that he knows it full well), Glavin reveals just how central the novel is to our habits of reading.

A comic reading of *Pickwick*, however, inevitably disrespects the rules and conventions of the novelistic form. All of the loose ends, dead ends, contradictions, questions, and inconsistencies that are characteristic of *Pickwick* as monthly serialization are welcomed in a comic reading. Readers accustomed to the exigencies of serialization, whereby installments must accumulate rather than build and must proliferate rather than point in a coherent and logical way (endward), were perhaps less inclined to think of their readings as "provisional," less interested in restructuring what they already read in light of new readings. One might say that the first readers of *Pickwick* did not necessarily care where Mr. Pickwick and company were going, they simply loved watching them go.

Contemporary readers, however, are less inclined to the idea of settling into a perpetual middle. We read on in order to get *out* of the middle, knowing that the middle is unjustified and meaningless without the end. Peter Brooks rightly argues that the end-determined plot, "moving toward full predication of the narrative sentence, claiming a final plentitude of meaning" (314) is more likely to be found in popular narrative fiction, such as cinema, rather than in experimental narrative fiction, such as the metanovel. Still, our fear of the "illusory middle" remains (142). In a not unrelated point made by Sharon Willis, audiences of *Thelma and Louise* (dir. Ridley Scott, 1991) were perhaps unaccustomed to a plot that zoomed carelessly ahead, with no regard to ends. "At every turn," argues Willis, "the film displaces its energy from narrative justification and explanation to other, less comfortable seductions—those of the road, the traveling, the speed of motion, and those of the image" (123). While some viewers may have responded to these displacements favorably,[13] most "have insisted tenaciously enough on giving Thelma and Louise a narrative reason for winding up on the lam" (124). More than this, they have stubbornly forgotten the thrill, the joy, and the wild, kinetic energy of the film's middle. For most of us, the film's final image—of the two women driving their Ford Thunderbird into the abyss—determines the film's overall meaning; we effectively rewrite the middle and "repress the partiality and disruption that make [the heroines'] journey so compelling" (124). Zooming carelessly ahead with no regard to ends becomes, retrospectively, lethal. But why must the lasting image be the last image? Why isn't the lasting image of *Thelma and Louise* the image of Brad Pitt's cute little ass? Sharon Willis says it is. For Willis, "the while film seems to come down to Thelma's lusty appreciation of JD's buttocks as he walks away form their car. 'That's him goin',' she tells Louise, 'I luuuuve watchin' him go.' This is a film that wants us to be able to say the same thing: we love watching it go, not watching it get somewhere" (124). From this point of view, the "end" of *Thelma and Louise* is very much like the "end" of *Pickwick Papers*: in the latter, we simply run out of pages; in the former, we simply run out of road. Even better, those who read comically prefer rear ends to novelistic ends.

   Those who read novelistically are unable to ignore the shift mid-way through *Pickwick*, a shift they assume is, without a doubt, *in the text*; it is a shift that *must* be dealt with. "The central fact of the novel," says James Kincaid in uncharacteristic form, "is that Mr. Pickwick does change: he must be educated. He must first learn the nature of the real world and, without becoming cynical or despairing, discover the limits of benevolence and innocence as effective agents in that world" (22). The language used here to describe the guidance and preparation Mr. Pickwick needs is, of course, the same language used to describe the way we drive our children into the future—the same language used to sustain the myth of childhood and of "growing up." Psychoanalysis, specifically, has been "quintessentially reactionary in its acceptance and promotion of this dismayingly comforting progress myth," argues Adam Phillips. "We are born in turbulent love with the world, which is assumed to be made for us, of a piece with our wishes; then we suffer the humiliation of disillusionment, in which our rage is the last vestige of our hope. And then, if we are lucky—if we have the character, or the right parent, or both—we accommodate to the insufficiencies" (39–40). If we are lucky, we become a hero like Mr. Pickwick. We become, in Phillips's words, "masters of absence"—a fine echo of Glavin's own view of Mr. Pickwick as a man without a phallus. *Pickwick* is a guide to becoming wise, a "how to" book that makes us "serene in our adaptation to the way the world is" (Phillips, 40).

But even if we were to insist on a singular, pivotal change in Pickwick's character, it is one that does not fit comfortably into the familial paradigm, the homology of child/play : adult/reality. Not only does *Pickwick* show us how y (adult : reality) will not follow x (child : play) in any necessary or natural way, it shows us that the two variants are wholly unreliable, and that no assertion of any logical or symbolic pattern will enable these variants to signify to us directly. In his essay on the subject of daydreaming, Freud nudges us away from the comfortable zone of myth even as he tries to account for its power. "There is," Freud maintains:

> another consideration for the sake of which we will dwell a moment longer on this contrast between reality and play. When the child has grown up and has ceased to play, and after he has been labouring for decades to envisage the realities of life with proper seriousness, he may one day find himself in a mental situation which once more undoes the contrast between play and reality. As an adult he can look back on the intense seriousness with which he once carried on his games in childhood; and by equating his ostensibly serious occupations of to-day with his childhood games, he can throw off the too heavy burden imposed on him by life and win the high yield of pleasure afforded by *humour.* ("Creative Writers and Daydreaming," 437)

Freud seems to be granting an enormous power to a thing he calls "the adult." The adult indulges in play not simply as a way of disassociating itself from reality, but from play as well—or, more specifically, "child's play." One can only assume that the games in childhood of which Freud speaks are those in which rules are taken seriously, victory is more self-ishly obtained, and tantrums abound. As the adult takes on a far more serious view of reality, its view of play becomes less so. Of course, we can only assume that although a child's view of play is very serious indeed, its view of reality is far less serious than the adult's (to be fair, the seriousness with which it views reality is "improper").

What Freud clarifies here is not the boundary between "the child" and "the adult" (on the contrary, he's making a bit of a mess of it), but the power of "humor." Forget, for a moment, who has access to it (the child when it views reality? the adult when it views reality as well as the seriousness of its child's play?). Consider instead that, in *Pickwick*, the characters tumble and bounce around these various positions, but gravitate ultimately towards humor. Humor is the force that gets people together, it's what everyone is moving towards—although obstacles stand in the way. Furthermore, no one obstacle is more grave or serious than another when humor is your aim. Barbara Hardy has referred to the early chapters of *Pickwick* as "unsuccessful horseplay" (What sort of horseplay is unsuccessful? Adult's play?). What I have been suggesting is that we might think of the entire book as horseplay—even at its seemingly darkest moments. Think of "horseplay" as "humor," the way Freud sees it, the way I've been presenting it. Humor is not simply a thing in and of itself; it changes the way we look at the serious, the grave, the adult, the child, the knowing, and the naïve. All of these things are blasted into the air in the eyes of the humorist—they may settle, but only temporarily. Best of all, the humorist fears nothing. "Even when, on his return to London, Pickwick is imprisoned in the Fleet," says Anny Sadrin, "he does not seem to care what is going to happen to him and whether he will stay there for ages or not. He just looks about him. The present makes him sad, but the future does not worry him" (25). Nothing—not suffering, not anger, not even death—will cause the humorist the slightest bit of worry. Recall the dialogue between Tony and Sam when the elder speaks of Mrs. Weller's passing: "'Vell,' said Sam, venturing to offer a little homely consolation after the lapse of three or four minutes, consumed by the old gentleman in slowly shaking his head from side to side and solemnly smoking, 'vell gov'nor, ve must all come to it one day or another.' 'So we must, Sammy,' said Mr. Weller the elder. 'There's providence in it all,' said Sam. 'Of course there is,' replied his father with a nod of grave approval. 'Wot 'ud become of the undertaker vithout it, Sammy?'" (792–793). This is not a refusal of seriousness, of death, but a loving, whole-hearted humorous acceptance of death into the world. This is "grave approval," so to speak. Where would the undertaker be without death? Where would *we* be without death? We would be in half of a world, in a world different only in kind from the world without life. Tony and Sam allow only "three or four minutes" to pass before it's time for the entire world to resume, and it is reborn by way of humor, of laughter. Death is a sort of soporific, it makes people drowsy, and it dulls the senses—but only temporarily. Death does not end the story, it only completes our experience of the world. Laughter restores death to the story in full, not as an end ("Wot 'ud become of the *living*," asks Sam the elder). "True ambivalent and universal laughter," claimed Mikhail Bakhtin, "does not deny serious-ness but purifies and completes it (122). According to Bakhtin, laughter forbids seriousness to shrink away and to be isolated from one being, "forever complete." Laughter restores this ambivalent wholeness. "Such is the function of laughter in the historical development of culture and literature" (*Rabelais and His World,* 122–123).

Conclusion

Bakhtin once described Mr. Pickwick's "fat little paunch" as far too ambiguous for his liking, preferring instead the fleshy barrel of wine that is Gros Guillaume (Fat William). The latter "was unusually obese and had to make well-planned contortions to reach his own navel. He was girt with two belts: one under his chest, the other under his belly, so that this body resembled a wine barrel. His face was thickly powdered with flour, which he shed on all sides as he gesticulated. Thus his figure was the symbol of bread and wine in bodily form" (292). Why Bakhtin did not hold Mr. Pickwick's belly in as high regard as Fat William's (or Fat Jack's, or Sancho Panza's, or Friar John's for that matter) isn't entirely clear. It is well known that Bakhtin preferred *Little Dorrit* to any other Dickens novel, but this is largely due to the utility of Dickens's 1857 novel in illustrating the finer points of heteroglossia ("Discourse in the Novel," 303–308). Perhaps Bakhtin sensed that the English comic novel in general was reducing the potency of carnival forms to mere parody, satire, and irony. To Bakhtin, Mr. Pickwick is nothing more than a popular clown whose figure was the symbol of one-way laughter, typical of the reduced period in which he wrote. As Morson and Emerson point out, "Bakhtin himself, for all his neglect and apparent disdain…was never-theless writing from a 'reduced' period in the twentieth century" (444). Perhaps, the authors conclude, Bakhtin "feared that his own conceptual structures for understanding…were themselves reduced" (445). This is a generous pardon, to be sure. More generous still is the suggestion that the significance of Pickwick's night in the pound, with all its overtones of carnival debasement ("You an't got no friends. Hurrah!") was not lost on Bakhtin. After all, Bakhtin was speaking less of Mr. Pickwick himself than of his reception among readers in England: "The English applaud Pickwick and they will always applaud" (292). The ambiguity of Pickwick's fat little paunch lies in what we throw at it. So let us not applaud his seeming passage from immaturity to maturity. And let us not pity Mr. Pickwick as he cries out for his friends. Let us instead hurl a ripe tomato at his face. He an't got no friends! He don't need no friends!

Notes

1.   J. Hillis Miller speaks of the "inalterable permanence of the characters" in *Pickwick* (27).

2.   "Talking furniture always reminds me of Dickens," a friend once told me after having watched Disney's *Beauty and the Beast*.

3.   Put another way, I am not promoting the notion that characters in Dickens are largely one-dimensional and certainly lacking the complexities and contradictions recent scholarship has given them; rather, I am using this claim in order to wedge my way into a different notion altogether. I am not inclined to gravitate toward the structuralist view that a character is, as Brian Rosenberg puts it, "wholly defined by the needs of a particular literary structure" and has "no significance or even existence outside of textual language" (158–9). I am more inclined to take issue with our habits of reading, which we inherit from "institutions with histories and sets of needs" (Kincaid, *Annoying the Victorians*, 4). Right now, in this current critical and theoretical moment, we tend to read novelistically, not comically. I think Chesterton and Orwell prod us into reading Dickens in a different context than the one to which we're accustomed—not a better, truer context, but a different one. I see reading novelistically as the search for what Jonathan H. Grossman calls "system and underlying intrigue" as opposed to the reveling in the fluid and fragmentary and the acknowledgment of "only the temporary unity of vignettes" which, I will argue, constitutes the comic plot (175).

4.   I see reading novelistically as the search for what Jonathan H. Grossman calls "system and underlying intrigue," as opposed to the reveling in the fluid and fragmentary and the acknowledgment of "only the temporary unity of vignettes" that constitutes the comic plot (175).

5.   On this point, however, a Shakespeare critic will be quick to remark that Falstaff's banishment, at the close of *2 Henry IV* is *not* "but a colour" (a necessary charade, a fiction) but indeed an ending, and one cannot fully experience the character of Falstaff without bearing this in mind. I do not suppose it would be of much use to argue, in response, that this banishment is important only from a certain point of view, namely Hal's, and that we have such endings only because we desire them ("There must be conclusions," says Nym in Act II of *Henry V*).

6.   We aren't always complaining, of course. Sometimes we're delighted by the change mid-way, if only because the numbers in the first half of the book are a bit disappointing. Writing to a friend in June 1837, Mary Russell Mitford says: "[Pickwick] is rather fragmentary, except the trial (No. 11 or 12), which is as complete and perfect as any bit of comic writing in the English language" (in Grossman, 171).

7.   For a useful analysis of Pickwick in terms of this movement, see Jonathan H. Grossman, "Representing Pickwick: The Novel and the Law Courts," *Nineteenth Century Literature* 52 (1997), 171–197. Grossman argues, quite nicely, that the

book takes on a new coherence mid-way not because it discovers a "plot" for itself (the trial of *Pickwick v. Bardell*, the legal machinations of Dodson and Fogg), but because this "plot" simultaneously produces a double—the fluid, fragmentary, anecdotal "anti-plot"—and that this doubling in turn "conjures up doubles of the plotting author within the shape of lawyers" (176). In other words, the self-reflexive doubling Grossman describes not only provides the narrative coherence of the book, it simultaneously announces the emergence of the novelistic, legalistic tradition within Victorian fiction through the figure of Dickens.

8.   James Kinsley. *Introduction to Charles Dickens, Pickwick*. ed. Kinsley. (Oxford: Clarendon Press, 1986), xlvii.

9.   *Dickens and the Rhetoric of Laughter,* (20–49).

10.   In Chapter 17 of *Oliver Twist,* Dickens referring to what he calls "murderous melodramas," suggests that "sudden shiftings of the scene, and rapid changes of time and place, are not only sanctioned in books by long usage, but are by many considered as the great art of authorship" (169). He even speaks of the reader's hunger for the "regular alternation" of ups and downs as if these things were "layers of red and white in a side of streaky bacon" (168). Yet, the heightened expectations and sudden halts that characterize the melodramatic plot are perhaps better understood as the machinery with which we veer towards each chapter's resolution. There are, says Dickens, "good and substantial reasons" for journeying back to the town in which Oliver was born. This is a novelistic expedition, one that shall provide vital textual evidence for the reader who wishes to produce some significant resolution to the book. Our diversion, the artificial dance backwards to Oliver's place of birth, is as important as the novel's overall plot and no more. Although it appears that it is the author's duty to account for each narrative diversion, for each dance incontiguous with destiny, so that some kind of coherence and unity of design may be produced. It is my suspicion, and perhaps Dickens's as well, that some readers may be content with the bacon. Of course, some readers may *not* be content—at least not entirely—though they may never bother to say so, their mouths being too full. At the very least, we can say Dickens reveals to us two different ways of reading: for plot and for bacon (see James R. Kincaid, "Fattening Up on Pickwick" in *Annoying the Victorians* [New York: Routledge, 1992], 21–33).

11.   See James R. Kincaid's "Fattening Up on Pickwick" in *Annoying the Victorians.* (New York: Routledge, 1995), 21–33. "The Pickwick Papers," claims Kincaid, "makes no demands on us; it does not push us into a strenuous adult world, all sweat and muscle and cartilage. It gives us a world of infinitely yielding, cushiony flesh" (22).

12.   See, too, Peter Brooks. "Repetition, Repression, and Return: the Plotting of Great Expectations," *Reading for Plot*. 113–142.

13.   See, for instance, Peter N. Chumo II, "*Thelma & Louise* as Screwball Comedy," from a Film Quarterly round table, *The Many Faces of Thelma & Louise* Vol 45, no. 2 (Winter, 1991–92), 20–31. Report in *Film Quarterly: Forty Years—A Selection*. Ed. Brian Henderson and Ann Martin. (Berkeley: University of California Press, 1999), 548–550.

6

Reading and Repairing the Grotesque

[T]he workingman, who turns his attention partially to art, will probably, and wise-
ly, choose not to do that which he can do best, and indulge the pride of an effective
satire rather than subject himself to assured mortification in the pursuit of beauty.
—*Ruskin*, Stones of Venice

We might say that the predominant theme of failure in Kafka's writings functions for us the way the Gothic grotesque did for Ruskin. Were we to employ the language of *Stones of Venice* (1851–1853); we might say that a text by Kafka invites us either to play wisely with its sublime and terrible forms, or to endure them only for an instant so that we may embrace that much more strongly the beauty found elsewhere (whether it may be found in more fulfilling relationships with friends, family, and God, or in future professions). To play wisely with Kafka's objects of horror is to contemplate them "in their true light, and with the entire energy of our souls" so that these objects "cease to be grotesque, and become altogether sublime" (150). Sublime, Peter Heller would add, because these objects will remain forever beyond our grasp, eternally incommensurable with reason. In his essay "On Not Understanding Kafka," Heller suggests we admit:

> that we don't understand, that we cannot interpret...that generally, Kafka's fictions do not make sense in the way expected of most literary works, that they do not make up a world which makes sense...Kafka, himself, apparently, did not "understand" his works in the widely if vaguely felt sense of that term, and treated them as one might approach the interpretation of a dream, to surmise some intelligible aspects. "Do you find meaning in 'The Judgment'," he asks his fiancée. "I don't, and can't explain anything in it." (31)

On this point Heller sounds very much like Ruskin, who also claims that the highest or "noblest" works of art are "ungovernable," and "have in them something of the character of dreams" (Ruskin, 151). This is by no means a chance encounter; for although Heller may not have had in mind Ruskin's portrait of the wise man, it is clear enough that he treats Kafka's visions as if they are, by Ruskin's standards, the noblest forms of imaginative power. A vision of the noble grotesque, claims Ruskin, "comes uncalled, and will not submit itself to the seer, but conquers him, and forces him to speak as a prophet, having no power of his words or thoughts" (151). Heller's Kafka is a something like a prophet who is incapable, or unwilling, to explain his visions; he speaks to us in impenetrable truths that scratch "the wounds of our lives where they itch" (Heller, 35).

However, one could just as easily say that Kafka was simply a man who was incapable of confining his thoughts to what Gilles Deleuze and Félix Guattari call "territorialized language"—language that boldly asserts its significance, its relationship to worldly things. "Metaphors," Kafka confesses, "are one among many things which make me despair of writing." In other words, metaphor always returns language to some positive territory and, thus, shows a shameful dependence on the world. In Kafka's diary entries, one can find fragments of thoughts such as these: "Writing's lack of independence of the world, its dependence on the maid who tends the fire, on the cat warming itself by the stove; it is even dependent on the poor old human being warming himself by the stove. All of these are independent activities ruled by their own laws; only writing is helpless, cannot live in itself, is a joke and a despair" (*Diaries II,* 200–201). The burden of Kafka's writing is that it can never settle, can never compromise. His impulse is to call the world's bluff. From the same dated entry as above, Kafka writes (perhaps as a way of testing himself), "Two children, alone in their house, climbed into a large trunk; the cover slammed shut, they could not open it, and suffocated." Lines such as these are written precisely because others *cannot* be written. Suppose one were to write a very different set of lines—lines that would betray the dependence on things Kafka dreaded so much: "Two children, alone with the cat warming itself by the stove, stared curiously and wildly at a large trunk; what glorious mysteries lay within? what marvelous secrets? what magnificent treats for the eyes?" I have a strong suspicion that if Kafka caught himself writing lines like these, he would to quote from Woody Allen's *Hannah and Her Sisters* (1990), "never stop throwing up." Kafka must instead opt for a language capable of wrestling itself free of things, a language that can savagely parody this communion we have with the "real." What delivers comfort to Kafka is the absurd; it is both the source of Kafka's exhaustion and shame, and the promise of his glorious escape—the impossibility of not writing.

Perhaps, even, it is the impossibility of not writing within the form of the grotesque. Like Ruskin's noble man, Kafka turns to his art during his leisure time, during his hours away from the mindless toil. For him, his art is both a form of self-preservation and a form of grueling punishment. Writing is necessary, essential. It is also altogether unbearable. "Were his powers and his time unlimited," says Ruskin of the noble man:

> so that, like Fra Angelica, he could paint the Seraphim, in that order of beauty he could find contentment, bringing heaven down to earth. But by the conditions of his being, by his hard-worked life, by his feeble powers of execution, by the meanness of his employment and the languor of his heart, he is bound down to earth. It is the world's work that he is doing, and world's work is not to be done without fear. And whatever there is of deep and eternal consciousness within him, thrilling his mind with the sense of the presence of sin and death around him, must be expressed in that slight work, and feeble way, come of it what will. (141)

Ruskin is giving us a portrait of an artist who has no choice but to find the expression of his soul in the true grotesque. It is a portrait in which Kafka may have wanted to discover his own likeness. Like Ruskin's noble man, Kafka wished to escape the apathy awaiting him by wringing out his grotesque images with exquisite care and pains. But neither Kafka's powers, nor his time, were entirely unlimited—at least not consistently. He came home from work too tired to concentrate, and business trips denied him the "fire of consecutive hours" needed to write (in Mailloux, 270). Only rarely did Kafka refuse to allow travel to interrupt his writing.

I suggest there is some use in reading Kafka as if he were Ruskin's workingman, particularly if one's aim is to account for the high degree of comedy in the writings. As the epigraph from Ruskin suggests, the workingman (Franz Kafka, drafting clerk, Workers' Accident Insurance Institute for the Kingdom of Bohemia in Prague) "will probably, and wisely, indulge the pride of an effective satire rather than subject himself to the assured mortification in the pursuit of beauty" (Ruskin, 132). There is, in my mind, no question that Kafka's writings can be read as examples of the true grotesque. So many, Heller included, have constructed Kafka as a modern prophet of the most sublime and terrifying forms. What I hope to show, however, is that Kafka's grotesque images are as much ludicrous and sportive as they are fearful and terrible, and that it is precisely this neglect of the more sportive forms that has disabled our approaches of understanding and teaching Kafka's comic sense. This particular neglect, however, is only symptomatic of a much wider-reaching phenomenon endemic to our current critical practices: a reliance on skepticism and paranoia—two interpretive styles whose single-minded approach to the grotesque privileges the fearful and terrible and diminishes the ludicrous and sportive.

The Sportive and the Fearful: Two Meanings of the Grotesque

These categories of the grotesque were first defined by Ruskin, who, in his *Stones of Venice* (1851–1853), sought to classify its manifold strains within the Gothic and Renaissance periods. The "terrible" strain depicts a cold and estranged world in which we are tormented by abysmal forces beyond our control. Nothing in this world allows us to forget the true depths of our fear. We wander this terrifying province like the figure in Edvard Munch's *The Scream*, vomiting our shrieks of hopelessness and dread daily. The "sportive" strain, however, depicts a Dickensian world wherein we find the menacing figure of Quilp waiting, it seems, at every turn, to ambush us with his vicious reprisals. Here, as in the terrible strain, hope is strangled like a fragile little bird, leaving only our pathos. Yet the sportive grotesque, Ruskin admits, expresses sufficient playfulness so as to allow for laughter; for, unlike its sublime counterpart, the sportive grotesque often gives way to humor and "fits of erratic fancy." To put it another way, Quilp is not an abysmal force beyond our control; he's simply a nuisance.[1]

Yet another strain of the grotesque, one that is far less menacing, even, than the sportive, finds its source in what Ruskin calls the full exertion of a frivolous mind (143). Whereas Quilp is a source of perverse laughter, full of hostility and pathos, a figure of the false grotesque is so far removed from fear that what is left is nothing more than an elaborate toy (144). In a completely frivolous world, one ruled entirely by the false grotesque, we'd find ourselves matched with Marty Feldman's Igor (pronounced "Eye-gore"), rather than with Quilp. Low sarcasm governs the aesthetic sensibility of Mel Brooks's *Young Frankenstein* (1974), leaving little space or time for revelations of the sublime characteristic of the true grotesque. And though Brooks's grotesque images are wrought with care and skill—Gene Wilder's perfectly deranged hair, Marty Feldman's huge, bulging eyes and sneaky hump, even Peter Boyle's abnormally-crooned "Puttin' on the Ritz" are extraordinary expressions of the grotesque—together they weave nothing more than a "tissue of nonsense" (Ruskin, 144).

One cannot, with any degree of confidence, separate these categories so neatly. Even the least indulgent reading of Dickens's *The Old Curiosity Shop* will produce a Quilp who is capable of moving in and out of all three categories at any given time. One might argue that the reader's agility owes itself not strictly to Dickens's genius, but also to the full extent to which the various kinds of the grotesque reflect on one another. In this way, Ruskin's "all-embracing proportions" of the grotesque offer those who are interested in studying the grotesque considerably more freedom than more recent critical investigations (Barasch, lv). Our contemporary models of the grotesque tend to disregard laughing, playful, and sportive forms in favor of the claustrophobic, the uncanny, and the sublime. Nowhere are the social dynamics and political implications of this choice more keenly put than in Peter Stallybrass and Allon White's *The Politics and Poetics of Transgression* (1986). In it, the authors argue against nostalgic treatments of carnival history that mourn the "disappearance" of grotesque forms by claiming that the grotesque has not disappeared at all, that it has been "re-territorialized" within the symbolic domain as the political unconscious. Since the Enlightenment, powerful forces have sought to exclude the grotesque from official identity and to reject all transgressive and excessive invocations of the body. The reward for their efforts came in the form of a stable, bourgeois democracy. "As we have seen," conclude the authors:

> the carnivalesque was marked out as an intensely powerful semiotic realm precisely because bourgeois culture constructed its self-identity by rejecting it. The 'poetics' of transgression reveals disgust, fear and desire which inform the dramatic self-representation of that culture through the 'scene of its low Other'. This poetics reveals quite clearly the contradictory *political* construction of bourgeois democracy. For bourgeois democracy emerged with a class which, whilst indeed progressive in its best political aspirations, had encoded in its manners, morals and imaginative writings, in its body, bearing and taste, a subliminal elitism which was constitutive of its historical being. (202)

We may not know what happens when grotesque forms do not inspire "disgust, fear and desire," but it is clear *why* the more terrifying forms are so important to us. One may even be led to believe, after reading similar studies, that there exist no other forms of the grotesque but those that inspire disgust, fear, and desire, and that it is possible (and perhaps necessary) to speak only of a single category, "the Grotesque," as if the blanketing bulk of Ruskin's *Stones of Venice* could be gathered, tucked, and doubled over like a road map so that one's final destination is the only terrain there is.

The terrifying grotesque shares, with more sportive forms of grotesquery, the desire to explore "the possibilities of the ugly, the grotesque, the bizarre, to shake loose art from inherited restrictions" (Sokel, 22). These possibilities, however, are diminished by the modern oppositional belief that the grotesque is a world of radical alienation in which all that is familiar becomes hostile, in which all hope of liberation is foreclosed by trappings beyond our control, in which laughter is little more than an expression of fear.[2] Yet the grotesque, by its very nature, denies the capacity for reason that allows such hierarchies to be arranged. Put another way, the grotesque is defined by what Philip Thomson calls an *unresolved* conflict of qualities—a definition that is essential when distinguishing the grotesque from other modes or categories in art or literature (21). Ruskin himself wasn't terribly comfortable making clear distinctions between higher and lower forms of the grotesque, and for this reason devoted himself more confidently to the mind of the artist. Others, however, sought more totalizing definitions of the grotesques, definitions free from unresolved conflict of qualities Thompson finds in *Stones of Venice*, definitions that appeared, even, to be free from classification altogether. On this line of thinking, Wolfgang Kayser's account of the grotesque is perhaps the most formidable. For Kayser, the grotesque "is a structure" (184), an estranged world governed by a ghostly "It." Whether because of poor translation or rich misreading, Mikhail Bakhtin understood Kayser to mean *id*, not "It." Bakhtin argues, however, that Kayser's use of *id* is "not so much in the Freudian as in the existentialist sense of this word." Bakhtin continues: "*Id* is an alien, inhuman power, governing the world, men, their life and behavior. Kayser reduces many of the basic grotesque themes to the realization of this power, for instance the puppet theme. He also reduces to this power the theme of madness" (*Rabelais and His World*, 49). Such is the modern perception of the grotesque: a structured world of inhuman, transcendent power, of characters as mere puppets, of paranoia and sublime terror.

Although Kayser himself never invokes the "id," he does invoke Paul Ammann's third meaning of the word "It."[3] The grotesque is, first and foremost, the objectivation of the ghostly "It"—an absurd and alienated world that overwhelms us with forces that cannot be named. Although Kayser does not invoke this term either, it seems clear enough that *skepticism* is what the ghostly "It" compels us to experience, for, as Stanley Cavell has shown us, the condition of not having the world present to us in the way of knowing is also the condition of skepticism. Bakhtin's main concern, to put the matter one way, is that the modern grotesque, as defined by Kayser, is really little more than a form of skepticism. "The depth, variety, and power of separate grotesque themes," says Bakhtin, "can be understood only within the unity of folk and carnival spirit. If examined outside of this unity, they become one-sided, flat, stripped of their rich content" (52–53). The traditional themes of the modernist movement—themes such as skepticism, paranoia, the "spirit of existentialism," and "the opposition of life to death"—have fixed the limits of the modern grotesque (50). For if the grotesque guarantees possibility, liberation, and freedom because it discloses another world, another way of life, "how," asks Bakhtin, "is such freedom possible in relation to a world ruled by an alien power of the *id*?" (49). One could also ask how a world bereft of reason could still promote the truth of skepticism, the habitual privileging of failure, and the impossibility of freedom? Or, why are we compelled to assume that the logic of terror governs a world in which (presumably) anything goes?

Paranoia Did Destroy Ya

In an introduction to an anthology devoted to queer readings of fiction, Eve Sedgwick, borrowing a phrase from Paul Ricoeur, suggests that critical interpretation tends to be based upon a "hermeneutic of suspicion." The pursuit of knowledge is framed as a categorical imperative: "what is *really* going on, and how do we know?" The leading figures of this methodology have been Sigmund Freud, Karl Marx, and Friedrich Nietzsche. In the context of current theoretical writing here in the U.S., argues Sedgwick, where this triumvirate is "taken as constituting a pretty sufficient genealogy for the mainstream of New Historicist, deconstructive, feminist, queer, and psychoanalytic criticism, to apply a 'hermeneutic of suspicion' is, I believe, widely understood as a mandatory injunction rather than a possibility among other possibilities" (5). This certainly holds true within the context of Kafka criticism, which seems to be dominated almost exclusively by these three figures and their "intellectual offspring." It is perhaps the habitual privileging of this genealogy that has reproduced, time and again, "the transcendence of the law, the interiority of guilt, the subjectivity of enunciation"—what Deleuze and Guattari have described as the "three worst themes in many interpretations of Kafka" (44). What these themes share is not simply the "centrality of suspicion," as Sedgwick would describe it, but a "concomitant privileging of the concept of paranoia" (5). Sedgwick's tongue-in-cheek remark that paranoia is no longer just a diagnosis but a prescription as well seems especially provocative when one thinks of how often one encounters it in Kafka criticism.

I should point out here that I am not speaking of any literal or explicit invocation of paranoia[4] but of paranoia as an epistemological practice that can be best summed up with this maxim: never let the unthinkable get the best of you. Or, never be surprised by what your investigation turns up. Of course, the best way to forestall surprise is to plant the thing you fear *before* you discover it (or *so* you can discover it). At any rate, this is how some characterize the hermeneutics of suspicion. "The important point," writes Gerald Bruns, "is that what is disclosed (or exposed) is not any sort of truth or revelation—nor is it, indeed, any sort of sense, even of a negative persuasion; it is rather a purely formal condition in which the mind achieves something like a perpetual transport of suspicion" (*Inventions,* 92). The hermeneutics of suspicion is a "self-constructing" and "self-operating" system whose authority is "technical and intrinsic." It's as if, continues Bruns, "one can neither imagine that the thing never existed, nor that one could have ever been outside of it. It follows that to think systematically...is, in effect, to have your thinking done for you: one thing necessarily conducts to another, and so you are kept from going astray, or getting lost—anyhow there is no question of wandering around as if in the open" (92). And the fear of surprise is most intense when we are left alone, lost and wandering. One might say that Kafka's texts ask us to wander out in the open, forever bewildered. Why a critic should name this landscape a "landscape of failures," why we feel as if we've been *banished* to it, Lear-like, and, finally, why bewilderment is a condition of fear and anxiety, has everything to do with that exigency of the paranoid model of reading. "The first imperative of paranoia" argues Sedgwick, "is 'There must be no bad surprises,' and indeed the aversion to surprise seems to be what cements the intimacy between paranoia and knowledge per se" (9). Sedgwick then credits D.A. Miller who, in *The Novel and the Police*, observes that surprise is not only what the paranoid seeks to eliminate, but is "also what, in the event, he survives by reading as a frightening incentive: he can never be paranoid enough" (164). The paranoid model of inquiry is so attractive because it promises us that we'll all know better next time, that we won't be surprised to find that we've failed once again. We have, in this specific cultural moment, moved beyond surprise and now anticipate horror and pain. We will not be surprised to discover the children suffocated inside a trunk; we will not be surprised to find one morning we've all been transformed into giant insects; we will not be surprised to encounter unnamed enemies in the bowels of the earth. Such paranoid maxims have assumed the role as fitting descriptions of Kafka's own exigency of writing.

Intellectual Burrowing

"The Burrow," written during the winter of 1923–1924, only a few months before Kafka's death, is the story of a nameless creature who contemplates the success and failure of his underground burrow as he builds it. Not knowing whether or not the elaborate burrow is worth the trouble, the creature nevertheless continues to build—if only for safety's sake. "The world is full of diversity," declares the creature, "and is never wanting in painful surprises" (347). A true skeptic if there ever was one. Given his philosophical disposition, the creature cannot afford to relax his vigilance: "may I not be attacked from some quite unexpected quarter?" (326). So the terrain of the burrow must be familiar and secure. Outside the burrow, above the loose and easy soil, are robbers who threaten to sink their teeth into the creature's flank while he's desperately digging away. Inside the burrow, within "the bowels of the earth," are enemies who cannot even be named: "I have never seen them, but legend tells of them and I firmly believe in them. They are creatures of the inner earth; not even legend can describe them" (326). Kayser points out, quite rightly, that Kafka never attempts to "invoke and name the ominous forces" that are present in his stories (149). What little plot there is in "The Burrow" revolves around a mysterious whistling that comes from without and the creature's inability to bring it under conceptual control. The grotesque, following Kayser's line of thought, is the expression of our failure to protect ourselves from, or orient ourselves with respect to, strange forces. Somewhere, in the back of the creature's mind, there is not much chance for survival in a world as threatening as this one. But the creature offers some hope, however slight, and he simply cannot live without it.

The "primary purpose" of "The Burrow," according to Heinrich Henel, is to make the reader share the experience of this threatening world: "to enmesh him in [the creature's] dilemma, to make him feel the seriousness of his plight" (123). Of course as readers, says Henel, we know that the creature's fears are irrational; and thus we experience the senselessness of the creature's despair. Kafka's story, then, is really about "the ineluctable problems of man's inner and outer existence. Specifically, the conflict in 'The Burrow' is...between his intellect and its objects, an outer world of contingencies which defies rational planning and inner world so hidden that it eludes self-searching" (132). Malcolm Pasley sees this conflict as Kafka's own: "It seems possible...to accept the burrow both as an image of Kafka's work and as an image of his inner self" (421). More recently, "The Burrow" has been seen as a portrayal of absolute and inescapable anxiety (Mailloux, 545), even the internalization of Kafka's own doomed struggle with tuberculosis (Gilman, 236). One of the more interesting readings of Kafka's story, however, comes from Allen Thiher who, in "The Nachlaß: Metaphors of *Gehen* and Ways Toward Science," argues that "The Burrow" is really about giving one's self over to scientific investigation. The exterior world of Kafka's story "penetrates the burrow in the form of a mysterious noise, subject to multiple interpretations and explanatory hypotheses, as if it were some signal that might be decoded like a non-random noise: sometimes as whistling, sometimes a piping, sometimes with pauses, sometimes ubiquitously uniform, with the same strength throughout the day and the night" (262). Though Thiher never states this explicitly, his reading makes it possible to suggest that "The Burrow" is a parody of our own need for science, of our belief that for every violent imposition upon us, there can be a technical speculation that can account for it and defend us against it in the future.

What is needed, however, is no ordinary science. What is needed is a science of a paranoid style, a style that can eliminate the potential terror that is produced by the random production of meaning. According to Sedgwick, who in a happy coincidence invokes our Kafkaesque metaphor "[t]he unidirectional future-oriented vigilance of paranoia generates, paradoxically, a complex relation to temporality that burrows both backward and forward: because there must be no bad surprises, and because to learn the possibility of a bad surprise would itself constitute a bad surprise, paranoia requires that bad news be already known" (10). So the creature goes over his burrow again and again, back and forth, repairing and inspecting, so as to protect himself from the unknown. The creature's "constant preoccupation with defensive measures" is not a philosophical imperative, a mode of Being, or an essential spiritual condition. It is simply a craft, a systematic approach to things similar in kind to that of an engineer of a proposed subway system. Given its faults and shortcomings, given its disturbing cracks and hideous protuberances, given that the enormous labor behind it far outweighs the security it provides, this no ordinary subway system, this is the MTA Red Line of Los Angeles: a vast and costly joke, an idle *tour de farce*. "The Burrow" can be read as a subtle demystification of paranoia: it isn't something that defends *us*, it's a critical method *we* defend. Paranoia functions as interpretive control; and those who live within its scope function for it such that the pleasures of life come from how well one executes its will. "All this involves laborious calculations" says the creature, "and the sheer pleasure of the mind in its own keenness is often the sole reasons why one keeps it up" (325). In other words, the joy of paranoia is not found in the security it produces, but in its being produced. And when the creature suspects that his *joie de vivre* has been sapped, it is because he realizes that all his work has been misplaced: "The joy of possessing [the burrow] has spoiled me, the vulnerability of the burrow has made me vulnerable; any wound to it hurts me as if I myself were hit. It is precisely this that I should have foreseen; instead of thinking only of my defense—and how perfunctorily and vainly I have done even that—I should have thought of the defense of my burrow" (355). Ask not what paranoia can do for you; ask what you can do for paranoia.

If "The Burrow" is a grotesque tale, and indeed it is, it is as sportive as it is fearful. In fact, the story functions more interestingly as a travesty of the fearful grotesque than it does as an example of it. Certainly, "The Burrow" is a story about the objectification of anxiety and *angst*, as many people claim; and reading Kafka's story from a paranoid position means understanding this objectification as an absolutely essential defense against the unknown. It also means giving the creature a name or transforming, at Henel's suggestion, what would otherwise be some form of *Leporidae* or *Talpidae* into a version of ourselves. There is no need to find fault with those who are inclined to perform this textual metamorphosis, for it helps define Kafka's story as grotesque, which is our purpose here. The world of "The Burrow" isn't exactly fantastic, and the creature that inhabits it isn't terribly fabulous. But by portraying the former not as the ground beneath our feet but as a placeless world, and the latter not as a rabbit or a mole but as a version of ourselves, the story becomes more grotesque. But what sort of grotesque are we approaching? There is no ghostly "It" lurking in the dark, only the "small fry" who dig burrows too close for our creature's comfort: "What an indefatigably busy lot these small fry are, and what a nuisance their diligence can be!" (343). One could say that the "small fry"—of which our narrator is (unwittingly) one—are the only creatures inhabiting the world of "The Burrow." Now the story is a grotesque joke, made at the creature's (and our) expense. True, there are decidedly un-comic moments, moments of sheer terror. The story moves fluidly between the fearful and the sportive; noises and stirrings from without are at once an object of terror, and again simply a nuisance. Sometimes the creature is frozen with fear, at other times he is just overwhelmed with lassitude. There is tranquility even in his constant vigilance, and he calls moments such as this "[h]appy but dangerous hours" (331). The threats, in all shapes and sizes, come and go; moods and states of mind are in constant flux; the burrow is a happy success, and a money pit whose brilliance is only theoretical. What remains constant, however, is the creature's paranoia. Sure, there may be some fear. "But you do not know me if you think I am afraid or that I built my burrow simply out of fear" (325). No, the creature builds his burrow out of paranoia—which is quite a different thing.

Even if we admit a more than negligible degree of the sportive in Kafka's writings, we do so only to establish more firmly the paranoid style of reading. Even Jean Collignon, whose insightful investigation of Kafka's humor has inspired much of this chapter, does little to upset this cherished assumption:

> One truism stands out from the outset: if humor there must be, it does not correspond in the least to the variety exemplified by Rabelais, Fielding and good natured people who delight in after-dinner jokes. Kafka's humor must haunt the opposite pole: it is the humor of a man both oppressed and depressed who smiles not in order to forget but to assert his independence, and makes plain his determination not to be overwhelmed by hardships: he will be defeated, he knows it, there is no hope; he will be murdered "like a dog"; but he can keep smiling at the whole procedure and at himself into the bargain. (53–54)

If the reader is comfortable with the loud and smug assertion that "one truism stands out from the outset," she will likely already share Collignon's belief that visible traces of Kafka's laughter lead only to tragedy. Heinrich Henel, in a similar vein, argues that these traces "show what a writer of comedy Kafka could have been had he allowed the ironically detached view of his implied author to prevail over the tragically involved view of his protagonist" (125). But how does such a claim earn its confidence? After all, what does it mean for a text to produce this particular hierarchical arrangement? What compels a reader to accept that the one has prevailed over the other? What if we chose to ignore whatever presumptive evidence exists that the tragically involved view of the protagonist has prevailed and instead see it as unveiled? To pull something like this off, one would have to read Kafka as if he were a pre-Romantic (or, using Ruskin's criteria, as if he belonged to the grotesque pre-Renaissance). Let us choose an altogether different sense of the grotesque—a pre-Romantic comic perspective that destroys "all pretense of an extratemporal meaning and unconditional value of necessity," one that "frees human consciousness, thought, and imagination for new possibilities" (Bakhtin, *Rabelais*, 49). In what follows, I will attempt what Eve Sedgwick has termed "reading from a reparative position" and visit two stories by Kafka (*The Metamorphosis*, and "A Report to the Academy"). I will also illustrate how this approach to Kafka suggests that the comic is just as central to his stories and novels as other modes assumed to be more dominant.[5] The difficulty, as Wallace demonstrates, is that it is not entirely clear exactly what the comic in Kafka means, or what it is (Wallace speaks of Kafka's "funniness"; his "humor"; his "wit"; his "comedy"; even his "comedy-as-literalization-of-metaphor"). Thus, the subsidiary purpose of this chapter is to find out what we can learn from Kafka about the nature of the comic, and to make room in our understanding for a more *comic* Kafka, and for a more *comic* grotesque—an alternative to the logic of terror so often associated with modern grotesque forms. I emphasize the term comic because what these stories seem to do is play with comedy's basic theme (other human beings) and its basic movement (liberation). There will be casualties along the way, of course, because these stories don't hesitate to ridicule all that oppose comic liberation.

Many of Kafka's texts belong to a world where there is no surprise. But how should we understand such a world? Is Kafka trying to scare us away from our comforting paranoia by showing us what kind of world awaits us should paranoia achieve everything it promises? *Or*: is Kafka describing, simply, a different world—one in which paranoia isn't in- stinctual, where paranoia simply hasn't been programmed into us as an option? After all, how can we know better next time when the cause of Gregor Samsa's metamorphosis is never explained, or why Joseph K. is arrested one fine morning, or why a giant mole paid a visit to a small village?

"The Apple Went on Sticking to His Body": Comedy is Other People

Reading *The Metamorphosis* from both a paranoid position and a reparative position produces two very different stories. One who under- stands the grotesque as an eager-minded collaboration with skepticism may conclude that the moral of the Kafka's tale is this: maybe we *can* be paranoid enough. After all, Gregor Samsa is everything a paranoid wants to be. He is neither surprised nor horrified to find himself one fine morn- ing transformed into a giant beetle. His first thoughts, when he wakes to find his thin, struggling legs twittering beneath his sheets, are not "Oh God, I should have known" or "Oh God, I'll know better next time." His first thoughts, instead, turn to his work: "Oh God, he thought, what an exhausting job I've picked on! Traveling about day in, day out. It's much more irritating work than doing the actual business in the office, and on top of that there's the trouble of constant traveling, of worrying about train connections, the bed and irregular means, casual acquaintances that are always new and never become intimate friends. The devil take it all!" (90). We assume that Gregor Samsa should have known he'd wake up one morning and find himself transformed into a giant insect. This is not to say he has achieved everything the New Historicists want: never to be surprised again. Perhaps he is simply too concerned about his work. Perhaps he is so exhausted by his everyday affairs to be bothered with this never-ending determination to be one step ahead of the unthinkable. If one were to extend Ruskin's thesis, one could argue that paranoia is luxury only the noble man can possess. The workingman has far too much on his mind to indulge, full-time, in the "dark forces that lurk in and behind our world and have power to estrange it" (Kayser, 188). But then again, what would it mean to imagine Gregor Samsa as contemplating these dark forces rather than his job, his family, the possibility that his boss "would reproach his parents with their son's laziness, and would cut all excuses short by referring to the insurance doctor, who of course regarded all mankind as perfectly healthy malingerers" (91)? For starters, we would no longer have *The Metamorphosis*.

I have seen and read of interesting stage adaptations of *The Metamorphosis*, all of which insist that the actor playing Gregor Samsa tie himself up in a knot, like a contortionist, so that he effects some illusion of grotesque physical transformation. Never, as far as I know, has there been a theatrical adaptation of Kafka's story in which Gregor Samsa appeared as a normal, healthy human being, *sans* transformation. But such an adaptation could work and with great comic effect. After all, what Kafka has given us is not the tale of a human being who has become a giant insect (i.e., David Cronenberg's 1987 re-make of *The Fly*) but the tale of a giant insect who must function as if he were a human being—a dutiful son and salesman to be precise. Gregor Samsa's world is a humdrum world and nothing should change that. But a paranoid reader can't help but change it; one might even argue that the metamorphosis in *The Metamorphosis* belongs not to Gregor but to the reader. David Eggenschwiler has suggested as much in his essay "*The Metamorphosis*: Freud and the Chains of Odysseus." Readers of Kafka's story give in swiftly and happily to the temptation to transform the literal into the symbolic, and with good reason: "the obtrusively obvious images and actions, the patent juxtaposition of symbols with descriptions of Gregor's longings, frustrations, and guilt, even the coy asides that suggest a psychological possibility while pretending to deny it—these techniques coax from the reader a psychological interpretation" (203). Descriptions of Gregor's struggle are no longer of a bug's attempts to live in a human world, but of a human whose sublimations have gotten the better of him. In a particularly clever and convincing moment of his essay, Eggenschwiler describes the scene in which Gregor's father chases him from the room, brandishing a walking stick, waving a newspaper, and shouting so wildly that the voice no longer seems to come from just one father: "A brandished cane, a savage, multiplied father—the scene pushes irresistibly into a primal conflict, representing the unconscious infantile fears that Freud had already described in the famous and then highly controversial *Three Essays on the Theory of Sexuality*, published in 1905" (206).

But why, asks Eggenschwiler, do we fail to respond to the literal scene of a man shooing away a bug? "Can we be sure that we do not have a grotesque joke? And at whose expense would it be? And how much would it undercut the psychological themes? If, intellectually, the latent content is made almost too obvious by the manifest content, is it not, affectively, subverted by the manifest?" (206). There's no doubt Kafka baits us with "wonderfully loud and heavy-handed" variations on the Oedipal theme, but for what purpose? To show how some interpretive methods struggle to make familiar and human that which is strange and irrational. This is, Eggenschwiler claims, Kafka's explicit critique of psychological theory: "psychology pretends to describe in rational and observably human images an inner world that is indescribable, irrational, and inhuman; it profanes the sacred and makes the mysterious seem knowable" (203). It's as if Kafka wants to show us the degree to which the literal repels us. We distance ourselves from it as much as possible, visit it as seldom as possible. We throw apples at it, and we chase it away when it gets too close. We remove its furnishings and cut off all its ties to the world. In one of the most touching and hilarious passages ever written by Kafka, we are presented with the damage caused by this disgust:

> The serious injury done to Gregor, which disabled him for more than a month—the apple went on sticking to his body as a visible reminder, since no one ventured to remove it—seemed to have made even his father recollect that Gregor was a member of the family, despite his present unfortunate and repulsive shape, and ought not to be treated as an enemy, that, on the contrary, family duty required the suppression of disgust and the exercise of patience, nothing but patience. (122)

We are, one might say, as impatient as the Samsa family. We rush to psychological interpretation by transforming the literal into the symbolic every chance we get ("Psychology is impatience," says Kafka in one of his notebooks). Of course, we need not argue that the literal is finally incomprehensible just because there are limits to psychological interpretations. "Either to spell out a set of psychological patterns," says Eggenschwiler, "or to assert that Gregor's metamorphosis is entirely and intentionally incomprehensible is to miss the further pleasure of recognizing both and appreciating their interplay" (208). I would like add further pleasure by suggesting that these two interpretations, which are really nothing more than two different kinds of skepticism, are not our only options. The first is hell-bent on recovering meaning when it disappears. The second, more radical, form is satisfied knowing that the unknown cannot be known, only acknowledged. The former is the hermeneutic of suspicion as described by Sedgwick, the latter is the "truth of skepticism" as described by Cavell. The two indeed play off each other as Eggenschwiler has wonderfully demonstrated, but I would suggest that *The Metamorphosis* ignores skepticism altogether and offers the sportive grotesque as another way of looking at the world. Sure, bad things happen, things we don't quite understand, but what is far worse is how we respond to these things. Gregor's torture lies not in his being a giant insect. Gregor's torture lies in his family's disgust. His torture is that apple, stuck to his back.

The Metamorphosis reminds us that our world is a comic world, full of people rather than "ghostly Its."[6] The sheer, unexplainable terror of Gregor's transformation does, one may argue, inaugurate the great themes of tragedy: fate, the restoration of moral order through suffering, the guarantee of moral salvation through renunciation, sacrifice, death. Yet, these themes are set to what Susanne Langer calls "the comic rhythm." Being human means being aware of other humans—to be "consciously bound to people who are absent, perhaps far away, at the moment" (330). An individual's awareness of events, says Langer, "is far greater than the scope of his physical perceptions. Symbolic construction has made this vastly involved and extended world...The pattern of his vital feeling, therefore, reflects his deep emotional relation to those symbolic structures that are his realities, and his instinctual life modified in almost every way by thought—a brainy opportunism in face of an essentially dreadful universe" (330–331). The fact that Gregor is more concerned about others than his own buggy self suggests the incredible pull of this human life feeling, and this gives the story its comic pattern. The rhythm of Kafka's story is set to the comings and goings of other people: the mother and father, the sister Grete, the charwoman, the three lodgers, the chief clerk from Gregor's employer. One could even argue that Kafka's story delivers a typically comic ending, one that restores "a lost balance" and implies "a new future" (Langer, 335). As Mr. and Mrs. Samsa ride in the tram that takes them further and further away from the city, they are warmed as much by the sunshine as by Grete's "increasing vivacity" (Kafka, *The Metamorphosis,* 139). "They grew quieter and half consciously exchanged glances of complete agreement, having come to the conclusion that it would be time to find a good husband for her. And it was like a confirmation of their new dreams and excellent intentions that at the end of their journey their daughter sprang to her feet and stretched her young body" (139). One doesn't need to pay much attention to the ending in order to feel the story's comic rhythm (and who reads Kafka for plot anyway?). The point of reading Kafka from a reparative position is to remind ourselves of other people, to put them before any "queer, extra-human power that evidences itself murkily, menacingly"—however central such power seems (Gurewitch, 194).

"Head over Heels and Away": How the Grotesque Gives Us a "Way Out"

"A Report to an Academy," written in the summer of 1917 and published later that winter in the monthly *Der Jude*, begins like this: "Honored members of the Academy! You have done me the honor of inviting me to give your Academy an account of the life I formerly led as an ape" (250). And with that, we are taken head over heels and away. There's no way to explain, really, how we got here, and Kafka himself doesn't care to dwell on this matter. "A Report to an Academy" begins in the same way an improvisational troupe begins a skit: someone from the audience shouts towards the comedian on the stage: "You're an ape!" while a second adds "in a business suit!" followed, quickly, by a third: "giving a speech!" Stories such as this one begin with lightning-quick, absurd nonchalance.[7] However, by making the connection between improvisational theater and the stories of Kafka, I only wish to account for the suddenness with which we are given a comic perspective.[8] The point is simply this: we need not ask *why* there is an ape speaking to us, *why* Joseph K. is arrested, or *why* a village once celebrated a disgusting giant mole, and so on. There is no set-up, these worlds are just assumed; and to read the opening lines of stories like this one is not to be turned upside down (as it would be for Lewis Carroll's Alice), nor is it to be led, systematically, to another place altogether (though it is often easy to assume this is Kafka's purpose). "Report to an Academy" is about the impossibility of achieving liberation except by sheer will.

One cannot, with any claim of reason, account for this comic world—to do so would be a bit like explaining to the human perspective how you felt when you were an ape, or a giant insect, or a dog. "Of course what I felt then as an ape," writes Kafka, "I can represent now only in human terms, and therefore I misrepresent it, but although I cannot reach back to the truth of the old ape life, there is no doubt that it lies somewhere in the direction I have indicated" (253). This humble ape, however, has much to teach us. The lesson here, I hope to show, is that comedy does not liberate us from the rigid laws that contain us (in the sense that, once free, we can stand safely *here* while the rigid laws are *there*). In the same way, comedy does not subvert from *within* (because it never for a moment believed there was an "inside" worth acknowledging). The comic in Kafka is positive, regenerative, and creative. His grotesque images (of talking apes, of self-pitying beetles, and miserable vermin) seem to promise an entirely different world, another order, another way of life precisely because these images need not be understood as belonging to a conflict in need of resolution or to a hierarchy in need of arrangement.

Although the ape insists he is giving a report and nothing more, although his modesty ("I regret I cannot comply with your request to the extent you desire") gives the reader the impression that no expert knowledge is being imparted, one can nevertheless find in his a words an important lesson[9]: we can achieve strange things with a comic perspective; it can liberate us from the most confining of places. The necessity of this perspective occurs to the ape very early on in his life: he is captured by the firm of Hagenbeck and taken from the jungles of the Gold Coast back to Europe aboard a giant steamer. He is given the name Red Peter—or Rotpeter, as he's referred to in an unpublished fragment of the same story—because a gunshot wound to his cheek has left a red scar. "A horrible name, utterly inappropriate, which only some ape could have thought of, as if the only difference between me and the performing ape, Peter, who died not so long ago and had some small local reputation, were the red mark on my cheek" (252). It is from within the dankness of his cage that he begins to contemplate the limits of freedom:

> For the first time in my life, I could see no way out; at least no direct way out...Until then I had had so many ways out of everything, and now I had none. I was pinned down. Had I been nailed down, my right to free movement would not have been lessened. Why so? Scratch your flesh raw between your toes, but you won't find the answer. Press yourself against the bar behind till it nearly cuts you in two, you won't find the answer. I had no way out but to devise one, for without it I could not live. (252–253)

If the space in which the ape is trapped seems impenetrable, how does one "devise" a way out? It is always possible for an ape to gnaw and gnash his way through a cage, but Rotpeter did not do it. "What good would it have done me?" he says. "As soon as I poked out my head I should have been caught again and put in a worse cage" (255). What magic can the comic perspective perform upon the oppressive spaces we inhabit on a daily basis? It would seem that the magic lies in the ability to demystify not simply "real spaces," but the idea of freedom these spaces construct. It is through the grotesque creature-as-human performance (such that the performer is neither creature nor human) that lines of escape become most clear.

Take, as an example of this demystification, a scene from Steven Spielberg's 1983 film, *E.T.: The Extra-Terrestrial*. A more common space than the animal cage is demystified: the elementary school. In this space we find a young school boy, Eliot, who must dissect a frog for his biology experiment. Meanwhile, left alone at Eliot's house, E.T. is drinking beer and watching an old romance flick on television. As the alcohol affects E.T., so too does it affect Eliot (who, by some otherworldly phenomenon, shares E.T.'s thoughts, feelings, and physical condition). The two of them, under the soporific effects of beer and romance, begin to swoon. Neither one is entirely extra-terrestrial nor terrestrial, neither is entirely creature or human. Before any of his fellow classmates can notice the peculiar change that has overcome him, Eliot has risen from his desk and is seducing a fellow classmate. By way of clever crosscutting, the two schoolchildren kiss before our eyes precisely as John Wayne and Maureen O'Hara kiss before E.T.'s eyes. This passion goes viral and soon the exuberant children are freeing the frogs from their jars and racing through the hallways. This overflow of powerful feelings—that has no source of which reason may speak—spills out of the classroom. Doors blow open, frogs leap about, and children dance themselves head over heels and away.[10]

From one point of view, the school is no longer a school, and the metaphors of playground and classroom are no longer oppositional. The children's festival is a "way out," the same sort of "way out" our distinguished ape is searching for—which is to say, he is *not* searching for someone to lift him from his cage, the way the frogs are lifted from their jars. To put the matter another way, the children did not liberate themselves from the classroom by ditching school altogether, becoming delinquents, and in so doing acquiescing to the power of surveillance (truant officers, school administrators, angry parents, etc.). This line of escape, although not uncommon, is structurally oppositional and therefore temporary rather than transformative. *E.T.*, however, seems to tell a very different story—different than, say, the story told by *Rebel Without a Cause* (dir. Nicholas Ray, 1995), whose view of liberation as necessarily doomed seems far more familiar to us.

The structural logic of classroom/playground is discussed at length in Chapter 2 of this project so I will not address it at length here. I will, however, briefly suggest here the difficulties in speaking of the liberatory possibilities of the festive and the grotesque at the discursive level of literary theory. In his 1982 essay for the *New Left Review*, "Wittgenstein's Friends," Terry Eagleton illustrates the basis of Bakhtin's appeal by citing the latter's notion of carnival. Here, says Eagleton, "the Nietzschean playfulness of contemporary post-structuralism leaves the academy and dances in the streets" (79). Robert J. C. Young, however, claims that there is, for the institutionalized critic, "no easy passage from one domain to another—if only because Bakhtin has broken down the distinction between the two. The academic fantasy of moving out on to the streets is itself disrupted by the carnivalization of academic disciplines" (53). Eagleton's view, according to Young, is an example of an anxiety-driven search by radical intellectuals and rootless academics for an imaginary space positioned in ideological opposition to a sadly "all-too-real" space. It is to Eagleton, one might say, that Kafka's ape addresses his report. "I fear," says the ape:

> that perhaps you do not quite understand what I mean by "way out." I use the expression in it fullest and most popular sense. I deliberately do not use the word "freedom." I do not mean the spacious feeling of freedom on all sides. As an ape, perhaps, I knew that, and I have met men who yearn for it. But for my part I desired such freedom neither then nor now. In passing: may I say that all too often men are betrayed by the word freedom. And as freedom is counted among the most sublime feelings, so the corresponding disillusionment can be also sublime. (253)

The men this ape has met are likely men who speak, with appropriate skepticism, of the Nietzschean playfulness of post-structuralism, of "all-too-real" institutional spaces that construct imagined spaces of freedom, and the betrayal they feel after having consulted this freedom. Betrayal, argues Robert C. Young, seems to be precisely the feeling Terry Eagleton feels after having suggested that Bakhtin can send an academic dancing in the streets, which is why he follows up his initial praise of Bakhtinian carnival a year later with this bleak analysis that carnival "may be little more than the intellectual's guilty dues to the populace, the soul's blood money to the body; what is truly unseemly, indecent even, is the apparent eagerness of deans, chaired professors and presidents of learned societies to tumble from their offices into the streets, monstrous papier mâché phalluses fixed in place" (in Young, 53).

But the ape's notion of "human freedom" is fashioned not from his association with academia, but from his observations of local theatrics.

He recalls the trapeze artists who, with their fantastic acrobatics, seemed to have freed themselves from this earth and its demands upon them. Such a spectacle could be found anywhere and could dazzle anyone. Indeed, the figure of the acrobat, by the turn of the century, had become a privileged subject of representation by writers and artists—one which could even stand in for the artist himself (Russo, 35). Seeking the thrill of the spectacle, it would seem, had replaced the more participatory enchantments of the festival—in fact, it could be said that the rise of what the psychoanalyst Michael Balint would call "philobatism" marks the turning point in the history of festival. The glory of the festival loses its broad cultural force as it becomes internalized, subjectivized. Spectacle becomes the *interior infinite* of the nineteenth and early twentieth centuries (Bakhtin, 44). Why, if the actual event of carnival disappears, would the thrill, disembodied and dislocated, still survive? Balint would have it that the love of acrobatics, this amateur pursuit of thrills, is evidence of "residual, primitive reenactments of early sensations, phantasms, and psychic senses" (35). Perhaps, but not for Rotpeter:

> In variety theatres I have often watched, before my turn came on, a couple of acrobats performing on trapezes high in the roof. They swung themselves, they rocked to and fro, they sprang into the air, they floated into each other's arms, one hung by the hair from the teeth of the other. "And that too is human freedom," I thought, "self-controlled movement." What a mockery of Mother Nature! Were the apes to see such a spectacle, no theater walls could stand the shock of their laughter. (253)

If there is freedom to be found in the acrobatics of self-controlled movement, it is in the laughter it inspires, the laughter that no wall can withstand. The artifice of freedom, and the sublime effects it has on its spectators, is, for our ape friend, the object of a most powerful laughter. One could assume, then, that Rotpeter shares the same criticism for theatergoers that Eagleton shares for literary academics. "What a mockery!" they both can be heard saying. The difference between Rotpeter and Eagleton, however, is that Rotpeter knows there's another option and Eagleton does not. Eagleton understands Bakhtinian carnival as offering "a somewhat perilous 'way out' for Marxist criticism," but does little to question the efficacy of this understanding or to imagine a different set of options (Young, 53). Rotpeter, however, understands that the problem lies not with the "way out," but with how one imagines "way out." One could say that the trapeze artists have taught Rotpeter that there are limits to the "interior infinite" of spectacle and the freedom it provides. This is not to say, however, that the ape is performing an empiricist critique of subjective experience and the Kantian sublime, for he takes great pains to distinguish empirical definitions of freedom (as "the spacious feeling of freedom on all sides") from his own—a distinction that would seem to identify the ape as a formal idealist if there ever was one. His reference to a pure and simple "way out" sounds very much like an appeal to the transcendental (after all, this sort of freedom cannot be put into language, much less taught). Still, the ape appears critical of what Francis Ferguson calls "a temporary peculiarity in taste" (39), or what Thomas Weiskel calls the "predisposition to melancholy" as the remedy of choice to the "vague boredom" characteristic of Romantic and post-Romantic experience (97). Such is the melancholia of a Coleridge who, despite being stranded in his lime tree bower, is nonetheless able to transport himself and join his friends on their afternoon sojourn. The feeling of pleasure is produced not by the success of this flight, but by its failure.

But if the ape's definition of freedom is neither empirical nor transcendental, then what is it? One cannot produce an adequate answer to this question because the freedom the ape experiences is not produced by the sublime but by the grotesque. This may be what distinguishes Rotpeter from the academics to whom he addresses his report (Eagleton, Young, and the rest of us). For some reason, an ape who mocks human behavior has access to the absolute grotesque, a point of view that is simply different than the oppositional framework of post-structural thought. Only a sense of freedom that is created by a framework of confinement could appear so spectacular, so sublime; for once inside such a framework, one has more hope of escaping from an iron cage. Rotpeter's laughter, then, is enlisted in an all-out put-down of narrow-mindedness that sees freedom as always, necessarily, and finally, subject to control. Deleuze and Guattari's observations are quite apt here: "it isn't a question of liberation as against submission, but only a question of a line of escape or, rather, of a simple *way out*" (6). The trick is not to imagine freedom in terms of confinement (the way an acrobat's high-flying tumbles are the product of an always persistent gravitational pull, the way Joseph K.'s liberation from the court's charges depends on a mastery of its procedures, or the way K.'s strategy of challenging the authority of the Castle depends on his entering into its field of vision), but to simply see a way out, to allow the comic perspective to take you, immediately, head over heels and away.

This is the trick Rotpeter performs; he pretends to be a human (and why not? don't humans pretend to be apes all the time?). He learns their habits, their ridiculously slow movements, their coarse jests, their tendency to grumble and spit. Granted, this is not the more attractive of options, "Had I been devoted to the aforementioned idea of freedom, I should certainly have preferred the deep sea to the way out that suggested itself in the heavy faces of these men" (255). What is this "deep sea"? Perhaps the ape is referring to the waters upon which his captors sail. Is it not also possible that this "deep sea" refers to the sublime disillusionment of a Coleridge or a philobat? If so, then it would seem that Kafka is posing an absolutely comic alternative to what we generally assume to be the truth of his own writings: the "deep sea" the ape ridicules is precisely that "vast landscape of failures" we have been taught to read as Kafkaesque. And despite the lure of such sublime disillusionment, the ape opts for the rather crude tactic of mockery. He drinks schnapps to excess, breaks into human speech—not out of despair, but "as an artistic performer" (257). This is a spectacle indeed but not for its own sake. No, the ape has turned theory into practice: "I repeat: there was no attraction for me in imitating human beings; I imitated them because I needed a way out, and for no other reason" (257). He does not retreat to some imaginary space—free from all signification, yet still within the four walls of his cage.

On the one hand, "A Report to an Academy" is a sober recital of an unconventional theory of freedom, a personal narrative documenting a curious line of escape. On the other hand, it is much more than this. It can be read as an illustration of the radical alterity that makes Bakhtin's dialogics so unimaginable to those for whom "[t]he draw of the binary is too strong, its appeal too seductive," and so attractive to those who understand the disruption of closure as the potential basis of all criticism. It may even be a call for grotesque criticism. There can be no same and no other as such in dialogism, which is why Rotpeter's finds his "way out" through dialogism. His line of escape begins with the arrival of a teacher who hopes to solve the "enigma" of Rotpeter's being by having the ape mimic his every move: "He would slowly uncork the bottle [of schnapps] and then look at me to see if I had followed him...After the bottle was uncorked he lifted it to his mouth; I followed it with my eyes right up to his jaws; he would nod, pleased with me, and set the bottle to his lips" (256). The interesting thing, however, is that the teacher sees Rotpeter's escape not in a dissolution of difference between self and Other, inside and outside, but in the subsuming of the Other (ape) by the self through an antagonistic dialectical maneuver: "[the teacher] perceived that we were both fighting on the same side against the nature of apes and that I had the more difficult task" (257). The teacher assumes that the theoretical dissolution of difference is practiced by a monological drive to incorporate the Other within the self, hence, his enormous satisfaction whenever Rotpeter put the bottle of schnapps to his lips. The triumph, in the teacher's mind, comes only when the ape becomes human. And although Rotpeter is truly delighted by the theoretical dissolution of difference, he has neither the power to let go of his ape enigma nor the monological drive to seize his freedom by reversing the teacher's game. Rotpeter escapes not when he has become fully human, but when he has dissolved the difference between self and Other. The force of Rotpeter's dialogism is not lost on the teacher: "My ape nature fled out of me, head over heels and away, so that my first teacher was almost himself turned into an ape by it, had soon to give up teaching and was taken away to a mental hospital. Fortunately he was soon let out again" (258). The teacher, of course, doesn't expect to lose conceptual distinction in this transaction, and goes slightly mad when "sameness and difference become implicated within each other" (Young, 59).

The reason why the story is more than simply a fable is that what holds for Rotpeter and his teacher holds for critical theory as well. Young puts the matter this way, Bakhtin's dialogism is:

> tricky to use in conjunction with any conventional model of the other...As David Carroll has stressed, representation, narrative, or theory cannot encompass dialogism without it becoming monological; in this sense they have the same function as poetry, against which the novel is defined, and will only reduce heterogeneity to sameness. Unless, that is, they are themselves dialogized, in which case, those who say a 'way out' in Bakhtin were in a sense right after all. Bakhtin's position may conflict with the central tenets of many an orthodoxy, indeed of the very project of "theory" itself, but he does facilitate a move into the promised land of the social. (60)

What emerges through Bakhtin is a social that resembles nothing that critical theory has ever achieved; for, continues Young, "[if] Bakhtin enables and sustains this recognition of and identification with irreducible otherness, of sameness with difference, it also means that the social will not be recognizable as 'the social' anymore. It will rather have become... a form of 'the grotesque'" (60). What the ape does is restore the genuine liberatory possibilities of the grotesque. If Kafka can write about a man inexplicably put to death for a crime he didn't commit, surely he can write about an ape who inexplicably becomes human and walks free from his cage. We don't question why Joseph K. is arrested one fine morning, nor do we question why Gregor Samsa is awakened from uneasy dreams to find he has been transformed into a giant insect. To be precise, we have taught ourselves that asking why such horrible events occur only wastes critical energy. So we choose to ignore the question. Knowledge becomes acknowledgment, if by acknowledgment we mean "openness and acceptance of the other as such, that is, as other, as that which resists every effort on my part to reduce it to something containable within the legislation of my concepts" (Bruns, "Stanley Cavell's Shakespeare," 184). In other words, moving comfortably through a story by Kafka means being a good skeptic: the world can't be explained; it can only be accepted. By and large, Kafka critics are poor skeptics. They acknowledge the incomprehensible, but rarely read Kafka accordingly. This is because they are quite incapable of surrendering knowledge entirely. To illustrate this, consider Peter U. Beicken's claim that Kafka's "radically subjective narrative strategy defines the inevitable human failure of his protagonists as a modern predicament" (183). Being accepting of "inevitable human failure" does not constitute skepticism, for the radical skeptic should acknowledge that nothing is inevitable. To use Bruns's terminology, "openness and acceptance of the other as such" means the openness and acceptance of the other as sometimes menacing, and sometimes delightful—sometimes this, sometimes that.

The acceptance of failure as the *defining* characteristic of Kafka's stories owes little to radical skepticism. Instead, it owes everything to the centrality of paranoia to our own critical style: the willing acceptance of suffering in exchange for the guarantee of predictability and resolution. It is no wonder scholars are less interested in the incomprehensibility of the ape's miraculous escape than in the incomprehensibility of Joseph K.'s guilt, for the latter flatters our sense of paranoia, whereas the former does not. To be fair, Deleuze and Guattari *are* interested in the ape's escape. To be precise, they are interested in preserving the *meaninglessness* of the ape's escape: "it isn't a question of a well-formed vertical movement toward the sky or in front of one's self, it is no longer a question of liberty as against submission, but only a question of a line of escape or, rather, of a simple *way out*, 'right, left or in any direction,' as long as it is as little signifying as possible" (6). As little signifying as possible, lest the act of becoming an ape be reduced to something containable within the legislation has of a concept, such as the Oedipal complex. The act of becoming animal "has nothing to do with a substitute for the father, or with an archetype" (12). The acts of becoming an ape, a dog, or a beetle "are absolute deterritorializations...To become animal is to participate in movement, to stake out a path of escape in all its positivity, to cross a threshold, to reach a continuum of intensities that are valuable only in themselves, to find a world of pure intensities where contents free themselves from their forms as well as from their expressions, from the signifier that formalized them" (13). Rather than "stay with the negative," as

Heller suggests we do, Deleuze and Guattari insist that by reading Kafka we "stake out a path of escape in all its positivity." In this specific cultural moment, however, one is more likely to treat the very possibility of such a path with extreme suspicion. After all, sheer negativity is an easier pill to swallow that sheer positivity. We are more skilled in anti-essentialist readings than in those that presume liberation is no more essentialist a category than routinized dismissals of it. My point, of course, is not that reading Kafka is a matter of choosing between positivity and negativity, or choosing between fear and joy, or choosing, even, between "Oedi-palized neurosis" and the rejection "of all submissions to the ostensible ties of family and neurosis" (Bensmaïa, xxiv). At the risk of sounding too abstract, one *could* say that reading Kafka is really more a matter of choosing between possibility and impossibility. The latter leaves room for the former, whereas the former precludes the latter.

Several of Kafka's enigmatic parables suggest a similar logic. "On Parables," in particular, sets up the premise that no parable has ever said anything else except "the incomprehensible is incomprehensible"—something we know already. "But the cares we have to struggle with every day, the narrator suggests, "that is a different matter" (11). So the progress of modern culture, one might say, depends on how far removed we are from parable—if by "parable" one means "absolute possibility" (or, as our narrator defines it, "some fabulous yonder"). Similar suspicion is mimicked (though not in the least shared) by Sedgwick and Frank who enumerate "the broad assumptions that shape the heuristic habits and positing procedures of theory today" in the opening pages of their introduction to *Shame and Its Sisters: A Silvan Tomkins Reader.*[11] One could understand the skeptic of "On Parables" the way Sedgwick and Frank understand the contemporary critic; one might, using Sedgwick and Frank's words, characterize the reluctance of the skeptic this way: the distance of any account of our everyday struggles from something so axiomatic as, say, parable "will correlate near-precisely with its poten-tial for doing justice to" these same struggles (Sedgwick and Frank, 1). The modern skeptic *acknowledges* parable but is reluctant to *live* by it. "Concerning this," continues Kafka's narrator, "a man once said: Why such reluctance? If you only followed the parables you yourselves would become parables and with that rid of all your daily cares." To which a second man replies, "I bet that is also a parable" (11). Anthony Thorlby is right in thinking that "the advocate of the [parabolic] life does not actually live it; he knows its value by reference to a reality where for him too it does not prevail and is not true. While the unbelieving realist knows that the value of his winning common sense is—albeit 'unfortunately'—a [parabolic] one" (36).

Rotpeter is perhaps one of Kafka's most privileged figures, a comic hero of enormous flexibility and cunning. He is one of the few Kafka characters who actually lives the parabolic life: "Why such reluctance?" he tells himself. "If you only followed the humans you yourself would become human and with that rid of all your daily cares." In this way, the parabolic life is also the grotesque life; and it is, strangely enough, the work of Kafka that gives us the most beneficent and ameliorative form of the grotesque in modern literature. His work deals with the arbitrariness of suffering, of punishment, of imprisonment, it is true, but his work also deals with the arbitrariness of joy, of compensation, of escape. In this way, Kafka's world is a comic world—a world of people, not of Ids. This world is, of course, no less terrible because it made up only of people. After all, people (as *The Metamorphosis* suggests) can be our worst nightmare. They can, however, be our line of escape, our "way out."

Kafka's Laughter, Our Readings

"I have experienced over and over again," writes Max Brod, "that admirers of Kafka who know him only from his books have a completely false picture of him. They think he must have made a sad, even desperate impression in company too. The opposite is the case" (39). In fact, Brod speaks very flatteringly of Kafka's sense of humor: "There was no end to our joking and laughing—he liked a good, hearty laugh, and knew how to make his friends laugh too" (40). Reflecting on Kafka's character and mind, Brod describes a man whose "spiritual bent was not in the direction of the morbidly interesting, the bizarre or the grotesque, but in that of the greatness of nature, the curative, health giving, sound, firmly established, simple things" (39). Of course, we are talking about the social Kafka, here, but Brod assures us that the portrait he paints from memory must stand alongside Kafka's writings "and demands to be taken into account in any final judgment of him" (40).

The background of Brod's portrait is the "Worker's Accident Insurance Institute"—a very silly place indeed. In a letter to his close friend, Kafka describes his work environment as if it were straight out of a Chaplin film: "people fall, as if they were drunk, off scaffolds and into machines, all the planks tip up, there are landslides everywhere, all the ladders slip, everything one puts up falls down and what one puts down one falls over oneself" (87). All this slapstick makes it very hard to take anything—particularly one's own busywork—very seriously; do we necessarily shudder with horror at the very idea of clumsy girls in china shops who "incessantly hurl themselves downstairs with mountains of crockery" (87)? I'm not saying that Kafka didn't have his share of headaches, but he must have had his share of laughs as well. After all, is it not so that he was witness to the potential for subversive laughter on an everyday basis? Brod's appeals are to a very comic perspective on everyday life, a perspective that I suggest readers of Kafka should acknowledge. Let's keep Kafka in the funhouse for a moment, because the "Worker's Accident Insurance Institute" created the perfect conditions for the comic. Bergson reminds us that the key element in the comic is mechanical inelasticity (surely the bread and butter of any insurance company). "Take the case of a person who attends to the petty occupations of his everyday life with mathematical precision," says Bergson. "[W]hen he fancies he is sitting down on a solid chair he finds himself sprawling on the floor, in a word his actions are all topsy-turvy or mere beating the air" (67). Anyone who could work in a place like the Worker's Accident Insurance Institute and maintain a high degree of seriousness and sobriety was, quite simply, a boob. No doubt Kafka knew such persons—he was perhaps, from time to time, a boob himself. At any rate, he was certainly incapable of avoiding the comic or letting it undermine his duties. Brod describes Kafka's once having lost it in front of a supervisor:

> One day [Kafka] came to me in the greatest excitement. He told me he had just done the silliest thing—which might have cost him the wonderful job he managed to ferret out with so much trouble—and valued for his parents' sake. What had happened was he had been appointed drafting clerk. A high personage on the Board of the institute had summoned the new drafting clerks to his presence and given them a talk which was so solemn, and so full of fatherly sanctimoniousness, that he (Franz) had suddenly burst out laughing and couldn't stop. (87)

No doubt, Kafka had in mind the pratfalls of only a few hours before—the Laurel and Hardy spills and banana-peel flops. There is also no doubt that Kafka feared losing his job (to be perfectly fair, he did his best to repair—in the most diplomatic terms possible—whatever damage his uncontrollable laughter had caused) but surely this only added to the hilarity of situation. The needy needs of the parents, the all-essential, life-supporting job, the gratuitously grave lectures from his supervisors—these things only make the machine all the more inflexible and the laughter all the more loud.

What can such anecdotes tell us about the comic form in Kafka's writings? After all, one cannot without a certain amount of unease claim that Kafka's stories are comic because he himself had a marvelous sense of humor and expect the matter to be solved. Anecdotes from Kafka's personal life offer very little in the way of compelling evidence, despite the fact that critics often rely heavily on Kafka's diaries, letters, and biographies in order to promote a host of different interpretations. Susanne Langer says Kafka has evoked a flood of discussion that often neglects literary form. So much so that "one hardly hears a word about [his] literary powers but only about [his] alleged personal feelings and moral attitudes, [his] hopes and fears for the actual world, [his] criticism of life" (288). There are, after all, countless examples of Kafka's despair to be found, and one of the most telling comes from Kafka's early encounters with Isak Löwy, a member of a local Yiddish acting troupe. As we know, Kafka was fascinated by Yiddish theatre and, when he found that he thought almost incessantly of Löwy after each night's performance, began entertaining the idea of becoming a benefactor. As a gesture indicating his genuine interest in the career of the young actor, Kafka took Löwy to the National Theatre of Prague to see a Czech play. The evening, however, went very poorly and Kafka wrote in his diary that night: "I again demonstrated the misfortune that follows every undertaking that I begin myself" (in Mailloux, 183–184). Such are the fruits of the paranoid model: the satisfaction of being able to say, "I should have *known*" and the guarantee of knowing better in the future.

There is, however, a reparative reading of this scenario just begging to be told. Kafka had, in fact, no way of telling what would become of his relationship with Löwy; no way of telling that his benefactions would produce rewards for both Löwy and himself; no way of telling that, within months, he would deliver, despite initial and overwhelming stage fright, a "lovely and charming" introductory speech for a benefit performance for the impoverished Löwy—an event Kafka had orchestrated himself almost single-handedly. I do not mean to suggest here that Kafka would have been more *accurate* to forestall all paranoid critique of himself since everything *did* turn out all right in the end. For one thing, each of Kafka's efforts to help Löwy were marked by a host of triumphs *and* failures, both personal and professional (for instance, the benefit for Löwy did not make much money—a circumstance that, Mailloux points out, only worked to strain the relationship between the two gentlemen). Secondly, and perhaps as a consequence of the first, the reparative reading is simply one kind among many. "[F]or someone to have an mystified view of systematic oppressions," Sedgwick reminds us, "does not *intrinsically* or *necessarily* enjoin on that person any specific train of epistemological or narrative consequences" (7). Or the fact that Kafka was humiliated by his initial failure should not compel us to find only humiliation in each successive attempt. And yet we do; and I think this may be one reason why biographical criticism of Kafka is rich and profuse. A paranoid reading, claims Sedgwick, "takes its shape from a generational narrative characterized by a distinctly Oedipal regularity and repetitiveness" (25–26). Many of Kafka's diary entries are characterized by a "dogged, defensive narrative stiffness of a paranoid temporality," a condition that Sedgwick attributes to the hermeneutics of suspicion (25). Take, for example, the following entry from Sunday, July 19, 1910: "slept, awoke, slept, awoke, miserable life" (*Diaries: 1910-1913,* 14). Such entries make it difficult not to judge Kafka. Nevertheless, what biographical criticism contributes to our understanding of Kafka's aesthetic innovations remains entirely unclear. Milan Kundera and Stanley Corngold strongly argue that it contributes nothing. The works of these authors, "In Saint Garta's Shadow: Rescuing Kafka from the Kafkaologists" and *Kafka: The Necessity of Form,* respectively, are formidable efforts to restore the primacy of form over content—no matter how provocatively or vividly the latter draws from the author's social identity.

One must ask what happens to, say, feminist criticism in light of such a claim. Elizabeth Boa has asked as much in her book *Kafka: Gender, Class, and Race in the Letters and Fictions.* What good is any piece of feminist criticism that is forbidden to draw on extra-textual contexts? More importantly, however, Boa wonders if the hostility to interpretation can sustain anything more than just another *type* of extra-textual knowledge. She turns to Kundera's description of the character of Brunelda in *Amerika* as "the shadow of real experience" and asks if:

> to appreciate the strange beauty of the shadow...we must retain some sense of the familiar that has been transformed. Such recognition of the familiar heightens, yet may also provoke resistance to, aesthetic pleasure in Kafka's shadows by inducing the characteristic squinting vision of the feminist critic, who may well question why fat ladies are deemed funny or why a bachelor's body should be emblematic of art only when it has become thin, questions which immediately lead beyond the text to its contexts. (24)

One squints in order to aim one's vision toward that which is reduced, obscured, or blurry—in this case, toward the "ideological common currency" with which metaphors are traded (21). One also squints, however, in order to diminish the scope of one's vision. For instance, squinting may blind one's self to the vivid specificity of signs and meanings. Reading is, after all, a process of both exposing and obscuring meaning. The "characteristic squinting of the feminist critic," at its most paranoid, obscures one type of knowledge just as it exposes another. "The monopolistic program of paranoid knowing," argues Sedgwick, "systematically disallows any explicit recourse to reparative motives, no sooner to be articulated than subject to methodical uprooting" (22). What Sedgwick suggests is not that paranoid reading practices are seriously bent on punishing merely reformist, merely ameliorative readings, it's just that they are nonetheless structured as if they were. Does one really need to squint in order to see the ways in which a text does an enormous injustice to difference?[12] What is being risked by structuring a response to formalism with squinting vision? The reparative reader has her eyes wide open—even at the risk of having them unexpectedly poked.

The wide-eyed reader is the reader who, as Jonathan Culler aptly puts it, "tells a story of reading" (35). And if the reader of Kafka is subject to what David Foster Wallace calls "the exformative associations" that "are not intertextual or even historical," this is not necessarily a handicap (23). Wallace assumes that without extra-textual reference points, readers are unlikely to find anything comic in Kafka's stories. A reader who is interested in simply telling a story of her reading, however, may find the absence of associations quite liberating. Perhaps only a reader interested in producing the "true meaning" of a text will miss them. On the other hand, *all* readers find a way of fulfilling themselves. Some readers will find it extremely suggestive that Kafka would burst into laughter while reading *The Trial* to his friends. Others will not. Some readers will find it extremely suggestive that Kafka's diaries are full of suicide fantasies. Others will not. But the point of this chapter would be lost if I didn't claim that readers who insist that Kafka is a "poet of despair" will likely ignore his laughter, whereas reparative readers who insist Kafka is modernity's great comic spirit will likely accept his suffering—embrace it even—in spite of Wolfgang Kayser's warning that the grotesque is "not properly understood" when read this way (181), that the comic only renders the grotesque "innocuous" (118). But even John Ruskin is more than willing to allow the comic and the grotesque to freely conspire in sportive and playful forms. He knew better than anyone else that the grotesque excludes nothing.

Conclusion

At a 1998 symposium sponsored by the PEN American Center in New York City celebrating the publication of the new translation of *The Castle*, David Foster Wallace delivered a speech that captured a frustration shared by professors who teach Kafka: "it is next to impossible to get [students] to see that Kafka is funny" (23). This frustration is doubled by the unyielding belief that any attempt to explain *why* Kafka is funny can only make matters worse. As Wallace puts it, "We all know there is no quicker way to empty a joke of its peculiar magic than to try to explain it" (23). Such a notion suggests a hands-off approach to teaching Kafka: read him, don't explicate him. Wallace thinks himself into quite a snare; his only way out is to throw up his hands and lament that Kafka's "grotesque and gorgeous and thoroughly modern complexity" is a little beyond our students' capabilities as thinkers (26). It's not their fault, admits Wallace, the problem is that students have difficulty understanding anything that does not use "the particular forms and codes of contemporary U.S. amusement" (26).

After giving it some thought, however, one would have to submit that our current forms and codes of amusement are too numerous and diverse to exclude something even as strange as Kafka. Furthermore, if the question of Kafka's funniness urges itself with special force when posed as a question of pedagogy, one need not immediately assume that the problem lies entirely with the students. For instance, it appears as if Wallace would insist one first become acquainted with the predominant themes of modernity and the social context of Eastern Europe at the turn of the century before attempting a successful engagement with Kafka, since these themes offer valuable explanations of Kafka's work. They even offer, as Peter Heller has put it, "explanations of explanations":

> reasons why isolation should have been raised to the nth power for this outsider-artist and socially uprooted intellectual who is an alienated part of an alienated minority, a Czech German Jew, estranged from the Czech and German communities of Prague and almost equally from assimilated Jewry who are themselves alienated from their Jewish tradition—a man alienated from his daily work, his responsible and conscientiously performed job at the Worker's Insurance Company of the Kingdom of Bohemia, and consequently, perhaps, all the more eligible to experience and express the pervasive alienation of the individual in the declining phases of Capitalism, or in modern bureaucratic mass societies generally. There are philosophic explanations in terms of this poet's visceral and imaginative awareness of existential alienation and isolation in the confrontation with *nothingness* (for God is presumed to be dead). And these extend, in turn, to theological explanations in terms of the essential alienation and isolation due to a lack of any religious faith which could provide the basis for a lasting human communion. (25)

And so on and so on. No explanation is sufficient and no interpretation is entirely satisfactory. But not explaining Kafka is, for Heller, "*the* or at least *a* major point of reading Kafka. He is drawn into, and draws the reader into, the dramatization of the—guilty—failure to arrive, to communicate, to understand" (32). And Heller is more than willing to share this guilt, to "stay with the negative" (33). Perhaps Wallace's students aren't willing. Margit M. Sinka's students certainly aren't. In her essay, "Kafka's *The Metamorphosis* and the Search for Meaning in Twentieth-Century German Literature," she tells us that "[t]hough deeply affected by Kafka, most students envision a far more satisfactory life for themselves and continue to formulate specific goals related to future professions and to happiness with people" (112–113).[13] Is it perhaps in fear of readings such as this that Kafka insisted, finally, that Max Brod should burn all of his writings?

Notes

1. James R. Kincaid knows Mr. Daniel Quilp as well as anyone, and it his informed opinion (informed, to a large degree, by Gabriel Pearson) that this sinister fellow is a force, "mostly isolated...toward energy, violence, surprise, rebellion, and motion" (*Dickens and the Rhetoric of Laughter*, 81). He is a powerful force indeed. Yet the force of Quilp exaggerates the "primary relation between human beings," rather than the relation between human beings and some alien power beyond our control (96). Quilp, the "elemental naughty boy" whose evil "is often merely mischievousness," does everything in his power to remind the other characters in the novel of the centrality of human relations (96). As powerful as Quilp may seem, he is only as powerful as he wants to be. Such a statement appears confusing to someone who assumes (as Quilp himself does) that power is something natural, that is granted to us from above:

    > Quilp supposes, as we suppose, that power is not a metaphor. We both think that power is in the world independent of our finding or putting it there. We think power is not a creation of discourse; we think discourse is a creation of power. Paradoxically, Quilp is so deeply entrapped by the metaphor of power that he is powerful; that is, he sees nothing but power and therefore is not bamboozled as are others by explanations which do not proceed from power, which mix in inauthentic doses of morality or sentiment, for instance, as Quilp would never do. (*Annoying the Victorians*, 42)

    As powerful as Quilp may be, he is necessarily vulnerable. In other words, Quilp is ultimately defenseless against the fear and folly produced by human relations no matter how strongly he feels he is control.

2. I'm thinking, here, of Baudelaire who conjures the phrase "the wise man laughs only with fear and trembling." In his essay, "Of the Essence of Laughter," Baudelaire argues that this maxim, whose origins are unknown to him, is an expression of the "primeval law" of laughter. Laughter is always the expression of one's superiority over one's fellow human being, and is therefore the expression of the satanic. Baudelaire draws from Charles Robert Maturin's "Melmoth" to illustrate this point:

What could be greater, what more powerful, in relation to poor humanity than this pale, bored Melmoth? And yet he has a weak, an abject, anti-divine and anti-luminous side to him. And so, how he laughs and laughs as he constantly compares himself with human caterpillars, he so strong and intelligent, he for whom a certain number of the physical and intellectual laws that condition humanity no longer exist! And this laughter is the perpetual explosion of his wrath and his suffering. It is, be sure and understand me, the necessary product of his dual and contradictory nature, which is infinitely great in relation to man, infinitely vile and base in relation to absolute truth and righteousness. Melmoth is a living contradiction. He has left behind the fundamental conditions of life; his bodily organs can no longer support his thought. That is why this laughter of his freezes and wrings the guts. It is a laughter that never sleeps, like a disease for ever on its stealthy way, in executions of a providential command. And so, Melmoth's laughter, which is the highest expression of pride, is always fulfilling its function, as it tears and scorches the lips of the laughter beyond hope of pardon. (147)

A wiser Melmoth would not laugh without trembling before the absolute knowledge of his own dual and contradictory nature. Baudelaire extends this idea of duality to the grotesque, which he refers to as "the absolute comic"; whereas the ordinary comic's laughter is the expression of the idea of superiority over other human beings, the absolute comic's laughter is the expression of the idea of superiority over nature. If one were to read "Of the Essence of Laughter" and "The Painter of Modern Life" together, one would note that both essays are working toward the same end: a formulation of modernity and the artist's relation to it. The last lines of "Of the Essence of Laughter" anticipates "The Painter of Modern Life," written four years later: "Artists create the comic; having studied and brought together the elements of the comic, they know that such and such a creature is comic, and that he is comic only on condition that he is unaware of his own nature; just as, by inverse law, the artist is an artist only on condition that he is dual and that he is ignorant of none of the phenomena of his dual nature" (161). It is because of this emphasis on the dual nature of the artist that many critics refer to Baudelaire as one of the key figures in the history of modernity. "If we go back to Baudelaire's formulation," writes David Harvey in *The Condition of Postmodernity* (Cambridge, MA: Blackwell, 1990), "we find him defining the artist as someone who can concentrate his or her vision on ordinary subjects of city life, understand their fleeting qualities, and yet extract from the passing moment all the suggestions of eternity it contains. The successful modern artist was one who could find the universal and the eternal, 'distil the bitter or heady flavour of the wine of life' from 'the ephemeral, the fleeting forms of beauty in our day'" (20). David Harvey's Baudelaire formulates not simply the essential character of modernity, but the relative perversity of post-modernity as well.

3.   "But who effects the estrangement of the world, who announces his presence in this overwhelming ominousness? Only now do we plumb the final depth of the horror that is inspired by the transformed world. These questions remain unanswered. Apocalyptic beasts emerge from the abyss; demons intrude upon us. If we were able to name these powers and relate them to the cosmic order, the grotesque would lose its essential quality. We have discussed such instances in connection with Bosche and E.T.A. Hoffmann. What intrudes remains incomprehensible, inexplicable, and impersonal. One could use another descriptive phrase and characterize the grotesque as the objectivation of the 'It,' the ghostly 'It' —in contrast to the

psychological 'It' (*es freut mich*: it pleases me = I am glad) and the cosmic 'It' (*es regnet*: it rains)—the 'It' which Ammann defined as the third meaning of the impersonal pronoun" (*The Grotesque in Art and Literature*, 185). In a note, Kayser refers also to K. Ph. Mortiz who, in his *Magazin zur Erfahrungsseelenkunde*, says "that by means of the impersonal 'it' we seek to express that which exceeds the sphere of our concepts and which language cannot name" (in *The Grotesque in Art and Literature*, 209).

4.   See, for instance, Ruth V. Gross's "The Paranoid Reader and His Neighbor: Subversion in the Text of Kafka" in *Kafka and the Contemporary Critical Performance: Centenary Readings*. Ed. Alan Udoff. (Bloomington: Indiana University Press, 1987), 150–157.

5.   In *Kafka: Toward A Minor Literature*, Deleuze and Guattari refer to negative theology/theology of absence, the transcendence of the law, and the *a prioriness* of guilt as the most dominant themes in Kafka interpretation (43).

6.   In "Tragic Thoughts at the End of Philosophy: Martha Nussbaum's Ethics of Particularity," Gerald Bruns claims that "[t]he comic's relation to the world is a relationship of thinking, thinking as reception, or in other words not of knowledge but acknowledgment, where the world is not just made of sensible objects or situations calling for perception but it is rather made up of other people" (122). This, as I argued earlier, is the position occupied by Daniel Quilp.

7.   Here I'm thinking, in particular, of *The Metamorphosis*, "The Village Schoolmaster," and *The Trial*—but there are certainly others. The first begins with this line: "As Gregor Samsa awoke one morning from uneasy dreams he found himself transformed in his bed into a giant insect" (89). The second begins like this: "Those, and I am one of them, who find even a small ordinary-sized mole disgusting, would probably have died of disgust if they had seen the giant mole that a few years back was observed in the neighborhood of one of our villages" (168). And the last begins: "Someone must have slandered Joseph K., for one morning, without having done anything truly wrong, he was arrested" (3).

8.   In an essay entitled "Kafka's Humor," Jean Collignon says "there remains in the mind of the Kafkan hero at least a doubt to his innocence, and he himself is aware that to have not done anything does not necessarily entitle a man to an honorable discharge. Of course the hero does not know why he is found guilty or of what. And the readers are not told why Joseph K. is arrested, why K. is never officially admitted into the castle, why the employers, relatives, and friends of Karl Rossmann keep suspecting him, or why Gregor Samsa is transformed one morning into an enormous cockroach. But we would not maintain to the bitter end that they are all the victims of unprecedented injustices. Strangely enough, however, the heroes preserve their sense of humor and we are expected to smile with them" [*Yale French Studies* 16 (1955), 54]. Collignon's essay is one of earliest attempts to explore the theme of humor in the work of Kafka, and it has greatly influenced my scholarship here.

9.   Elizabeth Boa indicates how difficult it is to interpret the ape Rotpeter's deferential tone. Although for some "[h]is mimicry of the academic manner turns the humor against the academicians," and thus functions as potent satire, for others such mockery does little to deflect the essential offensive image of the ape as a representative of the Western Jew. "But in my view," says Boa, "it is finally undecideable how far these stylistic features are signs of a naive autodiadact who has inadequately internalized his oppressors' values or how far they are sly mockery which deflects the barb from the mimicker to turn it against the mimicked: the ape plays a part of an ape in accord with the expectations of the academicians that an

ape aping men will be ridiculous; just so does the Irish peasant masquerade as a stupid Paddy in subterranean mockery of the English gentleman" (*Kafka: Gender, Class, and Race in the Letters and Fictions*. [New York: Oxford University Press, 1996], 162). Boa brilliantly turns to Bakhtin on this matter: "As Bakhtin puts it, 'Stupidity (incomprehension) in the novel is always polemical; it interacts dialogically with an intelligence (a lofty pseudo intelligence) with which it polemicizes and whose mask it tears away'" (162).

10.   James Kincaid referred me to this film and pointed out the way this particular scene transgresses the physical boundary that separates classroom from playground. What Kincaid suggests (personal comments) is that the kissing scene perfectly embodies the carnival spirit. When asked if the classroom isn't really, finally, after all, still a classroom in spite of the dancing and prancing of the children, Kincaid replied (with typical coyness) "only from a certain perspective." Like Collignon, Kincaid's work has influenced my scholarship here, as well as elsewhere throughout this project.

11.   "[T]heory not in the primary theoretical texts, but in the routinized critical projects of 'applied theory'; theory as a broad project that now spans the humanities and extends into history and anthropology; theory after Foucault and Greenblatt, after Freud and Lacan, after Levi-Strauss, after Derrida, after feminism" (1).

12.   I think Boa would agree with me on this point. Although she invokes the especially paranoid metaphor of "squinting" as knowledge in the form of exposure, she herself is not interested in characterizing Kafka's portrayals of gender and sexuality as visible only as hidden traces. After all, her argument is that these portrayals are already hyper-visible.

13.   Sinka, Margit M. "Kafka's *The Metamorphosis* and the Search for Meaning in the Twentieth Century." *Approaches to Teaching Kafka's Short Fiction*. Approaches to Teaching World Lit. 51. Ed. Richard T. Gray. (New York: MLA, 1995), 105–113.

Epilogue: Last Words

The rhetorician's art in its glory and power has silently faded away before the stern tendencies of the age; and, if, by any peculiarity of taste or strong determination of the intellect, a rhetorician en grande costume were again to appear amongst us, it is certain that he would have no better welcome than a stare of surprise as a posture-maker or balancer, not more elevated in the general estimate, but far less amusing, than the acrobat, or funambulist, or equestrian gymnast. No; the age of Rhetoric, like that of Chivalry, has passed among forgotten things.
—*Thomas De Quincey, "Rhetoric"*

Rhetoric and comedy are alike in ways that we haven't really begun to recognize. De Quincey touched on the problem so many years ago; like Bozo the Clown at a debutante's ball, the rhetorician's appearance before us is curious at best, annoyingly irrelevant at worst. Presented this way, De Quincey's argument creates a mood not unlike the one created by Charles Lamb in the Elia essay on artificial comedy, and very much like the one created by Bakhtin in his writings about carnival: those were the days. Nevertheless, it should be stressed that the likening of the age of rhetoric to the age of chivalry isn't terribly apt—and not simply because the rhetorician *en grande costume* will always look a bit like Don Quixote and not at all like Lancelot or Percival. De Quincey may have had the age of chivalry in mind when he glorified the art of rhetoric, but comedy is what he had on hand. Consider that De Quincey's description of Roman rhetoric comes very close to a description of comic thinking: "To hang upon one's own thoughts as an object of conscious interest, to play with them, to watch and pursue them through a maze of inversions, evolutions, and harlequin changes, implies a society...at leisure from the agitations of eternal change" (97). And when he anticipates the public reaction to rhetoric "on a formal scale," he invokes Shakespeare's clowns: "Falstaff on the field of battle presenting his bottle of sack for a pistol, or Polonius with his quiblles, could not appear a more unreasonable *plaisanteur* than a rhetorician alighting from the clouds upon a public assembly in Great Britain met for despatch of business" (98). Consider that comedy, like rhetoric, has been defeated by the stern tendencies of the age—that is, by philosophy, science, and "the necessities of everyday business" (97). Both rhetoric and comedy seek to restore all that the stern tendencies of the age seek to banish: leniency, indulgence, mercy, and so on.

The ease with which comic terms and imagery can emerge in a treatise on rhetoric may suggest that one cannot be rhetorical without also being comic, or vice versa. De Quincey's rhetorician *en grande constume* appears as if from another age, but it may be more realistic to suggest that he is from another world. After all, rhetoric is (like comedy) a way of viewing the world, a way of living in it—a way that is so very different than the stern tendencies of philosophers, lawyers, politicians, and scholars that it might appear to be other-worldly. That rhetoric can be understood as more than just the art of persuasive talk (and comedy as more than just the art of frivolity) need not be an unusual stretch. Shelley, taking a familiar "poet as priest" line of thinking to magnificent extremes, could argue that poetry is much more than the production of meter in language, that it "acts in another and diviner manner" when it "awakens and enlarges the mind itself by rendering it the receptacle of a thousand unapprehended combinations of thought" (796). Were we to accept Shelley's terms, we, too, would see poetry as everything and everything else as nothing without it.

But Shelley was legislating from the bench, as it were. And that, we are told, is a no-no. As our own Justice Antonin Scalia has forcefully put it in his book *A Matter of Interpretation: Federal Courts and the Law*, interpretation should follow this basic rule: "Words do have a limited range of meaning, and no interpretation that goes beyond that range is permissible" (24). Discovering what a text "really means," then, is not a choice between what the text says and what the author intended, but a matter of considering "what a wise and intelligent person *should* have meant." Comedy, on the other hand, should follow *this* basic rule: find the loophole.

I invoke Justice Scalia here not simply because his thoughts about meaning and truth are so uncomic (in the sense I'm invoking here) and, therefore, may demonstrate to us the need for reading comically, but also because I'd like to give the last word to someone who really *believes* in last words. Consider Scalia's example of bad interpretation. In the case of *Church of the Holy Trinity v. United States*, a New York City church appealed a district court's ruling that it pay a fine for violating a federal statute that forbids a person to encourage the importation or migration of any alien to perform labor or service of any kind in the United States. The church had contracted an Englishman to be its rector and pastor and had, therefore, been in violation of the statute. The Supreme Court, however, reversed the district court's decision, stating that: "we cannot think Congress intended to denounce with penalties a transaction like that in the present case. It is a familiar rule, that a thing may be within the letter of the statute and yet not within the statute, because not within its spirit, nor within the intention of its makers" (in Scalia, 19). In other words, Congress had no intention of forbidding a church from importing pastors from abroad. That's not the "spirit" in which the law was written.

Scalia wastes no time giving us his opinion of this ruling: "Well of course I think the act [of contracting the Englishman] was within the letter of the statute, and was therefore within the statue: end of case" (20)—or, as Begbie says in *Trainspotting*, "End ay fuckin story." Scalia sticks to his guns on this one, despite the fact that he also concedes that the law itself is just plain foolish. He reminds us that "Congress can enact foolish statutes and wise ones, and it is not for the courts to decide which is which and rewrite the former" (20). To acquiesce to the logic of the Supreme Court's ruling—that is, to look for "life-giving legislative intent" rather than the "deadening text of the statute"—is, quite simply, "an invitation to judicial lawmaking" (21). For Scalia, the text (what *he* takes to be the text—and he knows!) *is* the law. To paraphrase Justice Jackson, whom Scalia approvingly quotes, "who cares what the legislators meant? We care what the statute means." This, Justice Scalia reminds us, is a philosophy of interpretation widely known as textualism. And any good textualist will tell you that "[a] text should not be construed strictly, and it should not be construed leniently; it should be construed reasonably, to contain all that it fairly means" (23). In defense of this dictum, Scalia refers us to a case decided in his own court back in 1993. A defendant was subject to an increased jail term because he used a firearm while committing a drug-trafficking crime. But the defendant did not "use" the firearm the way one "normally" does in a drug-trafficking crime. "The defendant in this case had sought to purchase a quantity of cocaine; and what he had offered to give in exchange for the cocaine was an unloaded firearm, which he showed to the drug-seller" (24). The text of the law states that "use of a firearm" is reason for increased jail sentence. But rather than close the case on *this* one, Scalia instead cast a dissenting vote, pointing out to his colleagues that "when you ask someone, 'Do you use a cane?' you are not inquiring whether he has hung his grandfather's antique cane as a decoration in the hallway" (24). The difference between Scalia's ruling here and the ruling in the case of the Holy Trinity Church is that, in the former, what is a matter of interpretation is the text of the law.

The defendant didn't "use" the gun the way we believe the word "use" is meant to be taken here. In the latter case, what is a matter of interpretation is the intent of the lawmakers. Congress didn't *mean* for the courts to deny the church the ability to contract an alien to perform religious services. The two rulings, we are told, are not at all similar—despite the fact that both produced the same "desirable result" (22).

The textualist approach, which assumes that what matters most is the "text" of the law, represents what many critics argue is a very dangerous (though very old and powerful) approach to modern legal doctrine. Scalia's philosophy of textualism is really nothing more than a kind of formalism, perhaps the worst sort in that it assumes not only that the law is "fixed," but that the law "fixes" us (repairs and adjusts our judicial enterprise; compels us, by way of its insistence that it can mean only one thing, to interpret "correctly" and rule impartially). Advocates of the Critical Legal Studies movement will quickly tell us, as Peter Goodrich does, that it's high time we exposed this assumption and make the legal doctrinal community "explicitly accountable for the political choices underlying the development of the law" (219). Scalia will have none of it: "Long live formalism. It is what makes a government a government of laws and not of men" (25). One could assume that this is a good thing, were we a government of wise laws. But we are also, as Scalia admits, a government of foolish laws. Or more precisely, we are a government of laws that appear foolish in one situation and wise in the next. Or, more honestly, we are not a government of laws at all, nor are we a government of men (thank heavens). The distinction between "law" and "men" is just high-sounding bullying. We are a government of rhetoricians—which is to say we are a government of people behaving as best we can, as openly as we can, and as self-consciously as we can *as if* we were a government of laws.

As you may have already guessed, I was being disingenuous when I said that I would give Scalia the last word. I'd give the last word to myself if I thought it existed. But I don't, so I'll just give myself the *next* word, which isn't really mine at all but Don McCloskey's, and Don Mc-Closkey isn't Don McCloskey, she is Deirdre McCloskey. And Deirdre McCloskey isn't a judge, she's a professor of Economics. In her book, *The Rhetoric of Economics*, Deirdre McCloskey raises up the possibility of understanding not just economics, but also science and the law as founded not on evidence but on *enthymemes*—the Aristotelian notion of incomplete syllogism (93). In this modern age, we like to think that our methodologies (whether economic or other) can produce "knowledge free from doubt, free from metaphysics, morals and personal conviction" when really, no such knowledge can ever be delivered (152). Or, as Hans Blumenberg puts it, because we can seldom afford to wait for the seemingly endless processes of scientific method and rationality to play themselves out, instead, by way of discussion, we produce something that stands in for evidence. Something that allows us to act and act soon. Something more like consensus or "provisional truth." Using Blumenberg's anthropological approach (and this comes from his magnificent essay "An Anthropological Approach to Rhetoric"), we say that we are poor creatures, or creatures of deficiency who, despite our lack of self-evident truths, are nevertheless compelled to act in the world. And to make up for this lack, we turn to rhetoric because rhetoric doesn't hesitate to acknowledge that we live in a world of doubt, metaphysics, morals, and personal conviction—and of nothing else. Rhetoric gives us an emergency solution to the problem at hand. That this should be the state of things not just in everyday matters of importance, but in such truth-governed institutions as science, the law, the liberal arts college is a possibility awkwardly embraced (for some). That it should be the state of things in literary studies is a possibility easily embraced (for most). As Gerald Bruns puts it, most literary criticism is rhetorical by nature. Nevertheless, perhaps due to its deep philosophical desires, literary criticism often proceeds scientifically and methodically (*Inventions*, 1). As comfortable with the contingency of meaning as a literary critic may be, he or she will likely pay homage to textual evidence at some point. That is, when pushed hard enough.

But our hearts tell us something else: there may be no getting around the fact that, due to the insufficiency of textual evidence, we are poor creatures indeed. And the rational way of coming to terms with the condition of our deficiency is to ignore it altogether. *Or to see it as a positive boon.* Noting a parallel condition in the world of economics, McCloskey cheerfully declares, "Truth is a fifth wheel" anyway (181). We're much better off with earnest and intelligent conversation and our workaday utilitarian practices (what McCloskey calls "plain method"—lower-case "m") than with our truth-seeking Methodology (capital "M"). Leave the latter to middle management, where green-suited boobs "share the strange Cartesian notion that practice according to the whatever-it-is below conversation and above plain method is possible, and will yield a harvest of truth" (161). The emphasis here on everything but the center—the learned talk from upstairs, the useful tools stored below—shows that McCloskey is a good rhetorician. And there are, claims McCloskey, various reasons for a rhetorical approach to a text:

to understand it, to admire it, to debunk it, to set it beside other works of persuasion in science, to see that science is not a new dogma but is thoroughly and respectably part of the old culture. Rhetorical sophistication is an alternative to reading scientific texts the way the implied reader does, a reader who believes for example in talking bears. If we are to get beyond nursery school as scientific readers we need such a rhetoric applied to economic science. (19)

And McCloskey's idea of the proper way to get things done in economic science begins with the rhetorician's premise that "there are," again in Blumenberg's words, "rational decision rules that do not resemble science in their form" (449). These decision rules instead resemble something more like what necessarily arises from dialogue. Not just any kind of dialogue, but a Bakhtinian dialogue—one that is open-ended, is irreducible to a single voice, and proceeds from the very unscientific idea that "no word relates to its object in a *singular* way" (Bakhtin, *The Dialogic Imagination*, 276). Justice Scalia's idea of interpretation differs in that he regards a word as fixed and motionless. As you approach it, you get warm. As you drift too far from it, you get cold. The colder you get, the less rational your decision rules will appear. Bakhtin, however, sees the word not as fixed, but as "overlain with qualifications, open to dispute, charged with value, already enveloped in an obscuring mist—or, on the contrary, by the 'light' of alien words that have already been spoken about it. It is entangled, shot through with shared thoughts, points of view, alien judgments and accents" (276). Bakhtin's notion of meaning is gamelike. As in a festive round of Blind Man's Bluff, what is warm quickly becomes cold, and then warm again, and then cold once more, then colder still, and so on. This is not to say that it is impossible, in such a tension-filled environment, to make the proposition that a word *does* relate to its object in a singular way. "But," Morson and Emerson argue, "once this enunciation takes place, the truthfulness of the thought is entirely separable from the person who utters it. The proposition is 'repeatable,' as a scientific experiment is repeatable, by others" (235). Or, as Bakhtin himself puts it, "[t]rue judgments are not attached to a personality, but correspond to some unified, systematically monologic context" (*Problems of Dostoevsky's Poetics,* 81). Only error is individualized. We become, in Justice Scalia's words, a government of laws and not of men.

Another model—the one with which we have been concerned throughout this book, that the world is open to dispute rather than subject to laws—is not a strictly Bakhtinian idea, nor is it strictly the axiom of rhetoric. It is also a main feature of the comic attitude. One might even say that rather than resembling each other, rhetoric and comedy are one in the same (at any rate, rhetoric is more sensitive to comedy than philosophy or science). At the center of the comic world one finds only people—not systems, laws, metaphysics, God, power, etc. And people are inherently poor creatures: wanting of self-evident truths, we turn to our own talk in order to live and act in the world. This fundamental lack is a boon, not a curse. Comedy is always about talk, and lots of it, because comedy believes that, in the end, talk is all we really have. We do not possess anything like, say, "honor." And it's a good thing too, since the man who possesses honor is the dummy who got himself killed last Wednesday. Honor, Falstaff tells us, is just a word. It is "a mere scutcheon"—which may not mean that heroes are all talk (for such an attitude would suggest something like contempt for rhetoric), but may mean instead that heroes think they are doing something more than just talk, but aren't. From this point of view, Falstaff knows that all we have are words filled with air. Falstaff knows we are poor creatures.

No doubt, there exist people who believe we are not. They're the ones who wage war and believe in parking enforcement. They invoke their own personal convictions by renaming them as morality, ethics, science, or truth. They are often heard saying, "But I have the facts to prove it!" When bad things happen to them, they behave as if some greater Being, who for some reason tends to look unfavorably upon us, had a hand in things. They think nothing is outside the reach of power. They believe in heroism, not luck. They speak only with straightforward words. They're school principals, middle managers, deans, and legal clerks. They take everything seriously and tell us it's not fair to cheat. They tell us that we shouldn't laugh at other people's misfortunes. They insist on dividing the tab evenly, even though you ordered only the salad. They think we're a government of laws and not men. They think a story with no end is meaningless. They believe in family values. They're us, most of the time.

And judging by the standards of most ancient rhetoricians we're total morons. In a collection of essays on the state and direction of advanced composition in the university, William Covino reminds us that rhetoric— at least from the classical perspective—assumes that only the dullest of minds prefer the quick understanding of known laws to the "meandering irresolution" of dialogue (64). The problem with most writing programs, according to Covino, is that they buy too cheaply into the prevailing idea that "the mastery of closure and conventions" is the only sign of advanced knowledge. But this idea is hardly exclusive to writing programs; one can find it in service, to greater and lesser extents, of most forms of academic scholarship. For instance, Roderick P. Hart and Joanne Gilbert are writing largely for the student of rhetoric but their brief analysis of the film *Thelma and Louise*, which appears in *Modern Rhetorical Criticism*, is well within the tradition of serious academic criticism. They sound less like Covino, who champions the playful refusal of endings, and much more like Antonin Scalia: "Thelma and Louise kill a potential rapist, lock a police officer in a car trunk, and finally hurl themselves into the Grand Canyon rather than face capture. While the film addresses some of the oppressions modern women endure, its final message has a familiar, binary flavor: oppression or death. This is hardly a feminist message" (299). Is this an example of advanced knowledge from the perspective of classical rhetoric? Or is this what Scalia would call a reasonable exercise of judicial power, a wise and intelligent interpretation of a text, a careful consideration not of the film's potential meanings but of what the film *ought* to mean?

The issue is this: Do we want to treat our objects of inquiry seriously or rhetorically? I borrow Richard Lanham's terms here—terms that Stanley Fish invokes in his book *Doing What Comes Naturally*—to define two very different worldviews, that of serious man and that of rhetorical man. The former:

> possesses a central self, an irreducible identity. These selves combine into a single, homogeneously real society which constitutes a referent reality for the men living in it. This referent society is in turn contained in a physical nature itself referential, standing "out there" independent of man. Man has invented language to communicate with his fellow man. He communicates facts and concepts about both nature and society…When he is communicating facts or concepts, success is measured by what we call clarity. (in Fish, 482)

The latter, on the other hand:

> is an actor; his reality public, dramatic. His sense of identity, depends on the reassurance of daily histrionic reenactment. He is thus centered in time and concrete local event. The lowest common denominator of his life is a social situation…He assumes a natural agility in changing orientations…From birth, almost, he has dwelt not in a single value-structure of the world; much rather, to prevailing in the game at hand…He accepts the present paradigm and explores its resources. Rhetorical man is trained not to discover reality but to manipulate it. Reality is what is accepted as reality, what is useful. (in Fish, 483)

And as Thomas De Quincey notes, we tend to regard the rhetorician *en grande costume* as more or less a clown (97). And nothing is more irritating—from serious man's perspective, that is, than a clown. This is precisely why we need to do more clowning. "What serious man fears—the invasion of the fortress of essence by the contingent, the protean, and the unpredictable—is what rhetorical man celebrates and incarnates...the 'improvising power of the rhetor' is at once all-creating and the guarantee of the impermanence of its creations" (Fish, 483). I would add that the improvising power of the rhetor is, by nature, comic. After all, one can't really be rhetorical without being, at the same time, comic. The words of the rhetorician are frivolous, meandering, laughing. They seek to keep the game going so as to prevent thought and language from ossifying.

Although the invocation of Greek sophistry is indeed an apt (if not a bit too standard) illustration of the art of game-making and meandering irresolution, I have in mind something (slightly) less ancient: the famous "Why a duck?" scene from The Marx Brothers film, *The Cocoanuts* (1929). Groucho is owner and manager of a Florida resort, the exotically named Hotel de Cocoanut. An auction is to be held on the grounds of the Cocoanut Manor, and Groucho hatches a scheme to dispose of all the lots on his property at inflated prices. He enlists the aid of the shifty Chico, who has come to Florida to make a few bucks in the big real estate boom. Groucho's plan is rationalized; it depends wholly upon organized spaces, detailed diagrams, calculations of mathematical formulas ("This is a map and diagram of the whole Cocoanut section. This whole area is within a radius of approximately 3/4 of a mile..."). His operation cannot proceed without the guarantee of utmost certainty such information provides ("No matter what you say, this is Cocoanut Manor..."). Groucho's plan, Michel de Certeau would say, is strategic: "It postulates a place that can be delimited as its own and serve as the base from which relations with an exteriority composed of targets or threats (customers or competitors, enemies, the country surrounding the city, objectives and objects of re-search, etc.) can be managed" (36). Groucho plays the military strategist, the scientist. Chico plays the opportunist, the trickster:

Groucho:	Now here is a little peninsula, and over here is a viaduct leading to the mainland
Chico:	Why a duck?
Groucho:	I'm all right, how are you? I say, here is a little peninsula and over here is a viaduct leading to the mainland.
Chico:	All right, why a duck?
Groucho:	Well I'm sorry the matter ever came up. All I know is that it's a viaduct.
Chico: why	Well look, all right, I-ya catch on why a horse, why a chicken, a this, why a that, I no catch on why a duck.
Groucho:	I was only fooling, I-I was only fooling. They're gonna build a tunnel there in the morning. Now is that clear to you?
Chico:	Everything but the why a duck.

The point of this pointless scene from *The Cocoanuts*, for our purposes anyway, is that "why a duck?" isn't simply the thing that eludes Chico, it is elusiveness itself. It is a way out of the straightforward word. Everything is clear, we are told, but the "why a duck?" which endures, always, as a loophole. It is, in the words of Bakhtin, "the retention for oneself of the possibility of altering the ultimate, final meaning of one's words" (*Problems of Dostoevsky's Poetics,* 233). Groucho wishes to give "viaduct" a precise meaning; or better, he wishes to attribute analytically its proper place within an ensemble of spatial elements. Better than the military strategist or the scientist, Groucho is playing the Supreme Court Justice. Better still, he is (when he spars with Chico, that is) playing the grammarian, the one who knows the rules and watches over the propriety of terms. (Groucho: "You do know what an auction is, don't you?"). Chico, as we all know, has little knowledge of—or no use for—grammar. ("I come from Italy on the Atlantic auction.") He communicates according to what de Certeau calls "rhetorical alterations"—metaphorical drifts, elliptical condensations, and metonymic miniaturizations. Chico doesn't want to know "Why a duck?" he simply wants to celebrate the right to ask "Why a duck?"—the need, even, for asking this question of ourselves, again and again, in the hopes of creating new ways out of the critical dead-ends we produce with our suspicion and sloth; the need for choosing correctly between "homo-serious" and "homo-rhetoricus."

But the choice for us isn't really between one or the other, between Groucho and Chico. As this scene neatly illustrates, the opposition of serious man and rhetorical man, between knowledge and endless inquiry, between truth and truth-effects, is a false one "because the rhetorical effect is not an alternative that one can choose instead of insight that one could also have, but an alternative to a definitive evidence that one cannot have, or cannot have yet, or at any rate cannot have here and now" (Blumenberg, 436). Philosophy opposes rhetoric, banishes it as mere costumery. Rhetoric, on the other hand, excludes nothing; it treats philosophy as simply another manner of speaking. We reintroduce the opposition every time we fail or choose not to see ourselves as already rhetorical. As McCloskey puts it, "Economists are scientists who don't even know that their science has become a boy's game in a sandbox" (xiv). One could also put it this way: Groucho and Chico are not oppositional forces but are part of the same game. The playful tetherball match between the serious and the frivolous is both comic and rhetorical—never concluding, stopping only because dinner is ready and it is time to go home. One would hope we would use rhetoric to slow down, as much and as best as possible, the processes by which we reach conclusions. In this way, comic readings may prove too useless to those of little patience. Bruno Latour, in his recent book *Reassembling the Social*, notes a similar impatience with Actor-Network-Theory, and his insistence on the "more costly and painful" approach is instructive:

> I want to break the habit of linking the notions of "society," "social factor," and "social explanation" with a sudden acceleration in the description. When sociologists of the social pronounce the words "society," "power," "structure," and "context," they often jump straight ahead to connect vast arrays of life and history, to mobilize gigantic forces, to detect dramatic patters emerging out of confusing interactions, to see everywhere in the cases at hand yet more examples of well-known types, to reveal behind the scenes some dark powers pulling the strings. (22)

Reassembling the social means resisting the temptation to discipline and categorize too hastily. One might say I have been proposing that we reassemble the comic with similar patience. To borrow from Latour, reassembling the comic means we will "travel somewhere else and with very different kinds of gear" (22). As we travel, we may begin to question (comically, lovingly) the value of conclusions and results, the value of knowing exactly what we are doing, where we are going, and why. Criticism rarely proceeds this way, though. We want conclusions and results, and to get them we must put unusual epistemological stress on matters at hand: "what is *really* going on here?" We seek out "underlying elements"; we "unveil truth" and "reveal (sub)texts." We speak from inside theoretical models so as to guarantee error-free thinking, to give the impression that what we are doing is not mere talk, and to keep us from wandering around aimlessly in the open or from discovering there's no ground beneath our feet.

I've already implied that reading seriously means investing too much in method, so much so that other possibilities are excluded. But reading comically should not be taken to mean the blatant disregard of method. As the preceding chapters have shown, I immerse myself in methodology as often as any other (and a lot more than some). Reading comically should instead be understood as a way of putting methods, and the readings they produce, into a critical dialogue with more frivolous, fruitless, and even implausible readings. The former come to us naturally—too naturally to my mind. The implausible readings sneak up on us whether we like it or not—like rascals who trail us from behind, never ambushing us. They have no other intention but to keep the game going, the way Chico's ridiculous question, "Why a duck?" keeps Groucho from closing the deal in the 1929 film *The Coconuts*. The point is not to take such a question seriously—comic readings aren't critical ends in themselves, but being attentive to them and allowing them to nudge us from our comfort zones into areas of surprise, uncertainty, indecisiveness, and irresolution is precisely what reading comically is all about.

To be clear, reading comically is not an anti-theoretical activity. Our theoretical proceedings are often comic, particularly when they are at their weakest. Consider Sedgwick's distinction between "weak" and "strong" theory. The latter, "because of its wide reach and rigorous exclusiveness" risks becoming tautological, "in that it can't help or can't stop or can't do anything that proving the very assumptions with which it began" and "may be experienced by the practitioner as a triumphant advance toward truth and vindication." The former, because its proceedings are occasional and situational, does not aspire to mastery and control. But "weak" theory is not without its pleasures. Sedgwick asks whether or not we would be surprised to hear that "the main argument, or 'strong theory' of D.A. Miller's *The Novel and the Police* is entirely circular: everything can be understood as an aspect of the carceral, therefore the carceral is everywhere." Miller's theoretical operation is "strong" precisely because of its wide generality. But, asks Sedgwick, "who reads The Novel and the Police to find out if its main argument is true?" Within the "breadth of reach" of Miller's strong theory, we can find space for his "tonal nuance, attitude, worldly observation, performative paradox" and so on (14).

Strong theories aren't tyrants. We allow them to govern because we mistakenly believe that we must always know exactly what we are doing, and where we are going—in spite of the nagging possibility that, as Hans Blumenberg puts it, "the circumstantiality that goes with the claim to know what one is doing is not in itself a guarantee of humane or moral insight" (446–447). Perhaps it is no guarantee because the better we get at knowing exactly what we are doing and why the less conscious we are. "Action shrinks to reaction the more direct is the path from theory to practice that is sought" (446). Eve Sedgwick and Adam Frank refer to this phenomenon when they speak of the automatic thinking routines of current theory and the resistance to other forms of thought.[1] Terry Eagleton would say that the easiest way to break from these routines is to slow things down a little. "This means asking first not what the object is or how we should approach it, but why we should want to engage with it in the first place...It is not a matter of starting from certain theoretical or methodological problems: it is a matter of starting from what we want to do, and then seeing which methods and theories will best help us to achieve these ends" (183). All of this sounds perfectly sensible.

But what if we were to say that the best way to break the routines of current theory is to have absolutely no idea of where one is going and why? "We must increasingly abandon the idea of a model of education or culture [Bildung] that is governed by the norm that man must always know what he is doing" (Blumenberg, 446). Of course, if we abandon this idea, we lose our ability to get instant results. But we may gain an understanding of we mean by "results" and why "results" sometimes don't get us anywhere. Perhaps the best thing for critics to do is to behave less like scientists and philosophers and more like rhetoricians, who not only believe that the best results are produced by talk, but who also believe that sometimes the best results are talk. Lots of talk. Talk that seems to go nowhere. Frivolous talk. And there's really only one sort of world where such an attitude is welcome: the comic world.

Unscrupulous Irresolutions or Dark Laughter Reprised

I have tried, in this book, to explore what may be comedy's most crucial, though unacknowledged, aspect: its critical function. Comedy can be understood—though it rarely is nowadays—as a way of positioning ourselves theoretically, a position where certain questions occur to us and provide us with new ways of seeing matters that we hold dearest; it can provide us with new stories to tell about our own laughter; it can help us make strange the rules of scholarship and find new things to say; and it can equip us with alternatives to the literary and cultural metaphors that shape our thinking. Comedy, however, has seldom been associated with insight and understanding. This is largely because, in life and letters, the only truths worth knowing are the terrible truths. Comedy, we are told, avoids terrible truths. Remember how Baudelaire put it, "The wise man laughs only with fear and trembling" (141). Tragedy tells the story of the fool who denies the hold that terrible truths have on him. It's not that Oedipus has no knowledge of the situation in which he finds himself. What he lacks is insight, which Hans Georg Gadamer says is "more than the knowledge of this or that situation," that it "involves an escape from something that deceived us and held us captive" (356). On the one hand, this idea sounds gloomy. The thought that we are capable of gaining insight—into ourselves and our everyday lives—only after we first have been deceived (or self-deceived) suggests that insight is reserved solely for those who choose to live their lives as if it were a Greek tragedy. Even those of us who have not read Gadamer may come to the same conclusion: the highest form of understanding available to humans—insight—is available only to those who have suffered. It's a philosophy designed to prohibit comedy from having the final word on things not that it would. Jocasta's advice to Oedpius is to move on, to forget the matter entirely. There are worse things, she says, than murdering your father and marrying your mother. She instructs Oedipus to stop suffering, but of course, he will not. There's nothing noble in avoiding suffering, and so Jocasta is denied the last word.

But there is insight to be found in Jocasta's words. To find it, however, one would have to (mis)read Gadamer and de-emphasize the idea of suffering, how central it is to the experience of reality, and so on in order to play up the more pleasant side of insight: escape.[2] Such a misreading, however, misses very little in the traditional view since it still takes suffering as fundamental and implicitly berates any evasion of it. Jocasta does not deny Oedipus's situation or evade it, she simply tells Oedipus to accept it and move on. Again, Oedipus already knows, as does Jocasta, that it is he who is guilty. So what, precisely, is Oedipus after? Why is acceptance an impossibility? To clarify this matter, one could turn once more to Stanley Cavell. He nudges us away from the traditional view of tragic knowing as an act of exposure, as a will-to-certainty, and wonders if perhaps what tragedy demands of us is the will to abandon knowledge. But how, asks Cavell, "do we learn that what we need is not more knowledge but the willingness to forgo knowing?" (*Disowning Knowledge,* 94). To put it another way, how does one convince Oedipus that it is possible stop, to give in, to simply shrug his shoulders and accept who he is and not discover, expose, reveal, or unearth himself. It may very well be that, should Oedipus have chosen instead to disown knowledge, or abandon reason, Sophocles would not have a tragic drama on his hands, but a musical comedy. Imagine what Mel Brooks could do with *Oedipus the King*: "Incest? Patricide? Who knew?"

The thought I'm thinking here is not that all tragedies really aspire to be comedy, rather that comedy—the will to uncertainty—is what opens up tragedy or any sort of text for that matter, to new possibilities, new ways of understanding. What if we said that Gadamer's appeal to "learning through suffering" could also be understood as comic thinking, since comedy is happiest when it's escaping from foregone conclusions, dead-ends, fate, the police, covert assumptions, impenetrable riddles, death—anything that would have us believe it has held us captive.

One might think, here, of Dickens's Pickwick Papers. In Chapter 5, I suggested that we needn't read the tragic events in the pound, the Fleet episode, or Sam Weller's grim expressions, as consequential. Mr. Pickwick emerged from the torment and indignities of the pound with laughter, not fear and trembling. This is not to say that our Mr. Pickwick needn't take things seriously, that he (and we) shouldn't be aware, as Susanne Langer reminds us, that the oncoming future is fraught with danger and suffering. Comedy questions not the seriousness of the world, but the importance we grant to it. What holds us captive is the idea that suffering makes us know better. This may seem like a paradox (what do we learn through the experience of suffering? that suffering teaches us nothing at all?). But if we tend fully to Gadamer's reading of the phrase "learning through suffering," as Gerald Bruns does, we find that what is learned is not "this or that particular thing, but insight into the limitations of humanity" (in "Tragic Thoughts," 121). Insight comes with the knowledge that we can't know better. A comic perspective if there ever was one, and not without its rewards. Recall what Susanne Langer says about the comic rhythm: "This ineluctable future—ineluctable because its countless factors are beyond human knowledge and control—is Fortune. Destiny in the guise of Fortune is the fabric of comedy; it is developed by comic action, which is the upset and recovery of the protagonist's equilibrium, his contest with the world and his triumph by wit, luck, personal power, or ever humorous, or ironical, or philosophical acceptance of mischance" (331). To be open to the ineluctable future is to be open to bad fortune—and to good fortune as well: "Here's a game!" roar the goons in the pound; "Here's a game. Hooray!" shouts Sam Weller.

A more harrowing example presents itself in the recent terrorist attacks on the World Trade Center in New York City. One might say the dominant narrative that emerged in response to the attacks was not much different than the one we (lazily, uninspiringly) attribute to Dickens's book: before 9/11, the United States of America was a kind of Dingley Dell, cozy and innocent. The story goes something like this: Americans were comically unconscious of the true (and sometimes evil) nature of the world out there. To our ears, the distant sound of suicide bombers blowing up public busses was little more than a rude interruption. All of this calls to mind the scene in *Pickwick Papers* in which Mr. Pickwick takes a morning stroll along Rochester Bridge: "Bright and pleasant was the sky, balmy the air, and beautiful the appearance of every object around" (82). He is roused from this "agreeable reverie" by a dismal man who reminds him that "the morning of the day and the morning of life are but too much alike." True enough.

"God!" continues the dismal man, "What would I forfeit to have the days of my childhood restored or to be able to forget them forever!"

"You have seen much trouble, sir," said Mr. Pickwick compassionately.
"I have," said the dismal man hurriedly; "I have. More than those who see me now would believe possible." He paused for an instant and then said abruptly,
"Did it ever strike you, on such a morning as this, that drowning would be happiness and peace?"
"God bless me, no!" replied Mr. Pickwick, edging a little from the balustrade."
(83)

As James Kincaid points out, Pickwick safely absorbs the trite observation that all good things must come an end, but when the threat of real death, in the form of testimonial suicide, imposes itself on him, his instinct is to run away: "Pickwick readily assents to the abstraction—he can easily live in a world of triteness, where death exists only in a Pickwickian sense—but he violently resist its application to himself" (*Dickens and the Rhetoric of Laughter*, 28). The point of this scene, we assume, is to show just how ill-prepared Pickwick is for disaster. A few months in the Fleet will change him, just as the terrorist attacks on the World Trade Center and the Pentagon will change us. On the two-year anniversary of the attacks, Alex Chadwick, the host of National Public Radio's "Day to Day," read from his essay "A Changed World After 9/11":

> What I recall vividly from the East Coast, from the time after 9/11 two years ago, was the achingly beautiful quality of the days. The air so fresh and clean, the sky a perfect blue, the sun, the warmth, it lasted and lasted. The finest autumn in memory, utterly joyless. The afternoons glowing with a kind of clarity that felt like an added cruelty. Now I think of that time as being brought about by a kind of national psychic refusal to move on from the moments just before the planes struck New York, Washington, that field in Pennsylvania. And when we did finally relinquish that moment, something dim settled in the air. I've not seen days like that again, or clarity either.

Chadwick's words are hardly exceptional. The vision of a pre-9/11 Anywhere, U.S.A., rapt in an eternal Indian Summer, is an essential ingredient in this cultural narrative, one that relies heavily on the idea that benevolence and innocence are ineffective agents in a world full of terror and suffering. Like Pickwick, the U.S. must emerge from adolescence into full adulthood, from innocence into experience, from Eden into the New Jerusalem. This is a profoundly uncomic narrative—one that is, of course, merely the index and the result of a specific, socio-historical temperament in our culture. In other words, Chadwick is just singing a familiar tune: "moving on" is seen not as the indulgence in new possibilities and new days ahead ("Here's a game!" roar the goons in the Pound. "Here's a game. Hooray!" shouts Sam Weller), but as the necessary abandonment of the comic spirit which, in the end, is nothing more than "a refuge from the harshness of the world and…a source of easy and comforting identity"

(Kincaid, 28). The question is: How do we position ourselves in such a way that a genuinely comic reading of something like the events of 9/11 might present itself? How might we speak of "befores" and "afters" in ways that suggest, if not improvement, at least some kind of significant change? How do we find a loophole out of the dangerously reactionary (and paranoid) attitude that although our innocence is lost forever, we are much smarter now? Are there other stories available beside this hackneyed one? How do we take comic action?

Let's begin from this risky position, that comedy needn't be seen as an escape from disaster, death, and decay; that, instead, it can be seen as escape from the oppressive narratives that assert that all that comes before the acknowledgment of death, disaster, and decay is illusory and that everything that follows is clarity. The general attitude that there's always a way out comes from what Langer's idea of "the basic biological pattern" that all animals share—the impulse to survive, to seize opportunities, to adapt, to overcome disasters and obstacles. When the life rhythm is disturbed, argues Langer, "the organism as a whole is out of balance. But the within a wide range of conditions, it struggles to retrieve its original dynamic form by overcoming and removing the obstacle, of if this proves impossible, it develops a slight variation of its typical form and activity and carries on life with a new balance of functions—in other words, it adapts itself to the situation" (328). The will to survive, which Langer argues is the underlying feeling of comedy, is so intense that those who witness it either laugh or go mad—perhaps because such an elaborate process of self-realization is what separates us from the apes.

At any rate, we have come close to what this book has taken as its guiding assumption: comedy is not about happy endings and satisfying resolutions, but new opportunities, new ways out in a world that has no endings, no resolutions. Traditionally, the wedding feast is seen as vital to the overall coherence of the comic narrative. The typical comic pattern consists of beginning, efflorescence, and end. One needs only to look to Shakespeare or the Screwball Comedy's remarriage plot to know this. To speak, then, of openness as the underlying feeling of comedy, seems counterintuitive. We tend to think of comedy the way we think of all dramatic forms: it has a distinct rhythm, one which corresponds with the rhythm of a living organism: "its life has a definite beginning, ascent, turning point, descent, and close" (332). The accepted wisdom in literature and philosophy is that comedies, like tragedies, always come to an end. In the case of comedy, the end is marriage. Still, one could argue that the wedding feast (the remarriage, the spring festival, the triumph, the birthday, the initiation, or whatever scene you choose) is not an end, but "an image of human vitality holding its own in the world amid the surprises of unplanned coincidences" (331). Think of any Screwball Comedy—Capra's *It Happened One Night* (1934) and *You Can't Take It with You* (1938), Sturges's *The Lady Eve* (1941) and *The Miracle of Morgan's Creek* (1944), or Hawks's *His Girl Friday* (1940). The ending of each of these films is indeed a union (or reunion) but each ending may be taken to be an unscrupulous *ir*resolution. "We do not really know," says Stanley Cavell of Howard Hawks's *His Girl Friday*, "that the pair are going off together unmarried; probably they do not, as we see them leave, know either. The speculation is pertinent. It is a premiss of farce that marriage kills romance. It is a project of remarriage to refuse to draw a conclusion from this premises but rather to turn the tables on farce, to turn marriage itself into romance, into adventure, which for Walter and Hildy means to preserve within it something of the illicit, to find as it were a moral equivalent of the immoral" (*Pursuits of Happiness*, 186). With this in mind, comedy "may be taken as escape (in which case you must keep on escaping); in another way it may be taken as refreshment and recreation (in which case you are free to stop and think)" (187). In other words, the ending of a comedy isn't an ending at all but a celebration of new beginnings.[3]

Speaking of a celebration of new beginnings, let me turn to a classic New York story, Leonard Bernstein's 1944 musical, "On the Town." It tells of three sailors during World War II who visit New York City on twenty-four-hour shore leave. While his buddies Ozzie and Gabey pursue the elusive (and fictional) Miss Turnstiles, Chip, the shy and skinny naïf, decides to spend the day seeing as many tourist spots as possible. A cabdriver named Hildy, who is smitten with Chip, offers to drive him to the best spot in town: her apartment. In the number, "Come Up to My Place," Chip points to his sadly out-of-date sightseeing map and sings:

Chip: My father told me "Chip, my boy, there'll come a time when you leave home; if you should ever hit New York, be sure to see the Hippodrome."

Hildy: Did I hear right? Did you say the Hippodrome?

Chip: Yes you heard right, yes I said the Hip- [Hildy slams on the brakes]. Hey what did you stop for?

Hildy: It ain't there no more, Aida sang an 'A' and blew the place away!

On and on the song goes, and one by one the things we associate with grand 'ol New York disappear: "Tobacco Road" (a successful Broadway play that ran from 1933-1941), the Aquarium, (which was closed from 1941 to 1957), and Woolworth Tower (which in 1931 was overshadowed by the taller, grander Empire State Building which, in turn, was overshadowed by the World Trade Center). In the 1949 film version starring Gene Kelly and Frank Sinatra, the lyrics were changed slightly so as to include another marvel long since gone (the infamous Floradora Girl—Evelyn Nesbit, also known as The Girl on the Swing—replaces the somewhat irrelevant "Tobacco Road"), and to indicate that the Hippodrome wasn't blown away (who was Aida anyway?), but torn down. No matter, because the song continues to celebrate not only an ever-changing urban landscape, but the general comic idea of "moving on." The turnstiles, we are told, will keep turning; and after all the Floradora Girls have faded away, after all the lights have been turned off for good, after the towers have crumbled to the ground, there's still the possibility of another story: the one that leads to Hildy's cozy, loving arms.

That such a story seems an unlikely alternative to the moralism that characterizes Chadwick's romance and others like it is due in large part to our willingness to embrace catastrophic insight at the expense of everything else, especially comedy. In Woody Allen's *Crimes and Misdemeanors* (1989), a celebrity filmmaker and outrageous narcissist named Lester tells his brother-in-law and documentarian, "comedy equals tragedy plus time!" A pedestrian observation, to be sure, and one that inspires us all to vomit—not just Woody Allen (and Steve Allen, whom Lester has plagiarized). The film is designed to make us loathe Lester and everything for which he stands. But were we to set aside our customary loyalty to Allen's loveable nebbish character, we'd be more willing to admit that Lester is simply parroting our own empty-headed notions. His idea of comedy is familiar, safe, above ground. We are more than willing to consent to the dubious idea that an exploding space shuttle joke is far more offensive the day of a NASA mission disaster than, say, two or three years afterward. Only a monster would laugh at such a tragedy. Like Lester, we betray "an acquiescence to the most smothering of political conservatisms. By coupling tragedy with the sublime, the ineffable, the metaphysical, and by aligning comedy with the mundane, the quotidian, and the material, we manage to muffle or even erase the most powerful narratives of illumination and liberation we have" (Kincaid, *Annoying the Victorians*, 92). It is strange how time makes us bolder.

In a piece for the March 13, 2005 issue of the *New York Times*, Frank Rich tells us of the dirtiest joke ever told—no surprise that it is tied, somehow, to the events of 9/11. I'd like to draw our attention to the rhetoric. Two weeks after the terrorist attacks, Rich went to the Hilton on 6th Avenue, where the Friars Club was roasting Hugh Hefner. "The ensuing avalanche of Viagra jokes did not pull off the miracle of making everyone in the room forget the recent events," Rich tells us. Last on the bill was comedian Gilbert Gottfried, who "delivered what may have been the first public 9/11 gag: He couldn't get a direct flight to California, he said, because 'they said they have to stop at the Empire State Building first'" "There were boos," Rich recalls, "but Mr. Gottfried moved along to his act's crowning joke," known to comedians from California to the Catskills as "The Aristocrats"—a joke whose rich history is the subject of a recent documentary. But back to the Hilton: "As the mass exodus began," continues Rich, "some people were laughing, others were appalled, and perhaps a majority of us were in the middle. We knew we had seen something remarkable, not because the joke was so funny but because it had served as shock therapy, harmless shock therapy for an adult audience, that at least temporarily relieved us of our burdens and jolted us back into the land of the living again...I have often reflected upon Mr. Gottfried's mesmerizing performance," Rich says. (The Greatest Dirty Joke Ever Told").

Rich should be commended for asking us to join him in this a risky positional shift, to acknowledge we tell 9/11 jokes (exploding space shuttle jokes, Holocaust jokes) not to get grisly kicks, but to transgress the cultural prescriptions that determine what can and can't be said in a given situation and, as Freud says, to "open sources of pleasure that have been inaccessible" (*Jokes and Their Relation to the Unconscious*, 123). But an even riskier positional shift is to *sustain* this pleasure-seeking attitude, bring it out in the open rather than keep it, as Eve Sedgwick argues, "as an always presumable, unexaminable, inexhaustible underground well-spring of supposedly 'natural' motive, one that presents only the question of how to keep its irrepressible ebullitions under control" (16). That is, why must we see such joke telling, such shaggy-dog tale tattling as "temporary relief"? It took Frank Rich three and a-half years to tell us about his response to the 9/11 joke; it's very likely that Gilbert Gottfried had to wait two weeks *just to tell it*—two weeks longer than he wanted to wait, no doubt. For Frank Rich, comedy equals tragedy plus time. For Gottfried, no time is like the present.

But the point of good comedy is not in the timing, or in the timeliness. Comedy does not attend to befores and afters. Remember, Hildy doesn't care about the Hippodrome. But we do. Our stories depend on it, or its absence, just as our stories depend on the absence of the Twin Towers.

Before and after. What comes before can only take on significance when the "after" strikes us. And the harder "it" strikes, the more knowledge we have "after."

And the knowledge we have "after" is saturated with tragic seriousness. In this state, comedy functions as nothing more than relief. At first glace, the metaphor appears flattering. Relief is soothing, restorative, comforting, refreshing. It's the sort of thing we consciously seek out, or encounter unexpectedly but happily, when exposed to disaster, everyday stress, or just a really gloomy story. But relief is also what ensures that these things are taken as important, serious, and lasting, worthy of our tax dollars, our time, and our best thinkers. As Kincaid notes, the idea of comic relief doesn't do much more than remind us, or generate in us the feeling, of what really matters in this world: "Comedy is that which attends on, offers relaxation from, prepares us for more of—something else, something serious and demanding…Comic relief relieves the status quo, in other words, contains the power of comedy" (92). Relief is prescriptive and temporary.

From this point of view, comedy seems destined to achieve in our culture a status no higher than athlete's foot powder. But as mundane and pedestrian as the idea of comic relief may appear—Kincaid thinks it is generally met with "bemused contempt" (92)—it is actually quite sophisticated, and its strength and reach as a cultural metaphor should not be underestimated. We grant the notion of comic relief much explanatory power, and charge it with no less a task than of making the world around us intelligible. It influences the way we absorb everything from elementary school to revolutionary art. Of the latter, the metaphor of relief has taught us to remain cautious. A work of revolutionary art has a function that differs little from that of a carnival at the Abbey of Thélème in the thirteenth century; it is, says Terry Eagleton, "a licensed affair in every sense, a permissible rupture of hegemony, a contained popular blow-off" (148). Of the former, Allon White says this: "The serious act of growing up and acquiring knowledge begins by inculcating the child with a primary law of double exclusion: where knowledge is, play is not; where play is, knowledge is not. The provision of playgrounds in school puts games, exuberant jokes, and pleasure in an open enclave where they cannot contaminate the realm of 'pure' knowledge" (132). Comedy, then, is like recess; it's part of the social control ploy, not an escape from it. And like relief, escape seems to be a promising way of describing comedy. It seems, even, a more promising way of describing comedy because escape is seldom thought of as temporary, or at any rate a licensed affair. Relief means going on shore leave. Escape means going AWOL. More important, one needn't associate the idea of escape solely with the capsizing of institutional structures. Escape can also mean joyful liberation from all forms of constraint. Of course this is a very old way of viewing comedy, as "the movement from pistis to gnostis, from a society controlled by habit, ritual bondage, arbitrary law and the older characters to a society controlled by youth and pragmatic freedom," as the joyful progression "from illusion to reality" (Frye, 172). Robert M. Polhemus argues that this sort of movement is not restricted to the green worlds of Chaucer and Shakespeare; for him, the comic is a kind of insight or means of discovery by which one "deals in miraculous transformations and the instantaneous casting-off of burdens and sufferings" dealt by religious and cultural authority (7).

The lesson here is that it's not our fate, as critics, to be held captive by tragic discourse. There is hope. Kincaid, for instance, is optimistic not because he imagines the future differently than Eagleton does, but because he imagines history differently. We do what we do as serious-minded critics not because there's no other choice, but because we are "lazy half-wits getting by within a set of critical practices we have inherited, have found remarkably easy to use, and have never troubled to examine because it is nicer to sit by the fire (or in front of students, at conferences, in learned journals) and doze" (5). The critical practices Kincaid has in mind, the practices we find the easiest to use, are the ones that take their object of inquiry too seriously. But what does this mean? If we grant enormous import to the serious, we say it means all the wrong things, all the worst things. Not to take your subject matter seriously is to indulge in the most politically reckless, socially irresponsible, or, at the very least, useless critical practice. More likely, not to take your subject matter seriously is simply to produce bad writing. Anyone who has spent more than a couple of semesters teaching freshman composition will likely insist that bad writing comes not from dumb students, but from smart students who don't take the assignment "seriously" (a fine and flattering way to explain why, in spite of the sound pedagogy that cultivates it, there can arise from one's own pool of student writing witless lines like, "Entertainment films which have class conflict as an underlying theme often pit one class against another"). To say what is serious and what not is to classify what can and cannot be said in any given case. But seriousness, as Allon White has argued, has "more to do with power than with content" (128). That is, the ability to determine what can or cannot be said in any given case testifies not to the intrinsic cultural value of this classification, but to the powerful single-mindedness of our critical methods.[4] Those who are aware of this tendency and its dangers often claim that literary criticism is at its best when it's rhetorical rather then analytical, devoted to openness and irresolution rather than to rigor and method.[5] To put it one way, "a rhetorician might have occasion to wonder what would happen if you did not arrange your thinking into the traditional polarities: as, for example, between truth and falsehood, reality and fiction, inside and outside, presence and absence, literal and figurative, signifier and signified, and so on" (Bruns, *Inventions*, 88). A critic who thinks chiefly in method is likely to fear that, without these polarities, we'd run out of things to say. Or, more precisely, we'd run out of serious things to say. A rhetorician, however, is likely to expect that not only would there be a brand new inventory of things to say, including seemingly frivolous things, there would be greater opportunities to critically examine why we're so attached to method in the first place.

Why we're so attached to method and why we're so skeptical of anything else is largely because method is virtually risk free. It tells us what we can and cannot say in any given situation and therefore assures us that we cannot go wrong—or least astray. Method tells us what we already know.[6] The point I wish to make, however, is that what we know, and know very well, is how to treat something seriously. Our critical language is the high language of tragic knowingness. Uninterested in precisely how this came to be, Allon White assures us that it is an unavoidable fact: "Once the high language has attained the commanding position of being able to specify what is and is not to be taken seriously, its control over the language of its society is virtually assured. Bakhtin calls this manoeuvre 'the lie of pathos', which designates the insidious identification of 'important matters' with an idealism centered upon tragedy" (134). Kincaid, who believes seriousness retains its commanding position largely through our own sloth, would likely insist that the best way to deal with the "lie of pathos" and escape its so-called power is to offer up our own lies and produce them right in its face.

Consider, for example, Slavoj Žižek's powerful reading of what is commonly referred to as "the long nose"—an obscene gesture that requires touching your nose with your thumb and spreading the remaining four fingers out so as to resemble the erected phallus. As an apotropaic gesture (a gesture meant to divert evil) "the long nose" is, at best, a mixed signal (after all, what makes the act of mimicking the large and powerful phallus of an adversary so insulting?). In search of a less ambivalent reading of the gesture, Žižek turns to Otto Fenichel, whose solution "is that one has to read this gesture as the first part of a sentence, the second part of which is omitted." The whole of it reads, "Yours is so big and powerful, but in spite of that, you are impotent. You cannot hurt me with it" (157–158). "The long nose" disempowers the adversary whether he reacts or not. Should he choose not to react, he must concede his power. Should he choose to react, he can only confirm his powerlessness. In this way, argues Žižek, the power structure is caught in a trap, "The more violent its reaction, the more it confirms its fundamental impotence" (157–158). But Žižek's point about escaping power is, paradoxically, about the impossibility of escape. Such is the logic of phallic inversion: although the object of power (in this case, the phallic signifier) cannot be obtained in the strict sense (it is, argues Žižek, an index of its own impossibility, a sign of its own lack) and, therefore, has no command over us, it cannot be avoided either. We may trap our adversary in his own logic, but we trap ourselves as well. This is why Žižek believes that the liberating, anti-totalitarian forces of laughter, irony, and cynical distance are illusory, are, "so to speak, part of the game" (28).

I've chosen this example not to introduce a specific challenge to Žižek's reading of "the long nose." On the contrary, there's little in any of Žižek's writings on ideology and psychoanalytic theory that warrant challenge. Once were inside the model of the Lacanian Real, everything Žižek says makes perfect sense. This is not a judgment of Žižek, but a statement on the nature of systematic thought, on the power of method. What begins as an apotropaic gesture becomes, for Žižek, an apostrophic gesture—that is, one that indicates a lack (in this case, the lack, the only real lack, the symbolic lack). The once strange and perplexing gesture of "the long nose" becomes, more or less, a functionality of the Lacanian Real and nothing more ("one must read this as," says Žižek). In the end, there's really no debating whether or not an obscene gesture and a powerful adversary are both "part of the game" if one is already convinced it's the only game in town.

There is, nevertheless, a comic reading to be made here—a reading that is determined to keep ends loose and suggest there's more to say (and, therefore, hope for all). Instead of reading "the long nose" as a way of saying to your adversary, "Yours is so big and powerful, but in spite of that you cannot hurt me," one could read it as a way of saying, "I simply don't care, and because of that you cannot hurt me." The assumption here, in this second and more comic reading of "the long nose," is that one doesn't have to play the game. When Groucho is confronted by a bullying baritone in *A Night at the Opera*, he makes no indication that there exists any power, presumed or real, to debunk. Instead, he looks at the bully's Pagliacci costume and says, "Say, how do you sleep with such big buttons on your pajamas?" What Groucho shows us is that "escape" means playing a different game. Kafka's Red Peter, the caged ape from his story "A Report to an Academy," tells us that finding a way out is simply a matter of devising one "even should the way out prove to be an illusion" (254). Apes belong in cages? Then let's not be apes.

A text must be read this way? Then let's read it differently. Mikhail Bakhtin would call such a counter-maneuver "the gay deception." As Gary Saul Morson and Caryl Emerson put it, the gay deceiver "parodies and reprocesses discourses of falsity so as to reveal what is false about them and to rob them of their harmful power" (359–360). Take, as a fine example of the gay deceiver, the comic figure of Mr. Jingle, Dickens's foil to the pompous gentlemen of the Pickwick Club. When told that one of the gentlemen has a "strong poetic turn," Jingle swiftly replies, "So have I…Epic poem—ten thousand lines—revolution of July—composed it on the spot—Mars by day, Apollo by night—bang the field piece, twang the lyre" (34). The effect of all of this gay deception, of course, is that we love the Pickwicks more, not less. The comic spirit swells and, happily, the story moves on—not so much with serious consequences than with endless games. If we can at least acknowledge our own inherited sloth and want of invention, if we can begin to recognize the lies of pathos that dominate literary method and be moved to gaily deceive them, we may discover the endless games available to us as well. We may, in fact, experience what Gadamer describes as real insight.

Notes

1. See *Shame and its Sisters: A Silvan Tomkins Reader,* (Durham, NC: Duke University Press, 1995), 1–28.
2. "Sometimes," claims Bruns, insight is "emancipatory" and that "we can think of comedy as the form of discourse that celebrates these moments of freedom from mental bondage" (*Hermeneutics,* 217).
3. The Screwball does not promote reproduction, which is the end of sex. To the contrary, the Screwball displaces the possibility of reproduction in a number of ways. Consider the curious absence of children or the unusual or diminished roles that mothers play in the Screwball. *You Can't Take It with You* is perhaps the most interesting film in this regard, in that it proposes an alternative system of marriage and family. The heroine's mother, Penny Sycamore (played by Spring Byington), spends all of her time producing and reproducing not children but plays—albeit very bad ones. Unlike Earl Williams in Hawks's *His Girl Friday*, the Sycamores don't believe in production for use. Nor does the Screwball, which believes only in new beginnings and beginnings with no ends.

188 Loopholes: Reading Comically

4. See also Terry Eagleton's *Literary Theory: An Introduction* (Minneapolis: U. of Minneapolis Press, 1998), pp. 175–177.
5. See especially Eagleton, pp. 179–183; and Gerald L. Bruns's *Inventions: Writing, Textuality, and Understanding in Literary History* (New Haven: Yale U. Press, 1982), pp. 1–13.
6. Gerald L. Bruns puts it differently, though no less bluntly: "Method is a substitute for thought" (*Inventions*, 74).

Bibliography

Ackroyd, Peter. *Dickens*. (New York: Harper Collins, 1990).

Andrew, Dudley. *The Major Film Theories: An Introduction*. (New York: Oxford University Press, 1976).

Auden, W.H. "Dingley Dell & the Fleet." *The Dyer's Hand and Other Essays*. (London, 1956). Rpt. in *Charles Dickens: Critical Assessments, Volume II*. Ed. Michael Hollington. (East Sussex: Helm Information, Ltd., 1995).

Bakhtin, Mikhail. "Author and Hero in Aesthetic Activity." *Art and Answerability: Early Philosophical Essays by M.M. Bakhtin*. Trans. Vadim Liapunov. Ed. Michael Holquist and Vadim Liapunov. (Austin: University of Texas, 1990), 4–256.

—. "Epic and Novel." *The Dialogic Imagination: Four Essays by M.M. Bakhtin*. Ed. Michael Holquist. Tr. by Caryl Emerson and Michael Holquist. (Austin, University of Texas Press, 1981), 3–40.

—."Forms of Time and Chronotope in the Novel: Notes toward a Historical Poetics." *The Dialogic Imagination*. 84–258.

—. *The Problems of Dostoevsky's Poetics*. Trans. and Ed. Caryl Emerson. Introduction by Wayne C. Booth. (Minneapolis, MN: University Minnesota Press, 1984).

—. *Rabelais and His World*. Trans. Hélène Iswolsky. (Bloomington: Indiana University Press, 1984).

—. "Response to a Question from the *Novy Mir* Editorial Staff." *Speech Genres and Other Late Essays*. Ed. Caryl Emerson and Michael Holquist. Trans. Vern W. McGee. (Austin: University of Texas Press, 1986), 1–7.

—. "Toward a Methodology for the Human Sciences." *Speech Genres and Other Late Essays*. 159–172.

—. *Towards a Philosophy of the Act*. Ed. Vadim Liapunov & Michael Holquist. Trans. Vadim Liapunov. (Austin: University of Texas, 1993).

Barasch, Frances K. *The Grotesque: A Study in Meanings*. (Paris: Mouton, 1971).

Baum, Rachel. "'What I Have Learned to Feel': The Pedagogical Emotions of Holocaust Education." *College Literature* 23 (1996), 44–57.

Barber, C.L. *Shakespeare's Festive Comedy, a Study of Dramatic Form and its Relation to Social Custom*. (NJ: Princeton University Press, 1959).

Beicken, Peter U. "Kafka's Narrative Rhetoric." *The Kafka Debate: New Perspectives for Our Time*. Ed. Angel Flores. (New York: Gordian Press, 1977), 178–187.

Bell, Millicent. *Meaning in Henry James*. (Cambridge, MA: Harvard University Press, 1991).

Benjamin, Walter. "The Storyteller." *Illuminations*. Ed. Hannah Arendt. (New York: Schocken Books, 1969), 83–110.

Bensmaïa, Réda. "Foreword: The Kafka Effect." *Kafka: Toward a Minor Literature*. By Gilles Deleuze and Félix Guattari. Trans. Dana Polan. Theory and History of Literature. 30. (Minneapolis, MN: University of Minneapolis Press, 1986).

Bergson, Henri. "Laughter." *Comedy*. Introduction and Appendix by Willie Sypher. (New York: Doubleday, 1956), 61–190.

Bersani, Leo. *The Culture of Redemption*. (Cambridge, MA: Harvard University Press, 1990).

Birchall, Steve. "Modern Music is a Sick Puppy: A Conversation with Frank Zappa" *Digital Audio Magazine*. October/November 1984.

Blumenberg, Hans. "An Anthropological Approach to the Contemporary Significance of Rhetoric." *After Philosophy: End or Transformation?* Ed. By Kenneth Baynes, James Bohman, and Thomas McCarthy. (Cambridge, MA: MIT Press, 1987), 429–458.

Boa, Elizabeth. *Kafka: Gender, Class, and Race in the Letters and Fictions*. (New York: Oxford University Press, 1996).

Booker, M. Keith. *Joyce, Bakhtin, and the Literary Tradition: Toward a Comparative Cultural Poetics*. (Ann Arbor: University of Michigan Press, 1995).

Booker, M. Keith and Dubravka Juraga. *Bakhtin, Stalin, and Modern Russian Fiction: Carnival, Dialogism, and History*. (Westport, CT: Greenwood Press, 1995).

Bourdieu, Pierre. *Outline of a Theory of Practice*. Trans. Richard Nice. (New York: Cambridge University Press, 1977).

Brod, Max. *Franz Kafka: A Biography*. (New York: Schocken Books, 1960).

Brooks, Peter. *Reading for the Plot: Design and Invention in Narrative*. (Cambridge, MA: Harvard University Press, 1984).

Bruns, Gerald. *Hermeneutics: Ancient and Modern*. (New Haven, CT: Yale University Press, 1992).

—. *Inventions: Writing, Textuality, and Understanding in Literary History*. (New Haven, CT: Yale Universtiy Press, 1982).

—. "The Last Romantic: Stanley Cavell and the Writing of Philosophy." *Tragic Thoughts at the End of Philosophy: Language, Literature, and Ethical Theory*. (Evanston: Northwestern University Press, 1999), 199–217.

—. "Stanley Cavell's Shakespeare." *Tragic Thoughts at the End of Philosophy*. 181–197.

—. "Tragic Thoughts at the End of Philosophy: Martha Nussbaum's Ethics of Particularity." *Tragic Thoughts at the End of Philosophy*. 107–129.

Cameron, Sharon. *Thinking in Henry James*. (Chicago: University of Chicago Press, 1989).

Caputo, Donald. *Radical Hermeneutics: Repetition, Deconstruction, and the Hemeneutic Project*. (Bloomington, University of Indiana Press, 1987).

Cavell, Stanley. *Contesting Tears: The Hollywood Melodrama of the Unknown Woman*. (Chicago: University of Chicago Press, 1996).

—. *Disowning Knowledge in Seven Plays of Shakespeare*, *Updated Edition*. (Cambridge: Cambridge University Press, 2003).

—. *Must We Mean What We Say?* Cambridge: Cambridge University Press, 1969.

—. *Pursuits of Happiness: The Hollywood Comedy of Remarriage*. (Cambridge, MA: Harvard U. Press, 1981).

Chesterton, G.K. "*The Pickwick Papers*." *The Dickens Critics*. Ed. George H. Ford and Lauriat Lane, Jr. (Ithaca, NY: Cornell University Press, 1961).

Clark, Katerina and Michael Holquist. *Mikhail Bakhtin*. (Cambridge, MA: Harvard University Press, 1984).

Clark, John R. *The Modern Satiric Grotesque and its Traditions*. (Lexington: University Press of Kentucky, 1991).

Clines, Francis X. "Voices from the Holocaust Reverberate Across Time." *New York Times*. 6 May, 2000.

Cohen, Elisabeth. "Kids Who Died at My High School This Year." *Conjunctions*. 36 (2001), 200–203.

Collignon, Jean. "Kafka's Humor." *Yale French Studies* 16 (1955), 53–62.

Chumo, Peter N. II. "*Thelma and Louise* as Screwball Comedy." *Film Quarterly: Forty Years*. Ed. Brian Henderson and Ann Martin. (Berkeley: University of California Press, 1999), 548–550.

Critchley, Simon. *On Humour*. (New York: Routledge, 2002).

Culler, Jonathan. *On Deconstruction: Theory and Criticism After Structuralism*. (Ithaca, NY: Cornell University Press, 1982).

De Certeau, Michel. *The Practice of Everyday Life*. Tr. Steven Randall. (Berkeley: University of California Press, 1984).

De Quincey, Thomas. *Selected Essays on Rhetoric*. Ed. Frederick Burwick. (Carbondale: Southern Illinois University Press, 1967).

Deleuze, Gilles and Félix Guattari. *Kafka: Toward a Minor Literature*. (Minneapolis. MN: University of Minnesota Press, 1986).

Derrida, Jacques. *Writing and Difference*. Tr. Alan Bass. (Chicago: University of Chicago Press, 1978).

Des Pres, Terrence. "Holocaust *Laughter?*" *Writing and the Holocaust*. Ed. by Berel. Lang. (New York: Holmes and Meir, 1988), 216–233.

Dickens, Charles. *The Pickwick Papers*. (New York: Penguin, 1964).

—. "Preface to the First Cheap Edition." *The Pickwick Papers*. ix–xiii.

—. *Oliver Twist*. (New York: Penguin, 1983).

Eagleton, Terry. "Bakhtin, Schopenhauer, Kundera." *Bakhtin and Cultural Theory*. Ed. Ken Hirschkop and David Shepherd. (New York: Manchester University Press, 1989), 178–188.

—. *Literary Theory: An Introduction*. 2nd ed. (Minneapolis: University of Minnesota Press, 1996).

—. *Walter Benjamin: Toward a Revolutionary Criticism*. (London: Verso, 1981).

—. "Wittgenstein's Friends." *New Left Review* 135 (1982), 64–90.

Easthope, Anthony. *Literary into Cultural Studies*. (New York: Routledge, 1991).

Eckardt, A. Roy. *On the Way to Death: Essays toward a Comic Vision*. (New Brunswick, NJ: Transaction Publishers, 1996).

Eco, Umberto. "The Frames of Comic Freedom." *Carnival!/Umberto Eco; V. V. Ivanov; Monica Rector*. Ed. by Thomas A. Sebeok. (New York: Mouton, 1984), 1–9.

Edel, Leon. Rev. of *The Comic Sense of Henry James: A Study of the Early Novels*, by Richard Porier. *American Literature* 33 (1961), 87–88.

Eggenschwiler, David. "*The Metamorphosis*, Freud, and the Chains of Odysseus." *Franz Kafka*. Ed. Harold Bloom. *Modern Critical Views*. (New York: Chelsea House, 1986), 199–219.

Emerson, Caryl. *The First Hundred Years of Mikhail Bakhtin*. (Princeton, NJ: Princeton University Press, 1997).

Emerson, Caryl and Gary Saul Morson. *Bakhtin: Creation of a Prosaics*. (Stanford, CA: Stanford University Press, 1990).

Federman, Raymond. "Notes Scribbled in the Dark While Watching *Schindler's List*, or What Price Schindler's Pots and Pans?" *After Yesterday's Crash: The Avant-Pop Anthology*. Ed. by Larry McCaffery. (New York: Penguin, 1995).

Ferguson, Frances. *Solitude and the Sublime: Romanticism and the Aesthetics of Individuation*. (New York: Routledge, 1992).

Fish, Stanley. *Doing What Comes Naturally: Change, Rhetoric, and the Practice of Theory in Literary and Legal Studies*. (Durham, NC: Duke University Press, 1989).

Freud, Sigmund. "Creative Writers and Day–Dreaming." *The Freud Reader*. Ed. Peter Gay. (New York: W.W. Norton & Co., 1989).

—. "Humour." *Sigmund Freud: Collected Papers, Volume 5*. Ed. James Strachey. (New York: Basic Books, 1960).

—. *Jokes and Their Relation to the Unconscious*. Trans. James Strachey. (New York: W. W. Norton & Co., 1960).

Frye, Northrop. *Anatomy of Criticism: Four Essays*. (Princeton, NJ: Princeton University Press, 1957).

Gadamer, Hans-Georg. *Truth and Method* 2nd ed. Trans. Joel Weinscheimer and Donald G. Marshall. (New York: Crossroad Publishing, 1989).

Gard, Roger. "Introduction." *The Jolly Corner and Other Tales*. By Henry James. (New York: Penguin, 1990).

Gardiner, Michael. "Bakhtin's Carnival: Utopia as Critique." *Critical Essays on Mikhail Bakhtin*. Ed. by Caryl Emerson. (New York: G. K. Hall & Co., 1999).

Gilman, Sander. *Franz Kafka, the Jewish Patient*. (New York: Routledge, 1995).

—. "Is Life Beautiful? Can the Shoah Be Funny? Some Thoughts on Recent and Older Films." *Critical Inquiry* 26 (Winter 2000), 279–308.

Glavin, John. "Pickwick on the Wrong Side of the Door." *Dickens Studies Annual*, 22 (1993), 1–20.

Goodrich, Peter. *Reading the Law: A Critical Introduction to Legal Method and Techniques*. (London: Basil Blackwell, 1986).

Grossman, Jonathan H. "Representing Pickwick: The Novel and the Law Courts." *Nineteenth-Century Literature* 52 (1997), 171–197.

Gurewitch, Morton. *The Ironic Temper and the Comic Imagination*. (Detroit, MI: Wayne State University Press, 1994).

Gutwirth, Marcel. *Laughing Matter: An Essay on the Comic*. (Ithaca, NY: Cornell University Press, 1993).

Hall, Stuart. "Metaphors of Transformation." Introduction. *Carnival, Hysteria, Writing: Collected Essays and Autobiography*. By Allon White. (New York: Oxford University Press, 1993), 1–25.

Halpern, Richard. *Shakespeare among the Moderns*. (Ithaca, NY: Cornell University Press, 1997).

Hardy, Barbara. *The Moral Art of Dickens*. (London: The Athlone Press, 1970).

Hart, Roderick P. with Joanne Gilbert. "Feminist Criticism." *Modern Rhetorical Criticism*. 2nd. ed. Roderick P. Hart. (Austin: Univeristy of Texas, 1997), 285–309.

Hawes, Donald. *Who's Who in Dickens*. (New York: Routledge, 1998).

Heller, Peter. "On Not Understanding Kafka." *The Kafka Debate*. 24–41.

Henel, Heinrich. "'The Burrow,' or How to Escape from a Maze." *Franz Kafka*. 119–132.

James, Henry. "The Beast in the Jungle." *Selected Short Stories*. Introduction by Quentin Anderson. (New York: Holt, Rinehart and Winston, 1960). 215–262.

—. *The Portrait of a Lady*. Reissued with a new introduction and notes by Nicola Bradbury. (New York: Oxford University Press, 1995).

—. Preface to *The Portrait of a Lady*. 3–18.

Kafka, Franz. *The Complete Stories*. (New York: Schocken Books, Inc., 1971).

—. *The Trial*. Trans. Breon Mitchell. (New York: Schocken Books, Inc. 1998).

Kant, Immanuel. *Critique of Judgment*. Trans. J. H. Bernard. (New York: Hafner Press, 1951).

Kayser, Wolfgang. *The Grotesque in Art and Literature*. (Bloomington: Indiana University Press, 1957).

Kermode, Frank. *The Sense of an Ending: Studies in the Theory of Fiction*. (London: Oxford University Press, 1967).

Kincaid, James R. *Child-Loving: The Erotic Child and Victorian Literature*. (New York: Routledge, 1992).

—. *Dickens and the Rhetoric of Laughter*. London: Oxford, 1972.

—. *Annoying the Victorians*. (New York: Routledge, 1995),

Kincaid, James R., and James Phelan. "What Do We Owe Texts? Respect, Irreverence, or Nothing at All?" *Critical Inquiry* 25 (Summer 1999), 758–783.

Kristeva, Julia. *Desire in Language: A Semiotic Approach to Literature and Art*. Ed. Léon S. Roudiez. (New York: Oxford University Press, 1980).

Lamb, Charles. "On the Artificial Comedy of the Last Century." *Elia and the Last Essays of Elia*. Ed. Jonathan Bate. (New York: Oxford University Press, 1987), 161–168.

Langer, Susanne K. *Feeling and Form*. (New York: Charles Scribner's Sons, 1953).

Latour, Bruno. *Reassembling the Social: An Introduction to Actor-Network Theory*. (New York: Oxford University Press, 2005).

"Laughter at Film Brings Spielberg Visit." *New York Times*. 13 April 1994.

Lewis, Paul. *Comic Effects: Interdisciplinary Approaches to Humor in Literature.* (New York: Routledge, 1992).

Lipman, Steve. *Laughter in Hell: The Use of Humor During the Holocaust.* (Northvale, NJ: Jason Aronson, Inc., 1991).

Lodge, David. "The Art of Ambiguity: *The Spoils of Poynton.*" *After Bakhtin: Essays on Fiction and Criticism.* (New York: Routledge, 1990).

Mailloux, Peter. *A Hesitation before Birth: The Life of Franz Kafka.* (Newark: University of Delaware Press, 1989).

McCloskey, Deirdre N. *The Rhetoric of Economics.* 2nd ed. (Madison: University of Wisconsin Press, 1998).

McFarland, Thomas. *Shakespeare's Pastoral Comedy.* (Chapel Hill: University of North Carolina Press, 1972).

Matthiessen, F. O. *Henry James: The Major Phase.* New York: Oxford University Press, 1963.

Meredith, George. "An Essay on Comedy." *Comedy.* 1–57.

Miller, D.A. *The Novel and the Police.* (Berkeley: University of California Press, 1988).

Miller, J. Hillis. *Charles Dickens: The World of His Novels.* (Cambridge, MA: Harvard University Press, 1965).

Miller, Tyrus. *Late Modernism: Politics, Fiction, and the Arts between the World Wars.* (Berkeley: University of California Press, 1999).

Modleski, Tania. *Feminism without Women: Culture and Criticism in a "Postfeminist" Age* (New York: Routledge, 1990).

Morris, David. *The Culture of Pain.* (University of California Press, 1991).

Orwell, George. "Charles Dickens." *The Dickens Critics.*

Paul, William. "Charlie Chaplin and the Annals of Anality." *Comedy/Cinema/ Theory.* Ed. by Andrew S. Horton. (Berkeley: University of California Press, 1991), 109–130.

Phillips, Adam. *The Beast in the Nursery: On Curiosity and Other Appetites.* (New York: Pantheon, 1998).

Polhemus, Robert M. *Comic Faith: The Great Tradition from Austen to Joyce.* (Chicago: University of Chicago Press, 1980).

Poirier, Richard. *The Comic Sense of Henry James: A Study of the Early Novels.* (London: Chatto & Windus, 1960).

Purdie, Susan. *Comedy: The Mastery of Discourse.* (Toronto: University of Toronto Press, 1993).

—. "The Greatest Dirty Joke Ever Told." New York Times. 13 Mar 2005.

Rich, Frank. "'Schindler's' Dissed." *San Francisco Examiner.* 6 February 1994. E:17.

Rose, Margaret A. *Parody: Ancient, Modern, and Post-Modern.* (New York: Cambridge U. Press, 1993).

Rosenberg, Brian. "Character and Contradiction in Dickens." *Nineteenth Century Literature* 47 (1992), 158–159.

Rothman, William. "Cavell on Film, Television, and Opera." *Stanley Cavell.* Ed. Richard Eldrige. (Cambridge: Cambridge University Press, 2003), 206–238.

Russo, Mary. *The Female Grotesque: Risk, Excess and Modernity*. (New York: Routledge, 1994).

Sadrin, Anny. "Fragmentation in *The Pickwick Papers*." *Dickens Studies Annual*, 22 (1993), 21–34.

Scalia, Antonin. *A Matter of Interpretation: Federal Courts and the Law*. (Princeton, NJ: Princeton University Press, 1997).

Sedgwick, Eve Kosofsky. *Epistemology of the Closet*. (Berkeley: University of California Press, 1990).

—. "Paranoid Reading and Reparative Reading; or, You're So Paranoid, You Probably Think This Introduction is About You." Introduction. *Novel Gazing: Queer Readings in Fiction*. (Durham, NC: Duke, 1997), 1–37.

—. *Tendencies*. (Durham, NC: Duke University Press, 1993), 23–51.

Sedgwick, Eve Kosofsky and Adam Frank. "Shame in the Cybernetic Fold: Reading Silvan Tomkins." *Shame and its Sisters: A Silvan Tomkins Reader*. Ed. Eve Sedgwick and Adam Frank. (Durham, NC: Duke University Press, 1995).

Solomon, Eric. "The Return of the Screw." *The Turn of the Screw*. Ed. Robert Kimbrough. (New York: W. W. Norton, 1966).

Stallybrass, Peter and Allon White. *The Politics and Poetics of Transgression*. (Ithaca, NY: Cornell University Press, 1986).

Stewart, Garrett. *Dickens and the Trials of the Imagination*. (Cambridge, MA: Harvard University Press, 1974).

Sypher, Willie. "The Meanings of Comedy." *Comedy: Meaning and Form*. Ed. Robert W. Corrigan. (San Francisco: Chandler Publishing Company, 1965), 18–60.

Thiher, Allen. The *Nachlaß*: Metaphors of *Gehen* and Ways Toward Science." *Kafka and the Contemporary Critical Performance: Centenary Readings*. Ed. Alan Udoff. (Bloomington: Indiana University Press, 1987), 256–265.

Thomson, Philip. *The Grotesque*. The Critical Idiom 24. (London: Metheun & Co. Ltd, 1972).

Thorlby, Anthony. "Kafka's Narrative: A Matter of Form." *Kafka and the Contemporary Critical Performance*. 30–40.

Wallace, Ronald. *Henry James and the Comic Form*. (Ann Arbor: University of Michigan Press, 1975).

Weiskel, Thomas. *The Romantic Sublime: Studies in the Structure and Psychology of Transcendence*. (Baltimore: Johns Hopkins University Press, 1976).

Weston, Kevin. "Laughing Instead of Crying: Why Oakland Teens Had Disturbing Reaction to *Schindler's List*." *San Francisco Examiner*. 30 Jan. 1994. D:2.

White, Allon. "'The Dismal Sacred Word.': Academic Language and the Social Reproduction of Seriousness." *Carnival, Writing, Hysteria*. 122–134.

Williams, Linda. "Something Else Besides a Mother." *Home is Where the Heart is: Studies in Melodrama and the Woman's Film*. Ed. Christine Gledhill. (London: BFI, 1997), 299–325.

Willis, Sharon. "Hardware and Hardbodies, What Do Women Want?: A Reading of *Thelma and Louise.*" *Film Theory Goes to the Movies.* Ed. Jim Collins, Hilary Radner, and Ava Preacher Collins. (New York: Routledge, 1993).

Wimsatt, W. K. "The Criticism of Comedy." *Hateful Contraries: Studies in Literature and Criticism.* (Louisville: University of Kentucky Press, 1965), 90–107.

Young, Robert C. *Torn Halves: Political Conflict in Literary and Cultural Theory.* (New York: Manchester University Press, 1996).

Zappa, Frank and Peter Occhiogrosso. *The Real Frank Zappa Book.* (New York: Simon and Schuster, 1990).

Zizek, Slavoj. *The Sublime Object of Ideology.* (New York: Verso, 1989).

Index

Affects, 23-24, 27, 28, 29, 37, 39, 41, 45 n.1, 46 n. 6
Allen, Woody, 18 n. 8, 128, 181
Anti-Semitism, 25, 36, 40
Aristotle, xiv, 1, 5, 17 n. 5, 100,

Bakhtin, Mikhail 3, 8, 9-15, 19 n. 15, 19 n. 17, 20 n. 17, 23, 30, 35, 37, 38, 41-42, 46 n. 8, 47 n. 10, 49-53, 55-59, 61-66, 68, 70-73, 74 n. 2, 75 n. 6, 75 n. 8, 76 n. 13, 78 n. 17, 98, 104, 123-124, 132-133, 138, 146-147, 149, 150, 162 n. 9, 163, 168, 172, 185, 187; and carnival, 3, 10-11, 19 n. 15, 19 n. 17, 35, 37, 38, 41, 62, 68, 73 n. 1, 75 n. 8, 104, 123, 146, 147, 163; and dialogue *see* dialogue; and Dostoevsky, xvi, 49, 51, 52, 63, 66; and finalizability, 55, 57-59; and the grotesque xviii, 132-133, 138; and laughter, xv, 8-10, 12-13, 14, 15, 30, 42, 51, 61, 123; and Rabelais, Francois, xiv, xv, 9, 11, 13-14, 19 n. 14, 37, 38, 41, 42, 46 n. 8, 47 n. 10, 51, 61, 62, 64, 65, 68, 104, 123, 132, 138; and reduced laughter *see* laughter, reduced; and the novel, 19 n. 14, 61-63, 75 n. 6, 98, 123, 150, 162 n. 9; and unfinalizability, 30, 52, 53, 68, 77 n. 13
Barton Fink, 77 n. 15
Bataille, Georges, 7, 12, 18 n. 7, 18 n. 8, 18 n. 10, 21-22
Baudelaire, Charles, 104, 159 n 2, 159 n. 2, 175
Bazin, André, 94 n. 6
Beckett, Samuel, xviii, 63, 80
Benjamin, Walter, xviii, 100
Bergson, Henri 23, 26-27, 154
Body, the, xix, 1-2, 15, 26, 30, 131, 156
Blumenberg, Hans, 167-168, 172, 174-175

Booker, M. Keith, xiv, 11, 47 n. 10, 62, 75 n. 6, 75 n. 7
Brooks, Mel, 130, 176
Brooks, Peter, xvii, xviii, 93, 94 n. 9, 100, 115-116, 120, 125 n. 12

Capra, Frank, 180
Carnival, xiv, xvi, xix, 1, 10-11, 13, 17 n. 4, 19 n. 14, 19 n. 15, 30, 33, 35, 37, 45, 52, 61-64, 68, 73, 73 n. 1, 104, 123, 132, 146-147, 162 n. 10, 183; and history, 131; and laughter, 9-10, 12, 13, 19 n. 17, 37, 49; and the novel, 52, 61-63, 67, 75 n. 6, 75 n. 7, 75 n. 8, 123; as metaphor, 11, 30-34; Bakhtin and, xiv, 3, 10-11, 13, 19 n. 14, 19 n. 15, 35, 37, 49, 61-63, 68, 73, 73 n. 1, 104, 123, 132, 146-147 163
Carnival laughter, *see* laughter
Carnivalesque, the, 11, 12, 19 n. 14, 30, 32, 37, 44, 50, 68, 75 n. 8, 131
Cavell, Stanley, xii, xvi-xvii, 7, 74 n. 3, 77 n. 14, 79-95 *passim*, 132, 142, 176, 180
Chaplin, Charlie, 18 n. 10, 75 n. 6, 153
Clark, Katerina, 10
Comedy, the Hollywood comedy of remarriage, xii, xvi, 7, 79, 81, 82, 86, 89-91, 93, 94 n. 7, 179-180; as irresolution, xi, xiii, xix, 11, 118, 169, 171, 174, 175-185 *passim*; and liberation (see Liberation); as oppositional, ii, xii, 1-2, 7-14, 20 n. 17, 43; and power, xi-xii, xiv, xv, 2, 3, 6, 10-11, 17 n. 3; as relief, xii, xiv, xvii, 4, 18 n. 6, 85, 182-184; and Rhetoric (see Rhetoric); and sovereignty, xiii, xx, 2, 3, 7, 12, 14, 15, 76 n. 10; and suffering, xv, 5, 6, 35, 39, 46 n. 8, 65, 76 n. 10, 102, 104, 109, 176-178, 184; and tragedy, xiii, xiv, 1, 5-6, 14,

43, 81-82, 84, 93, 100, 105, 138, 142, 175, 181, 182; as trivial, xiii

de Certeau, Michel, xx n. 1, 1, 16 n. 1, 18, n. 11, 171, 172
de Quincey, Thomas, 163-164, 170
Death 6, 9, 13-16, 18 n. 7, 18 n. 8, 37-38, 41-42, 49, 61, 100, 122-123, 129, 133, 142, 176, 178-179
Derrida, Jacques, 7, 18 n. 8, 20 n. 18, 162 n. 11
Dialogue, xvi, xix, 9, 11, 13, 19 n. 17, 41, 45, 47 n. 10, 51-53, 55-56, 58, 61-62, 64, 67, 68, 70-73, 76 n. 12, 77 n. 15, 77 n. 16, 78 n. 17, 80, 98-99, 122, 149-150, 162 n 9., 168-169, 173
Dickens, Charles, xvii, xix, 18 n. 13, 62, 130-131, 159, 176-178, 187; *The Old Curiosity Shop*, xix, 130, 159 n. 1, 161 n. 6; *Oliver Twist*, 125 n. 10; *The Pickwick Papers*, 97-125 *passim*
Dostoevsky, Fyodor, xv-xvi, 11, 13, 20 n. 17, 49, 51-52, 61-64, 66, 72, 74 n. 2, 77 n. 16, 98

Eagleton, Terry, 33-35, 46 n. 8, 47 n. 10, 146-148, 174, 183-184, 188 n. 4, 188 n. 5
Elia *see* Lamb, Charles
Emerson, Caryl, 9, 19 n. 17, 42, 49, 51, 52, 57, 65-66, 72-73, 75 n. 7, 76 n. 13, 97, 98, 99, 104, 123, 168, 187

Feminism, 79-80, 156-157, 162 n. 11, 170, 87, 94 n. 11
Festive laughter, *see* laughter
Folk humor, *see* humor and the folk
Foucault, Michel, xiv, 20 n. 17, 162 n. 11, 30; repressive hypothesis, 11
Freud, Sigmund, xv, xviii, 11, 23, 53, 65, 121-122, 132, 133, 141, 162 n. 11; and humor, 38-39, 41, 110-113, 122; and jokes, 40, 47 n. 9, 182
Frye, Northrop, 184

Gadamer, Hans Georg, 76 n. 12, 77 n. 14, 175-177, 187
Grotesque, the, xviii, xix, 1, 2, 10, 17 n. 4, 19 n. 14, 30, 42, 127-133, 135, 137-151, 153, 155, 157-159, 160 n. 2, 160 n. 3
Gurewitch, Martin, 5, 143,

Hall, Stuart, 31-35, 46 n. 7
Hawks, Howard, 80, 90, 180, 187 n. 3,
Hamlet, see Shakespeare, William
His Girl Friday 80-82, 89-92, 180
Holocaust, the, 25, 46 n. 6; representations of, 23, 29, 38, 41-43
Holocaust jokes *see* jokes
Holquist, Michael, 10
Humor, xi-xii, xv, xviii, 17 n. 4, 21, 27, 38, 43, 75 n. 7, 104, 109-113, 114-115, 122-123, 130, 138, 139, 177; and the folk, 13, 50; and Freud (see Freud, Sigmund); and Kafka *see* Kafka, Franz

James, Henry, xvi, 13; "The Beast in the Jungle," 51-61, 64-73; and carnival 67-68; and the comic 49-51, 52, 64; and dialogue, 51, 53-61, 71-73; "The Figure in the Carpet," 54; and laughter 52, 64-67, 70; *The Portrait of a Lady*, 57-58, 61, 67, 71-72, 74 n. 2, 78 n. 17, 78 n. 18, 99; *The Turn of the Screw*, 54, 69, 74 n. 4; *What Maisie Knew*, 52
Jokes, xi, 13, 21; and the Holocaust, 38-41, 182-183; and Freud *see* Freud, Sigmund
Joyce, James, 30, 52, 62, 75 n. 6, 75 n. 7

Kafka, Franz, "The Burrow," xix, 134-138; and humor, 153, 155, 161 n. 8, 161 n. 9; and laughter 153-157; *The Metamorphosis*, xix, 138, 139-143, 150, 153, 159, 161 n. 7, 161 n. 8; "On Parables," 152; "Report to the Academy," 143-153, 161 n. 9; and suffering, 142, 151, 153, 157, *The Trial*, 157, 161 n. 7; "The Village Schoolmaster," 161 n. 7
Kant, Immanuel, 38, 77 n. 13, 102, 147
Keaton, Buster, 18 n. 10, 82
Kincaid, James R., 1-2, 6, 14, 18 n. 12, 20 n. 19, 30, 33, 103-104, 108, 120, 124 n. 3, 125 n. 10, 125 n. 11, 159 n. 1, 162 n. 10, 178-179, 181, 183-185
King Lear, see Shakespeare, William
Kristeva, Julia, 12, 20 n. 17

Lacan, Jacques, 23, 54, 162 n. 11, 186
Lamb, Charles, 2-8, 85, 163
Langer, Susanne, 14, 15, 16, 16 n. 2, 85-86, 104, 142, 155, 177, 179
Laughter, xv, xvi, xvii, xviii, 8-10, 12-16,

17 n. 4, 19 n. 17, 21-43 *passim*, 46 n. 5, 49, 51, 52, 61-66, 68, 70-71, 73, 73 n. 1, 75 n. 8, 76 n. 10, 92, 94 n. 9, 102-104, 123, 130, 132, 138, 147, 148, 153, 154, 157, 159 n. 2, 160 n. 2, 175, 177, 178, 186; and affect, 23-25, 27-29; dark, 15-16, 175-182; festive, xv, 9, 14, 35, 38, 42, 45, 61, 66, 73 (*see also* carnival laughter 9-10, 12-13, 19 n. 17, 37); and history, 46 n. 8; and the Holocaust, 23, 25, 29, 38-43; and morality, 16 n. 2; and power, 23; reduced, xv, xvi, xvii, 13, 46 n. 8, 51-52, 61-67, 123; and suffering, 28, 31, 35, 160; transgressive, 29-32
Legal Studies, 166
Lewis, Paul, 27-28
Liberation, xi, xviii, 10, 11, 14, 30, 36, 38, 42, 65, 77 n. 14, 93, 111, 132-133, 139, 143-148, 150, 152, 157, 181, 184, 186
Literary criticism, xii, xiii, xiv, xvi, 3, 7, 19 n. 16, 42, 47 n. 10, 49, 50, 62, 118, 133, 147, 149, 156, 167, 170, 173, 185
Loopholes, xix, 55, 60, 66, 70, 73, 77, 118, 164, 172, 179

Marx Brothers, the, 82, 171-172
Marx, Karl, 133, 147
McCloskey, Deirdre, 166-168
Melodrama, xvii, 80-82, 86, 89, 91, 93, 93 n. 5, 94 n. 7, 94 n. 9, 94 n. 10, 125 n. 10,
Menippean satire, 49, 62, 63
Meredith, George, 16 n. 2, 64
Method, 133, 136, 141, 166, 167, 173, 174, 185-187
Miller, D. A., 17 n. 3, 174
Miller, J. Hillis, 101, 118, 124 n. 1
Miller, Tyrus xv, 63-64
Modernity, xv, xvii-xix, 7, 9, 12, 14, 18 n. 12, 19 n. 14, 19 n. 16, 51, 52, 61, 63-64, 129, 131-133, 139, 151-153, 157, 158, 160 n. 2
Modleski, Tania, 79
Monologic, the, 9, 19 n. 17, 20 n. 17, 56-60, 62, 66, 70, 73, 76 n. 12, 77 n. 13, 77 n. 15, 149-150, 168
Molière, 17 n. 2, 64
Morson, Gary Saul, 9, 19 n. 17, 42, 49, 51, 52, 57, 65-66, 72-73, 75 n. 7, 76 n. 13, 97, 98, 99, 104, 123, 168, 187

9/11, 177-182
Nietzsche, Friedrich, 133, 146
Novel, the, xviii, 17 n. 3, 19 n. 16, 97-102, 106-108, 112, 116-120, 123, 124 n. 3, 124 n. 4, 124 n. 7, 125 n. 10; and carnival *see* carnival

Oedipus the King, 77, 81, 84, 175-176
Old Curiosity Shop, The see Dickens, Charles
Oliver Twist, see Dickens, Charles
On the Town, 180-181

Paranoia, xviii, 8, 25, 40, 65-66, 132-133, 133-140, 151, 155-157, 162 n. 12, 179
Parody, xii, 7, 12-13, 18 n. 8, 18 n. 12, 61, 62, 74 n. 4, 123, 128, 136, 187
Pickwick Papers, The, see Dickens, Charles
Plato, 13, 66, 76 n. 12
Post-structuralism, xiv, 7, 12, 20 n. 17, 41, 146, 148
Power, xi, xii, xiv, xv, 2, 3, 6, 11, 17, 17 n. 3, 16 n. 19, 20 n. 17, 21-45 *passim*, 46 n. 17, 57, 132-133, 145, 149 n. 1, 159 n. 1, 169, 173, 184, 185-187
Proust, Marcel, 52

Queer reading, 65, 76 n. 9, 133
Quilp (*The Old Curiosity Shop*), xix, 130, 159 n. 1

Rabelais, Francois, *see* Bakhtin, Mikhail
Racism, 43
Reading, xiii, xiv, xvi, xvii, xviii, xix, 3, 10, 11, 42, 53, 54, 66-67, 74 n. 4, 80, 82, 83, 87, 89, 93, 94 n. 9, 94 n. 11, 97-126 *passim*, 127-162 *passim*, 164, 173-174, 176, 177, 179, 185-187
Reduced laughter (see laughter)
Reparative, 24, 28, 41, 77 n. 15, 138, 143; and paranoid, 139, 155, 157
Rhetoric, 65-66, 76 n. 12, 163-175 *passim*, 185
Rose, Margaret, xii, xiii, 3, 7, 8, 12-14, 18 n. 12, 62
Ruskin, John, xix, 127-132, 138, 140, 157

Satire, xi, xv, 2, 8-9, 15, 17 n. 4, 21, 61, 63, 123, 127, 129, 161 n. 9; Menippean *see* Menippean satire

Schindler's List, xv, 22-29, 36, 41, 46 n. 4, 46 n. 5

Scalia, Antonin, 164-170

Schadenfreude, 22

Screwball comedy, the, xvi, xvii, 125 n. 13, 179, 180, 187 n. 3,

Sedgwick, Eve, xix, 45 n. 2, 46 n. 3, 53, 54, 57, 61, 64, 70, 76 n. 9, 76 n. 11, 133, 134, 136, 138, 142, 156, 157, 174, 182; and Adam Frank, xv, 23, 25, 31, 34, 41-42, 45 n. 1, 152

"Seinfeld", 29

Seriousness, xii, xiii, xv, xvii, xviii, 4, 6, 7, 9, 12-16, 18 n. 8, 22, 29, 30, 31, 33, 34-38, 42, 50, 65, 68, 85, 105, 115, 121-123, 135, 154, 170, 173-174, 177, 183-185, 187; Serious Man vs. Rhetorical Man, 170-172; true open seriousness, 13, 31, 50, 51 (*see also* comic seriousness, 50, 51; tragic seriousness, 13-14)

Shakespeare, William, xvii, 50, 64, 75 n. 8, 77 n. 14, 80, 82, 83, 85, 86, 124 n. 5, 163, 179, 184; *2 Henry IV*, 124 n. 5; *Hamlet*, 14, 64, 75 n. 8; *King Lear*, xii-xiv, 77 n. 14, 81, 82, 83, 86, 104, 134; *Macbeth*, 64; *Othello*, 6, 81

Sheridan, Richard Brinsley

Sholvsky, Victor, 97

Solemnity, 22, 24-25, 29, 41

Sophocles, 176 *see also Oedipus the King*

Spielberg, Steven, 2, 3, 5

Some Like it Hot, 84-85

Stallybrass, Peter, xiv, xix, 1, 2, 10, 17 n. 3, 20 n. 17, 23, 31, 33, 47 n. 10, 63, 131

Stella Dallas, 80, 82, 85-93, 94 n. 7, 94 n. 9, 94 n. 11, 95 n. 11

Sturges, Preston, 180

Structuralism, 7, 10, 12, 30, 31, 34, 124 n. 3, 146

Textualism, 165-166

Thelma and Louise, 120, 125 n. 13, 170

Theory, xii, 7, 25, 31, 33, 45 n. 1, 141, 146, 150, 152, 162 n. 11, 175; post-structuralist *see* post-structuralism; structuralist *see* structuralism; weak and strong, 174

Tragedy, xiii, xiv, xvii, 1, 5, 6, 14, 15, 18 n. 5, 18 n. 6, 76 n. 10, 77 n. 14, 81-84, 93, 94 n. 5, 94 n. 9, 100, 105, 138, 142, 175, 176, 181, 182, 185

Transgressive laughter, *see* laughter

Wit, xi, 21, 110, 139

Young Frankenstein, see Brooks, Mel

Zappa, Frank, 30, 43-45

Zizek, Slavoj, 40, 185-186